Inherited Wealth, Justice and Equality

Inherited wealth and the transfer of property rights on the occasion of death remain highly controversial issues. They cause not only heated debates in the public arena, especially when it comes to inheritance or 'death' taxes, but also intense discussions in academic circles. This book focuses on the present-day intellectual discourses on the subject of bequest and inheritance. It does so by bringing together views and analyses from a variety of disciplines.

The core of the book consists of a selection of papers presented at an international workshop where researchers from a variety of fields and countries discussed the connections between inherited wealth, justice and equality. The volume is complemented by a few other papers commissioned by the editors. The contributions cover historical, political, philosophical, sociological and economic aspects.

Whereas in most disciplines these issues tend to be discussed by reference to a literature internal to each of them, the book aims to encourage mutual engagement between disciplines that usually proceed in isolation. Besides tackling questions of principle with deep roots in philosophy and law, the papers also deal with more practical issues such as the effects of wealth taxes and the evolution of trustees into wealth managers.

John Cunliffe is Associate Fellow at the Department of Politics and International Studies (PAIS), University of Warwick, UK.

Guido Erreygers is Professor and Chair at the Department of Economics, University of Antwerp, Belgium.

Routledge frontiers of political economy

Inherited Wealth, Justice and Equality

Edited by John Cunliffe and
Guido Erreygers

LONDON AND NEW YORK

First published 2013
by Routledge

Published 2014 by Routledge
2 Park Square, Milton Park, Abingdon, Oxfordshire OX14 4RN

Simultaneously published in the USA and Canada
by Routledge
711 Third Avenue, New York, NY 10017

Routledge is an imprint of the Taylor and Francis Group, an informa business

First issued in paperback 2015

British Library Cataloguing in Publication Data
A catalogue record for this book is available from the British Library

Library of Congress Cataloging in Publication Data
Inherited wealth, justice and equality / edited by Guido Errygers and
John Cunliffe.
   p. cm.
   1. Inheritance and succession. 2. Wealth–Social aspects. 3. Equality.
   4. Social justice. I. Errygers, Guido, 1959– II. Cunliffe, John.
   HB715.I56 2012
   346.05'2–dc23   2012022554

ISBN 978-0-415-51692-1 (hbk)
ISBN 978-1-138-95800-5 (pbk)
ISBN 978-0-203-07799-3 (ebk)

Typeset in Times New Roman
by Wearset Ltd, Boldon, Tyne and Wear

Contents

Figures and tables

Figures

Tables

Contributors

Luc Arrondel is Research Director at the Centre National de Recherche Scientifique (CNRS), Associated Professor at the Paris School of Economics (PSE), and Scientific Advisor at the Banque de France, Paris, France.

Jens Beckert is Director at the Max Planck Institute for the Study of Societies in Cologne, Germany.

Matthew Clayton is Associate Professor of Political Theory at the Department of Politics and International Studies (PAIS), and Director of the Centre for Ethics, Law and Public Affairs, University of Warwick, UK.

Helmuth Cremer is Researcher at the Institut d'Économie Industrielle (IDEI), member of the Toulouse School of Economics and Professor at the University of Toulouse I, Toulouse, France.

John Cunliffe is Associate Fellow at the Department of Politics and International Studies (PAIS), University of Warwick, UK.

Guido Erreygers is Professor and Chair at the Department of Economics, University of Antwerp, Belgium.

Brooke Harrington is Associate Professor at the Department of Business and Politics of the Copenhagen Business School, Denmark.

Ran Hirschl is Professor of Political Science and Law and Canada Research Chair in Constitutionalism, Democracy and Development at the University of Toronto, Canada.

Robert Lamb is Senior Lecturer in Political Philosophy and Director of Education at the Department of Politics, School of Humanities and Social Sciences, University of Exeter, UK.

Virpi Mäkinen is Deputy Director and Academy Research Fellow at the Academy of Finland and Lecturer at the University of Helsinki, Finland.

André Masson is Research Director at the Centre National de Recherche Scientifique (CNRS) and the École des Hautes Etudes en Sciences Sociales (EHESS), and Associate Researcher at the Paris School of Economics (PSE), Paris, France.

Ann Mumford is Reader at the School of Law, Queen Mary, University of London, London, UK.

Pierre Pestieau is Emeritus Professor of the University of Liège, Belgium, member of the Centre for Operations Research and Econometrics (CORE), Louvain-La-Neuve, Belgium, and associate member of the Paris School of Economics (PSE), Paris, France.

Rajiv Prabhakar is Lecturer in Personal Finance at the Open University and an ESRC fellow at the LSE, London, UK.

Andrew Reeve is Professor of Politics at the Department of Politics and International Studies (PAIS) of the University of Warwick, UK.

Ayelet Shachar is Professor of Law and Political Science and Canada Research Chair in Citizenship and Multiculturalism at the University of Toronto, Canada.

Carine Smolders is Professor of Economics at the Hogeschool Gent, Ghent, Belgium.

Preface

The transfer of property rights on the occasion of death has been a controversial issue for a long time, and it continues to arouse strong emotions today. Interestingly, inherited wealth causes both heated debates in the public arena – the 'No Death Tax' movement in the US is a case in point – and intense discussions in academic circles. This book focuses on the present-day intellectual discourses on the subject of bequest and inheritance, and does so by bringing together views and analyses from a variety of disciplines.

Most of the papers contained in this volume are revised versions of those originally presented at the international workshop 'Inherited Wealth, Justice and Equality' organized by the University Centre Saint-Ignatius Antwerp (UCSIA) at the University of Antwerp from 4 to 6 March 2010. For various reasons, some of the papers presented during the workshop could not be included here. In order to arrive at a finely balanced set of contributions, we subsequently solicited a few additional papers from specialists on inherited wealth.

When we started planning the workshop, our aim was to invite people from different disciplinary backgrounds and to create a fertile environment for discussions across disciplinary boundaries. The workshop certainly gave rise to lively debates and offered plenty of opportunities to learn from the views and methods adopted in other disciplines. We hope this book conveys some of that spirit.

John Cunliffe and Guido Erreygers
Antwerp, May 2012

Acknowledgements

When we suggested the idea of organizing an international workshop on 'Inherited Wealth, Justice and Equality' to the staff of the University Centre Saint-Ignatius Antwerp (UCSIA), we got an enthusiastic response. We are very grateful that UCSIA gave us the means and the time to invite some of the leading specialists on bequest and inheritance, and to put together an appealing programme. We thank especially managing director Walter Nonneman, (former) academic director Christiane Timmerman, administrative coordinator Geert Vanhaverbeke and scientific collaborator Sara Mels; Geert and Sara were in charge of all the practical details and handled things extremely efficiently.

Throughout the process of organizing the workshop and preparing the book, we benefited from the backing of our home institutions, respectively the Department of Politics and International Studies (PAIS) at the University of Warwick and the Department of Economics at the University of Antwerp. Matthew Clayton and Andrew Reeve have given us invaluable support by acting as fellow travellers and interlocutors: for us they have been constant sources of inspiration, and their input has been of crucial importance. We are also grateful that Kristel Van Hilst gave us a helping hand during the last stages of the preparation of the manuscript.

Last but not least we thank Routledge's editorial staff for their continued and unconditional support, and for their admirable patience.

John Cunliffe and Guido Erreygers
Antwerp, May 2012

1 The debates about inherited wealth and its taxation

An introductory essay

John Cunliffe, Guido Erreygers and Andrew Reeve

The problem of inherited wealth

The chapters in this volume address the issue of inherited wealth from the perspectives of various academic disciplines, each offering assessments by reference to a literature largely internal to each of them. Historians of ideas demonstrate that disputes over inherited wealth have been central to theories of property over many centuries. Political theorists assess the normative significance of intergenerational transfers in the light of tensions between the ideals of liberty and equality. Economists consider inheritance taxation in the light of the conflicting demands of equity and efficiency. Sociologists point to the crucial role of inherited wealth in reinforcing social inequality across generations and analyse the reasons behind the intense public opposition to inheritance taxation. These different perspectives identify a set of points which help to explain the profoundly controversial issues involved. The first is that inherited wealth raises in an acute form the especially sensitive fact of our mortality. The second is that this inescapable fate links inherited wealth to concerns over family structures and values. The third is that the huge inequalities in inherited wealth constitute a problem for the ideal of equality of opportunity and other egalitarian ideas. These equality issues alone support arguments for various forms of inheritance taxation. In contrast, the interest in family values, and the emotional weight attached to inherited property, count against any such taxation.

There might be little wrong with inherited wealth if we all received something approaching an equal share. But obviously we do not: inherited wealth is an issue because it is so massively unequal, reproducing social inequalities across generations. Inherited wealth attracts the idea of its taxation to counter this inequality. Since most people would benefit from inheritance taxation, we might expect it to be a popular cause. But the popular cause in many countries is the precise opposite: the abolition of inheritance taxation. This is surprising because only a minority of wealthy individuals – or their heirs – are liable to it, and in any case there are numerous loopholes. Opposition to inheritance taxation is, however, far from being limited to a wealthy minority. There is little doubt that there is a widely shared and deeply felt aversion to any level of inheritance taxation across all social classes, including those who will never be subject to it.

This aversion reflects a strongly held view that this type of taxation is somehow grossly unfair. The challenge for scholarly investigation is to explain this curious anomaly. Of course, the aversion might be explained by ignorance, or the influence of powerful interest groups mobilized by the wealthy. Again, it might be attributed to the dominance of neo-liberal economic ideas, or suspicion of the state, especially as an agent of social change. Although none of those explanations is irrelevant or totally false, they fail to address the most fundamental point that inheritance taxation forces us to confront the inescapable reality of death, and its impact on those closest to us, both family and friends. Those who support inheritance taxation on egalitarian grounds might adopt the ethos of the rationalist Enlightenment, but they singularly fail to recognize that most people do not follow that ethos when reminded of their own mortality. If, as the saying goes, death and taxes are the only certainties in this life, then the combination of these two certainties is toxic. The very last chance to leave some tangible mark on the world becomes subject to interference by the state, which cannot or will not leave us alone at that last moment. Even if we can have no further use for what was our property, our final will regarding its future should be complied with. To do otherwise is to demonstrate a singular lack of respect for the recently departed in their capacity as agents who might have chosen to benefit those close to them. Apart from solidarity with family and friends over a lifetime, passing on property to them is a continued expression of that solidarity, extending the temporal horizon of the individual beyond death. As the French adage puts it, 'toucher à l'héritage c'est comme toucher à la famille' (interfering with inheritances is tantamount to interfering with the family). Of course, scholarly debates can and do present rational assessments of the merits or otherwise of inheritance taxation. When conducted in those terms, however, these debates fail to address the singularly poignant nature of the posthumous transfer of wealth – that it is, above all, *posthumous*.

Family values

Given this popular sentiment, inheritance taxes are viewed with suspicion because they threaten family solidarity and unity, at the especially sensitive time of the death of one of its members. Legal systems have reached different conclusions as to the specification of those members, together with the extent of their entitlement. Over time and across countries, disputes over the posthumous transfer of property titles reveal three quite different conceptions of the family unit. The first considers each family member as an independent property holder in her own right. This favours bequest and testamentary freedom which grant the present owner absolute discretion over the posthumous disposition of her property. That freedom has been criticized for potentially weakening the family unit, since the donor could act capriciously with the choice of unequal dispersal within the family, or altogether outside it. In that knowledge, donors might use their testamentary freedom as a means of control. Potential beneficiaries could respond as they thought appropriate, doing whatever they thought necessary to enhance their prospects of securing a legacy. The second considers the property of family members in varying degrees as jointly owned, restricting testamentary freedom in favour of a right to inheritance and particularly to equal inheritance within the direct line. This might be against the preferred disposition of the current owner. The lack of discretion is seen as strengthening the family unit. Most legal systems seek to balance the competing claims of bequest and inheritance by allowing some testamentary freedom subject to a guaranteed reserve share for family members. This third conception reflects a compromise between the Anglo-Saxon common law tradition which favoured testamentary freedom (at least for personal property) and continental civil law which preferred inheritance. In both traditions, nevertheless, the transmission of property was considered a matter of political and legal convention rather than an expression of some basic right to private property. Even if that right were recognized legally during the lifetime of property holders, it did not extend to the posthumous disposition of their holdings. Which form of intergenerational transmission should be legally required or permitted, and whether and to what extent it should be liable to taxation, were quintessentially *political* decisions.

The legal privilege accorded to the intergenerational transmission of property within families is traditionally seen as a crucial incentive to the accumulation of wealth over successive lifetimes. This holds in particular for a discretionary bequest regime: under an inheritance regime, the guarantee of a legacy substantial enough to provide economic security might reduce any ambition to work and save. Economists and other social scientists have constructed various models of inheritance but concede that empirical information about bequest motives and incentive effects is extremely difficult to establish. The models distinguish between 'accidental' and 'planned' transmission. The former occurs not because of any intention to transmit wealth, but because death occurs before precautionary savings to ensure independent financial security in old age are exhausted. There will be an estate even if accidentally: it will go to the family, if there is one, and otherwise to nominated beneficiaries. It appears doubtful whether individuals who have no children are any less inclined to make precautionary savings than those who do. It is equally plausible to argue that their savings might be greater precisely because they have no family to fall back on. The latter, 'planned' transmission, can take many forms. The stereotype is that of a capitalist motivation concerned with wealth accumulation across generations. Each successive generation considers its inheritance as a formal or informal trust, which should be passed on in at least an undiminished, and preferably enhanced, form. Planned bequests can take many other forms than the stereotype, according to the particular model of the family: relationship between parents and children can range from altruism, through egocentric manipulation to total unconcern, or any combination of them. In 'altruistic bequests', the transmission of property will be based on the preferences of the children; in 'paternalistic bequests', it will be based on the view of the parents on what is best for their children; and in 'strategic bequests', it will be based on calculations of the extent to which each child supports the parents. Despite the standard claims about the incentive effect of the transmission of property especially within families, the relevant empirical research based on these models is inconclusive. We simply do not know how bequest motives differ between countries or social classes or over time.

There are other traditions, nevertheless, which qualify or reject the privileged position of transmission within families. In a moderate form, charitable contributions might be encouraged by a favourable tax regime for dispersal beyond the family, whether during a lifetime or at death. These contributions express the particular values of the donor who might not regard the family – if there is one – as the most appropriate recipient, or the state as the most appropriate institution for realizing those values. In a more extreme form, philanthropic foundations might be promoted by preferential taxation, expressing the conception of the community held by their founders, rather than the state. Insofar as there is any dynastic ambition, this would be achieved not through wealth accumulation across generations, but by the founder's memory living on in the name of the institution. In the moderate form, charitable contributions might be regarded as complementing transmission within the family, whereas in the more extreme form, philanthropic foundations might be seen as a rival or substitute for it.

Equality concerns

Despite these connections between family structures and economic incentives on the one side, and intergenerational transmission on the other, there are traditions which point to the unacceptable inequalities it leads to. The most prominent of these traditions is that which values equality of opportunity but there are others which again seek to redress those inequalities albeit in different ways.

The strongest argument for inheritance taxation is that it counters unequal inheritances and unequal life chances which are the product of mere luck. Although opportunities are welcome at any stage in life, these unequal inheritances are received typically not when the beneficiaries are children or in early adulthood, but when they are in their fifties. If the concern is with equal starting points, these unequal opportunities occur at the wrong stage in the life cycle. The extent to which inheritance taxation might promote equal starts depends on the tax yield and whether the proceeds are disbursed especially to benefit those younger age cohorts.

The familiar objective in relation to inheritance taxation is that its rate should not exceed the revenue-maximizing level, in order to prevent the creation of perverse incentives against work and savings, or in favour of *inter vivos* transfers. Although there might be some punitive level which could generate those effects, it remains singularly unclear what the optimal level should be set at. Given that it is neither possible nor desirable simply to eradicate all forms of partiality within families, or between friends, the issue becomes one of the legitimate scopes of this partiality, when it is expressed through the transmission of material wealth. Of course, there are many other ways of expressing familial partiality, but it would be naïve in the extreme to minimize the significance of inherited economic resources. The problem is the extent to which the concern with equal opportunity can accommodate any privileged tax status for transfers especially within the family, either by exemption and/or a higher threshold. If that tax status is too restrictive, parents will resort to *inter vivos* transfers of material wealth to their children. If that tactic is countered by constraints on monetized gifts in their lifetimes, parents will resort to non-monetized gifts to seek a positional advantage for their children – especially through education. Given these avoidance tactics, and the cost of countering them, some egalitarians argue that there are other and better ways to promote equal opportunities than inheritance taxation, perhaps through increasing income or wealth taxes.

Aside from the question of yield, current advocates of inheritance taxation – like some earlier counterparts – have developed ambitious and sophisticated projects concerned with promoting the interests of young adults by the appropriate disbursement of tax funds. One way of doing this might be to provide a capital grant to all such adults as their private property, with no conditions attached to its use. Alternatively, the grant might be made conditional on a set of approved purposes. Another and opposed thought is that the proceeds should be earmarked and used to provide better public services directed not at material wealth but improving human capital, especially through investment in education and training. Again, the inheritance tax rate might be modified to promote skipping generations, with bequests to younger individuals being treated more favourably. Or, again, earlier dispersal might be promoted by reducing taxation on gifts *inter vivos* relative to tax on transfers at death.

In the light of these and indeed other difficulties, it would be optimistic to expect equality of opportunity to prevail over the intense aversion to inheritance taxation, based on the massive emotive weight aroused by the transfer of property at death, and its effect on families. Equal opportunities do not, of course, generate equal outcomes. Inheritance taxation at a sufficient level might prevent or reduce the cumulative transmission of those unequal outcomes across generations. It does not address them, however, over the course of a lifetime, especially if they result in destitution for some. Before the emergence of the modern welfare state with its multiple sources of tax revenue, the proceeds of inheritance taxation could be directed at ameliorating those *ex post* outcomes, rather than promoting equal opportunities. In the modern welfare state, by contrast, no special significance might be accorded to inheritance taxation, whether in terms of its level or the disbursement of its proceeds. In a more pragmatic manner, inheritance taxation might be regarded as only one component of the overall level of taxation required to fund state expenditure, including amongst other aims the promotion of equal opportunities and redressing unacceptable inequalities in outcome. Inheritance taxation would no longer be seen as a distinctive means of initially equalizing private property, or promoting equal opportunities through public services, or ameliorating those lifetime outcomes. The role of inheritance taxation in financing state welfare in general becomes an issue of political calculation along with the priorities accorded to each of these aims. Policy issues and funding mechanisms are regarded as separate not linked. Modern states have an antipathy to earmarked taxation.

As Jens Beckert (2008) demonstrates in the comparative analysis in his monograph, *Inherited Wealth*, the development of inheritance practices in different countries reflects the tensions between conceptions of the family, concerns with incentive structures, and egalitarian commitments. Diverse interpretations and combinations of these considerations amount to distinctive national traditions. In the US, the controversy has been dominated by those supporting an unqualified bequest regime including incentives to promote charitable foundations, on the one side, against others calling for inheritance taxation on the grounds of equal opportunity. In Germany, opposition to inheritance taxation has been based on the priority of the family unit, whereas support has been motivated by a concern to redress unacceptable inequalities in market outcomes. In France, however, the controversy has concentrated on the general issue of tax equity, with a defence of family property against the view that inheritance taxation could be an instrument of social reform.

An overview of the book

The chapters in this volume reveal that the tensions between the various justificatory principles, compounded by the emotional weight attached to inherited wealth, seem likely to provoke continuing and unresolved controversy across a range of academic disciplines. Nevertheless, there is also common ground – but before we identify the common themes, let us first outline what can be found in each of the chapters.

Historical perspectives

The controversies over inherited wealth are part of wider debates about property which, of course, have a very long history. Virpi Mäkinen considers the debates surrounding the Spanish arrival in aboriginal territory, a debate beginning in the early sixteenth century and lasting some 200 years, by examining Vitoria's contribution in *De indis*. To consider whether the newer arrivals could have any claim over Indian lands, possessions (or even their persons) required identification of the relevant legal framework; it also required specification of what was required for an entity to be capable of dominion. Vitoria discussed these problems in relation to *ius gentium* (the law of nations) but this was connected to natural law. Vitoria has been seen as developing a subjective notion of rights of dominion, contributing to the development of natural law by his conception of individual right in relation to *ius gentium*, although Mäkinen holds that he drew on both subjective and objective conceptions.

The question of what was required for an entity to be capable of dominion was critical if the legitimacy of claims arising from seizure and enslavement based on the denial of that capacity to Indians were to be rebutted. Mäkinen draws attention to three meanings of dominion in Vitoria's analysis: dominion strictly speaking (a type of superiority); dominion as ownership; and dominion as ability to use something in accordance with law. Vitoria concluded that the

Indians could not be denied the capacity for dominion because of unbelief, because sinners can have dominion; nor because of madness, as their affairs are ordered, although only humans could have dominion. Indeed, all humans had dominion over other creatures, a use right which was universal and prelapsarian.

How, then, could property be legitimately divided? Vitoria suggested three methods – by Adam; by an elected ruler; and by common consent. 'Common consent' was universally valid under *ius gentium* and the Indians held their lands by right of first occupancy. Vitoria was able to conclude that the Indians were the true owners of their lands (and could exclude the claims of Spaniards arriving later) and that they had individual dominion (rights to use, transfer and inherit) according to *ius gentium*. Mäkinen argues that Vitoria connected the objective and subjective rights traditions in this analysis, contributing to the development of *ius gentium* and natural law.

Robert Lamb examines the issue of inheritance in relation to natural law over 150 years later, in the work of John Locke. Lamb distinguishes two types of focus on Locke's theory of property. The first is the endeavour to analyse Locke's arguments in relation to his wider thought, and in particular his theological positions. The other is the attempt by libertarians to use Locke's approach as the foundation for a normative political theory. These libertarians are said to 'bracket off' Locke's theology, but Lamb maintains that examining the issue of posthumous transmissibility reveals that Locke's theory differs from that of the libertarians, and reveals a common hiatus in the theories.

Lamb proceeds by explicating the distinction between the right to bequeath and the right to inherit. Locke is said not to provide a convincing account of the legitimacy of the right to bequeath. The issue concerns what rights follow from an act of original acquisition, for Locke's account of natural law places at its centre the duty to preserve oneself and as many others as possible. Is posthumous transmissibility among those rights? Lamb shows that other natural rights thinkers, adopting a consequentialist approach to the ends of preserving life and maintaining peace and harmony, can more easily address this than Locke. Locke refers to a natural right to inherit, which potentially constrains what a parent may legitimately do with property when alive, as well as ruling out a comprehensive right of bequest. It is nevertheless true that Locke endorses a parental right to bequeath. The right to bequeath and the right to inherit may be rendered compatible by reference to a prior commitment – to the preservation of persons – if we take Locke to mean that parents can bequeath the property beyond that which their children have a right to inherit to guarantee their preservation. But Locke does not provide a convincing justification for the *existence* of a right to bequest – a failing, Lamb says, shared by libertarians who merely assume one.

Of course, disputes over natural law and natural rights are irrelevant if transmission is regarded as a pure convention, which should be fashioned with regard to a number of different principles. John Cunliffe and Guido Erreygers draw attention to some mid-nineteenth-century proposals for reform of inheritance of this pluralistic kind, motivated by a concern with inequality and especially with cumulative inequality. The three sets of proposals were those of the Belgian rational socialists, the French philosopher François Huet, and two radical Americans. Although these ideas were put forward independently, they all involved consideration of the proper balance to be struck between three principles: how, if at all, can these principles be woven into a coherent system to regulate intergenerational transmission? All the writers favoured a basic capital payment to young adults, and tried to integrate a concern with equal opportunity as individuals set out in adult life, consideration of the value and status of the family, and some attention to correcting the *ex post* inequality which would result from the choices those individuals made. The details of the way in which they attempted this integration form the matter of three separate analyses – but since these schemes were advanced independently, the similarities and differences, which Cunliffe and Erreygers analyse in their fourth section, are particularly interesting. Objections to their schemes are based on arguments still forwarded today – that they weaken the solidarity of families and reduce incentives to work and save – so their rebuttals also resonate. They claimed that freedom of bequest provided incentives for capricious and mercenary behaviour, and that equal shares distributed to young adults reduced dependence and were provided to them at an appropriate time in their lives. The other argument concerns the effects of inheritance taxation, even up to the 100 per cent level: some of the authors denied the alleged effect on work and savings, others acknowledged it and factored it into a moderated right of individual transmission. Just as these controversies about incentives continue in relation to inheritance tax, so too has the proposal of a capital grant been revived.

Social and political theory

Beckert's chapter identifies a current reaction against using inheritance law and inheritance taxation as instruments of social reform, and seeks to explain it. Until the early 1970s, there had been a climate of public opinion which endorsed the Enlightenment conception of modernity, in which social status was a function of individual achievement rather than being ascribed by birth. That conception was recognized in changes to three areas of inheritance law: greater equality in family structures; the abolition of entails; and the introduction of progressive estate taxation. Of these three areas, the modernization process continues only in statutory inheritance law relating to the family. By contrast, in many jurisdictions rules against dynastic control over property across generations have been abolished or modified, or bypassed through complex family trusts. Similarly, inheritance taxation has been abolished or severely restricted in many countries, and where it remains it has become deeply unpopular. The symbolic turning point between endorsement and rejection of inheritance law as an embodiment of modernity is located in the failed presidential campaign of George McGovern in 1972, when he wrongly assumed that his proposal for a progressive estate tax accorded with the prevailing political mood in the US.

Beckert readily concedes that this profound change in attitudes toward Enlightenment modernity cannot be explained easily. In economic terms, it is part of the dominant supply-side orthodoxy that taxation inhibits growth, together with the race to the bottom in a globalized setting. Politically, it reflects scepticism about a strong state as an instrument of social reform, following the collapse of the post-war consensus. Socially, it expresses the growing pressures on the middle class combined with the processes of individualization and 'desolidarization'. Given increased economic insecurity, the individualized response is to provide opportunities for one's own offspring through inheritance, rather than seeing the taxation of transmitted wealth as an appropriate collective response offering opportunities for all. Culturally, the legitimization of wealth distribution seems to be based on an idea of 'success' – whenever and however realized. And, whereas social scientists might be concerned with structures like inherited wealth that reproduce social inequality, according to their own studies that concern is not shared outside their own circle.

This weakened opposition to ascriptive status runs counter to a great deal of liberal and republican thought. In as much as birthright is the basis of ascriptive status, Ayelet Shachar and Ran Hirschl draw our attention to some analogies and an anomaly. The analogies are between the entailed estate in land and the transmission of citizenship by virtue of birthplace. The intergenerational transfer of property is paralleled by the intergenerational birthright of citizenship. The anomaly is that entail is the quintessential device by which a testator could 'reach into the future'. Indeed, at some particular periods, he could create a perpetuity (an arrangement which could never be changed). Given the attention paid to the justifications for inheritance, the republican hostility to the aristocratic device of entail, and the fact of its abolition, Shachar and Hirschl ask why the practice of familial transmission of citizenship by place of birth and blood line has not been similarly scrutinized as to its normative standing. They cite the evidence that freedoms, opportunities, access to services and levels of well-being vary dramatically across polities to demonstrate the distributional consequences of citizenship by birthright. The analogies between property and citizenship are developed by reference to the notions of inclusion and exclusion. A citizen has a right not to be excluded from the polity of which she is a member and to enjoy its attendant benefits; but citizens also exclude non-citizens from those arrangements. Similarly, property allows the holder to exclude others from the use and benefit of it, while securing her in its ownership. This leads to the thought that citizenship is a scarce and potentially valuable resource, similar to property. Having detailed the more specific analogies between entailed property and citizenship by place of birth and family, the authors point to a puzzle: republican and liberal thought are hostile to ascriptive status, and in many areas of modern life it has been rejected, but it remains in the inheritance of birthright and thus calls out for examination when we assert that all persons are born free and equal.

The broad problem to which Matthew Clayton's argument is addressed is how are liberal egalitarians, who value both liberty and equality, to respond to the apparent tension between testamentary freedom and inequality in inheritance? There are some radical arguments for regulation of inheritance practices which Clayton rejects as resting on perfectionist premises – that is, they are not neutral between different conceptions of the good, but rely upon one. The argument that the dead have no interests is identified as one such argument; the view that legitimate partiality towards one's family outweighs concerns about equality and endorses testamentary freedom is another.

Clayton's project is thus to examine the radical implications of resource egalitarianism for legislation (including, of course, taxation) regulating bequest or inheritance. This draws upon Ronald Dworkin's account of the envy test and of hypothetical insurance, but extends it significantly. In particular, the mental experiment grounding hypothetical insurance when applied to the specific policy under discussion is elaborated to take account of the life cycle of an individual as both child and adult. Clayton also disagrees with Dworkin's specific conception of the harm caused by inequality in inherited resources and with his specification of the way in which the proceeds of inheritance tax should be spent. We are invited to consider, then, the justifications for legislative interference with freedom of *post-mortem* transfers from the perspective of a liberal egalitarian who has an anti-perfectionist account of political morality. Dworkin illustrated his account of hypothetical insurance in a discussion of healthcare. Clayton explains this and then applies the hypothetical insurance experiment to bequests and inheritance.

What kind of protection against inequalities caused by bequests would equally situated individuals insure to provide? More elaborately, what scheme of insurance would persons favour at different stages in their lives if they were to relive those lives from birth to death? He concludes that they would have good reasons to favour steeply progressive inheritance tax on bequests to move towards equal inheritance; it would be rational to constrain inequality-generating bequests for the sake of children, which would limit the testamentary freedom a person might otherwise favour as an adult. In other words, in deciding what to insure, individuals need to take account of their ambitions about both giving and receiving. This is proposed as superior to the interest-based approach (for example, that of John Rawls) which will license restrictions on gifts and bequests that threaten important freedoms or rights. But if a person wants to benefit particular others as part of her conception of the good life, and this produces inequalities in opportunities, what is the position? Rawlsians seem to give priority to receiving over giving, violating anti-perfectionism. Clayton thus concludes that, although there are many other issues to consider, resource egalitarianism has significant implications for inheritance taxation, because it is itself an appealing approach to the integration of concerns with liberty and equality.

Economic approaches

There are other routes to the conclusion that inheritance taxation is desirable, despite its current unpopularity. In their chapter, Luc Arrondel and André Masson defend the 'iconoclastic' proposal that increased and progressive inheritance taxation should be implemented in France so as to create an incentive to earlier dispersal of assets within families through gifts *inter vivos*. They argue that inheritances are received typically too late in the life cycle to affect opportunities when they matter most. Their immediate concern (similar to that of David Willetts (2010) in the British setting) is to redress the imbalance in assets between the 'baby boomer' generation and its successors, for whom a wide range of opportunities for an independent lifestyle occur at a much older age – or are postponed indefinitely. They demonstrate that the proposal is feasible in France for three main reasons: many older households could afford to transfer assets *inter vivos* given a remarkably high saving rate and a generous social security system; such households have responded positively to previous tax incentives encouraging earlier dispersal; and these earlier transfers have not led to increased consumption by their recipients but to productive investment.

But, earlier dispersal within families does not address inequalities between them. In response to that issue, Arrondel and Masson suggest that tax incentives should promote dispersal beyond the family, especially in favour of those charitable foundations concerned with the education and training of children from deprived backgrounds. In terms of the typologies of the welfare state, the iconoclastic proposal is seen as a hybrid between three paradigms. The proposal to increase inheritance taxation and to make it more progressive aligns with the 'equal citizenship' paradigm which believes that the state should grant a high level of welfare to all citizens through redistributive taxation. The suggestion that dispersal beyond the family should be encouraged matches the liberal or free-agent paradigm with its suspicion of state welfare. The concern to speed up family transfers reflects the 'multi-solidarity' paradigm where intergenerational family solidarity and parental altruism are valued.

For quite different reasons, Rajiv Prabhakar also considers the case for increasing inheritance taxation. He insists that reformers should continue to defend inheritance taxation – despite its making only a relatively small contribution to overall public finances and being extremely unpopular – for two main reasons. The first is that particular forms of taxation should be assessed not only by the revenue they raise, but also by the requirements of equity. The second is that opponents of inheritance taxation view it as only one element in egalitarian policies. To admit defeat in this case would result only in further attacks on other redistributive taxes. Instead of retreating, the objective should be to extend taxation to other forms of wealth, notably the windfall gains in property prices over the period of a housing boom in the UK. In more immediate political terms, Prabhakar considers the significance of the issues of inheritance and wealth taxation in the current Conservative/Liberal Democrat coalition. As part of negotiations over the formation of the coalition government, the Conservative party had to drop its proposal to raise the threshold of inheritance taxation to £1 million – a proposal criticized by Gordon Brown as having been dreamt up 'on the playing field of Eton'. Within the coalition, some concern has been expressed over wealth inequality, with the Liberals proposing a 'mansion tax' on extremely valuable properties, and some Conservatives suggesting ways of responding to wealth inequality without resorting to further taxation. On the contrary, Willetts argues that inheritance tax should be reduced, leaving the possibility that the 'baby boomer' generation could pass on more to its less advantaged successors. The 'red Tory' analysis (Blond, 2010) adopts the familiar neo-conservative objection to welfarism, in which the solution to wealth inequality lies in less not more state intervention. Against this background, Prabhakar concludes pessimistically that the future does not augur well for any strengthened commitment to wealth taxes.

Helmuth Cremer and Pierre Pestieau similarly defend inheritance taxation strongly on the grounds that compared with alternatives it is efficient, fair and painless. In the first part of their chapter, they assess the current controversy over the US estate tax, which is surprisingly unpopular even amongst those who will never be subject to it. They assess explanations for this puzzle offered by others. These include the ways in which survey questions are framed; the intense lobbying activity of opponents of the estate tax; resentment over the numerous loopholes used to avoid it; and the perceived clash with family values favouring transmission within that institution. Cremer and Pestieau point out, however, that many of the critiques of estate tax are directed against the way in which it is administered rather than its underlying principle. Their second section adopts a more theoretical approach, exploring the normative desirability of an estate tax, a desirability which depends on the motives for wealth accumulation and transmission. These differ between individuals, and, in addition, any individual might have mixed motives. Their approach is to assess the effect of taxation on each of these different motives for bequest, whether accidental, altruistic, paternalistic or strategic. Cremer and Pestieau demonstrate through a rigorous technical analysis that there is a positive case on efficiency grounds for taxing bequests whatever the motives. The case becomes even stronger if redistribution is an objective. Despite that, they acknowledge that there is a sharp contrast between the general support for wealth taxation amongst public finance experts, and the widespread opposition to it in more popular circles. The appropriate response is not to abandon the principle of the taxation of posthumous wealth transfers, because of popular resistance, but to reform its administration to deal with various problems. These include poor tax yields resulting from avoidance and evasion along with the race to the bottom between countries and regions.

Sociological views

Ann Mumford's chapter aims to explain the particular issue of current resistance to inheritance taxation by reference to the broader perspectives of theoretical sociology exemplified by Pierre Bourdieu's work on the legitimacy of state power. The current resistance goes far beyond economic or financial concerns; it embraces *inter alia* gender issues, the political process and property law. These concerns confirm Bordieu's view that social existence cannot be segmented and organized into distinct spheres. Instead, resistance to inheritance taxation, like other issues, relates to the complexity of social reality in which symbolic power is crucial. That power rests on two main pillars: symbolic capital or the power acquired by ruling groups in past struggles, and symbolic efficacy or the affinities between the agents in the power structure which reproduce it over time. The issue to be addressed is therefore what is the symbolic capital on which state taxation depends? The long history of struggles over taxation reveals that its legitimacy has always been questioned alongside the power structure of the state. Those earlier struggles assumed violent forms and continue in a more subdued fashion in widespread tax avoidance or tax fraud. And, most significantly, both these practices are not only endemic, but seemingly tolerated by the public, the law being rendered singularly ineffective. In the specific case of inheritance taxation, resentment is especially marked because of the intimate connection to death. Those immediately facing that prospect have one last chance to challenge the legitimacy of the state by declaring control over the *post mortem* disposition of their property. Although the resentment might be long standing, the strength of recent opposition to inheritance taxation across many countries is indicative of a broader scepticism about the state in an era of globalization and privatization. Such opposition cannot be traced to a single cause or restricted to a particular sphere of social existence. Rather, it must be analysed through a multi-faceted approach in which the issues raised by posthumous wealth are integrated into the general Bordieusian concern with power and its fluidity.

Brooke Harrington demonstrates how the unpopularity of inheritance taxation translates into the avoidance mechanism of trusts, particularly attractive to the very wealthy. She examines the role of trustees – or wealth managers – in enabling families to maintain their fortunes across generations, and to avoid or minimize taxation and regulation. From its medieval origins, trusteeship has developed from a voluntary role to a distinct profession of wealth management, with its own worldwide association. Despite that change, Harrington claims that there remains a consistent objective: to defend large concentrations of private wealth from outside intrusion through an aristocratic code of service and discretion. This historical continuity follows from the fact that trusts themselves have remained unchanged in important ways over some seven centuries. Even so, there has been a radical change in the type of assets trusts protect. From their feudal origins as a device to avoid inheritance restrictions and taxes occasioned by the death of the landowner, trusts have become a mechanism for holding a diverse portfolio of financial assets – from antiques to art collections and yachts. On the rare occasions when trust structures have come to public notice, their scale and complexity is astounding: a 2002 legal case revealed that a family fortune of $15 billion was held in 2,500 different trusts. From the viewpoint of such extraordinarily wealthy families, the advantages of trust structures are threefold: they avoid or minimize taxation; they secure privacy; and they facilitate various ways of transmitting assets which bypass formal legal structures. As the forms of assets contained by trusts changed, so did the role of trustees. From the original passive duty of holding title to a piece of land, trusteeship assumed the function of active financial management. Legal changes allowed trustees more discretion over the investment of trust assets and recognized them as an emerging professional class of wealth managers. In turn, these professionals sought to confirm their status by promoting formal credentials and a demarcation of their role as distinct from accountants or lawyers, through their own organization (Society of Trust and Estate Practitioners – STEP). With the mobility of wealth and the diversity of its forms, the activity of sheltering it from multiple tax jurisdictions involving different rules over transmission has become more complex and demanding. This activity by STEP members extends even to advising offshore and other tax havens on financial laws, as well as supporting those jurisdictions in their ambition to retain their favoured status.

If another mechanism to avoid inheritance taxation is *inter vivos* dispersal, then gift taxes are apparently attractive. In an impressive empirical analysis based on personal interviews and records of registered transfers, Carine Smolders examines the impact of the reform of gift taxes by the Flemish government in 2004. Through lowering gift taxes on mobile property and building plots, the reform sought to realize three objectives: to increase revenue; to raise the number of officially notified gifts; and to encourage earlier transfers between age cohorts. In relation to the last of these, the concern was that although savings were high, they were concentrated (as usual) in older age groups, who favoured dispersal *post mortem* rather than *inter vivos*. Consequently, inheritances were typically received in later stages of life, too late to help young adults – especially in the housing market. The analysis reveals that whereas revenue and registered gifts increased, there was no acceleration in transfers *inter vivos*. Far from that being the case, the average age of donors after the reform was 79, with the number of gifts by donors aged 80 or over increasing massively, compared to a smaller increase in the age group between 50 and 70 years old. The average age of beneficiaries was 50; and among beneficiaries only 15 per cent were under 36. Younger beneficiaries received smaller gifts than older ones and most of them were direct relatives of the donor. Given this profile, the general belief that parents donated money mainly to help their children acquire a house is not supported. Smolders offers some admittedly tentative explanations for these rather surprising results. By the age of 80 donors might finally recognize (or admit to themselves) that their life expectancy is very short, and that continued precautionary saving is rather pointless. Alternatively, gifts might be motivated by the strategic consideration that they constitute a form of exchange in return for increasing dependence on the family as a care provider. Even so, it is surprising that these considerations come into play so very late in life. Perhaps it is simply that old habits of *post mortem* disposition die hard. Smolders' conclusion that further investigation is needed to unravel why and when older generations choose to donate *inter vivos* is appropriate not only in relation to her own research but for the many issues about inherited wealth.

Common themes

As the foregoing makes clear, any consideration of the institution of property – whether private or otherwise – has to take account of its central role in social life and thus the way in which it is the object of analysis for many academic disciplines. It is therefore not surprising that the same is true for the more specific consideration of the intergenerational transmissibility of property. Although each contributor to this volume addresses this transmissibility from a particular academic viewpoint, common themes readily emerge. In the remainder of this introductory essay, we draw attention to the most prominent of these.

Mäkinen's chapter raises the issues of rights and duties with respect to property in the light of natural law and natural rights: the conceptions of inclusion and exclusion associated with the idea of dominion, the characterization of the set of rights and obligations associated with it, and whether these rights and obligations extend beyond the grave. She also attends to the discussion at the time as to who or what could be a *dominus*. The theme of dominion beyond the grave is explored further in Lamb's analysis of the tensions in Locke's *Two Treatises of Government* between the right to bequeath and the right to inherit, which also raise problems about the relationship between natural law and positive law. If dominion does extend beyond the grave, then bequest might be justified; but if inheritance trumps bequest, then dominion is confined to a lifetime, and the freedom of action of the current holder is potentially reduced. As Beckert emphasizes, the problem of control beyond the grave is especially acute in the device of entail. That device extended control across multiple generations, reaching into the distant future. Designed to keep property in the family, entail facilitated a particular dynastic and familial ambition. Cunliffe and Erreygers assess the particular conflict between family values and equal opportunities over time, in some notable radical proposals to reform inheritance practices in the mid-nineteenth century. The objections to these practices were twofold: they favoured unequal transmission, and that those lucky enough to receive an inheritance received it rather late in life. The proposed reform was a form of socialized inheritance, which would realize an equal and earlier inheritance and for all young adults. In considering objections to these proposals, the issues of family values and incentive structures were assessed, to counter the objection that the social inheritance fund would tend to zero.

The issues of property entitlement are examined further in their connections to citizenship and political status in contemporary political theory. Just as Edmund Burke had argued that the political rights of Englishmen were an entailed inheritance, like family property, so Shachar and Hirschl argue that birthright citizenship and the intergenerational transmission of political membership might be conceptualized as a form of property. Citizens' receipts are then independent of family status: they are received *qua* citizen, not *qua* heir. Whether and to what extent testamentary partiality towards family members as heirs can be legitimized is central to Clayton's examination of a non-perfectionist liberal egalitarian approach to the apparent tension between testamentary freedom and inequality in inheritance. His response adopts a Dworkinian approach which leads him to propose a steeply graduated inheritance tax.

The fiscal desirability of inheritance taxation (and its preferability to other forms of taxation) from the viewpoint of public finance, despite public opinion to the contrary, is stressed by Cremer and Pestieau. If redistributive considerations are also included, the desirability is enhanced. To promote earlier dispersal of assets in the interests of younger age cohorts Arrondel and Masson advocate *increased* inheritance taxation. From a political viewpoint, as Prabhakar argues, to concede to popular opinion opposed to inheritance taxation would only open the door to anti-egalitarians: they would simply change their target to another supposed redistributive tax mechanism.

The opposition to inheritance taxation is also discussed by Mumford, who proposes that the concerns are that assets are not only appropriated, but appropriated by the state, and at death. The combination of these three aspects reinforces Bordieusian scepticism about the legitimacy of state power. This sociological assessment might confirm Beckert's historical analysis of increasing scepticism towards the state since the 1970s. Even when the state has taken action with the specific objective of accelerating *inter vivos* transfers, the outcome so far, at least in the Flemish case, as Smolders shows, is that *post mortem* disposition still remains the norm, and moreover that *inter vivos* transfers still favour older age cohorts. Another objective of the Flemish reform was to increase tax revenue by increasing the number of officially recorded gifts *inter vivos*. Even if there were to have been some success in that particular case, Harrington demonstrates that any general ambition to close tax loopholes is likely to meet with failure, because the devices of the modern trust promote international tax avoidance effectively shielding family fortunes from regulatory endeavours, just as the entail shielded estates from testamentary freedom. These issues of tax avoidance and dynastic ambition are two further examples which help to explain the intensity and persistence of the debates about inherited wealth and its taxation discussed in this volume.

References

Beckert, J. (2008) *Inherited Wealth*, Princeton: Princeton University Press.

Blond, P. (2010) *Red Tory. How Left and Right Have Broken Britain*, London: Faber and Faber.

Willetts, D. (2010) *The Pinch: How the Baby Boomers Have Stolen Their Children's Future – And Why They Should Give It Back*, London: Atlantic.

2 Dominion rights of the aboriginals in Francisco de Vitoria's *De indis*

Virpi Mäkinen

The rights of aboriginals in history

Before the arrival of the Europeans, the Native Americans lived in communities, tribes or nations. Their habits of living were based on gathering, harvesting, farming, hunting and/or fishing. Their lands were shared communally; however, the North-American aboriginals did not understand them as property, either common or private as the Europeans. Thus the possession of inherited land has been much more like a community or tribal trust than a property of an individual. Many tribes were patriarchal and patrilinear. In some Indian tribes, women dominated the use and tenure of land, and thus, inheritance also passed through the maternal side. The latter culture was new to the Europeans. Since the conquerors were especially interested in the Native Americans' lands and resources, they used different ways to seize the lands and enslave the aboriginals.[1]

Many communities or tribes were, for example, subjected either to the Spanish systems of 'encomienda' or 'repartimiento', which were established by the Spanish crown during the colonization of the Americas to occupy lands, to regulate Native American labour and to support Spanish missionary, military and civil institutions.[2] Other strategies to occupy lands were by purchasing them or moving the Indians to reservations. All these systems often violated the traditional habits and culture of the Indians, and ignored their traditional ways of seeing the land as something that was shared communally.

Going back to the fifteenth century and to the beginning of the conquest by the Spaniards, the Castilian Crown claimed rights to Columbus's 'discoveries' as well as to the Native Americans referring, on the one hand, to the Bulls of Donation promulgated by Pope Alexander VI (Pope from 1492–1503) in 1493. The Crown interpreted these bulls in the widest possible ways so that all the lands inhabited by non-Christians they might discover across the Atlantic belonged to their dominion.[3] On the other hand, the Crown referred to a Castilian statutory code called the *Siete partidas* (Third Part, Title 28, Law 29), which included the Roman legal idea of islands belonging to their first occupant.[4] One of the first far-reaching debates on the rights of the aboriginal people of the New World started during the colonization of the Americas in the early sixteenth century.[5] In Spain, King Ferdinand (1452–1516) convened a commission (*junta*) of theologians and lawyers to consider the matter in 1513. During the same year, they published the Laws of Burgos, which was the first colonial legislation in Spain. The discussion led to international contention and lasted until the end of the eighteenth century.[6] Importantly, this discussion led to the origins of international law offering both a legal and politico-theological terminology to organise the relations between Europeans and the natives.[7]

In these debates, among the central questions was whether the Indians were true masters (*domini*) and thus possessed dominion over those lands they occupied before the arrival of the Spaniards. The later popes supported the rights of the indigenous people to their lands and issued many bulls on the subject. In his declaration *Sublimus Deus* of 1537, Pope Paul III (Pope from 1534–1549), for instance, wrote about the land rights of the Indians as follows:

> Indians and all other people who may later be discovered by Christians are to be by no means deprived of their liberty or the possession of their property; ... should the contrary happen, it shall be null and have no effect.

Other questions were also raised relating to the ownership of lands, which concerned the rationality (and humanity) of the Indians as well as the right to enslave them. Pope Paul, however, declared that the aboriginal people were fully rational human beings with souls and rejected their enslavement. The Crown's legal advisor, Juan Lopez Palacios Rubios (*c.*1450–1542) argued similarly already in 1512.[8]

A Spanish Dominican theologian, Francisco de Vitoria (*c.*1485–1546) took part in the dispute over the legitimacy of the colonization of the Americas in the summer of 1523.[9] In this chapter, my main aim is to discuss Francisco de Vitoria's theory of rights in his *De indis* in general, and more particularly, his theory of property rights which is closely related to the discussion on the legitimacy of the aboriginals' rights to their lands before and after the arrival of the Spaniards. *De indis* considered current political questions of aboriginal rights under the Castilian Crown, which Vitoria had divided into three main titles: (1) On the dominion of the barbarians[10]; (2) By what unjust titles the barbarians of the New World passed under the rule of the Spaniards; and (3) The just titles by which the barbarians of the New World passed under the rule of the Spaniards.[11] I will also use his other work, the commentary on Thomas Aquinas's *Prima secundae* and *Secunda secundae* of the *Summa theologiae*, where he discussed the theory of *dominium*, rights and justice.[12]

Ius gentium and the idea of expansive universal law

In the introduction of the *De indis*, Vitoria stated his main starting point:

> Since these barbarians we speak of are not subjects [of the Spanish Crown] by human law (*iure humano*), as I shall show in a moment, their affairs cannot be judged by human statutes (*leges humanae*), but only by divine ones, in which jurists are not successfully versed to form an opinion of their own.[13]

Vitoria very clearly stated that the case of Indians should not be discussed under human law. Therefore the Spanish system of 'encomienda', for example, was invalid.[14] However, his reference to divine law and its statutes is not explicit. Vitoria seems to refer to a divinely created natural law that contained precepts which were imprinted into the human mind by God at birth.[15] Therefore, all people, including infidels such as Indians, were guided by same natural law.[16] What Vitoria tries to show is that the case of Indians should be discussed under such a law that firstly covers everyone (i.e. all humans whether they are Christians or infidels) and secondly is universally applicable everywhere. Later on, he often referred to *ius gentium* as such a law. However, he did not give any coherent definition of *ius gentium* and thus it remains a somewhat unclear conception in his theory.

The notion of *ius gentium* was adapted to medieval and early modern usage from ancient legal and philosophical thought where it was seen as one source of law in relation to natural law (*ius naturale*) and civil law (*ius civile*). The interpretation of the *ius gentium* varied in these texts and especially in Roman legal sources which were the main document for Vitoria. For example, a Roman lawyer, Ulpian (AD 193–235) defined *ius gentium* as the law common to all communities, whereas Gaius (fl. AD 130–180) interpreted it in relation to natural law (*ius naturale*) and sometimes identified these two sources of law. The definition of *ius naturale* was also inconsistent in these sources as well as in the medieval canon law sources. In Roman law, some saw it as a law common to all animals whereas *ius gentium* concerned only human beings or the non-citizens and *ius civile* confined only to Roman citizens. All these caused Vitoria difficulties in defining *ius gentium*,[17] and as Koskenniemi describes it, Vitoria 'is frustratingly unclear about its legal nature'.[18] He seems, however, to consider *ius gentium* more as a matter of custom (and therefore of positive law) than of natural law since the rules under *ius gentium* were often based on 'pacts and agreements' and on a universal custom (examples of the notions under *ius gentium* were private property, the right to travel and trade). Since *ius gentium* also consisted of rules to which all nations adhere and they had a certain moral foundation, Vitoria also considered it to be based more or less directly on natural law. In his lectures *De potestate civile*, Vitoria described *ius gentium* as a set of precepts enacted by the power of 'the whole world, which is in a sense a commonwealth'.[19] He termed these precepts as irrespective of the local legislative convictions, beliefs and customs of individual communities.[20] It has been argued that Vitoria's notion of *ius gentium* paved the way for the later notion of international law.[21] He seems to be at least an early developer of international law.

Vitoria and subjective rights tradition

As a Dominican theologian, Vitoria naturally operated within the Aristotelian–Thomistic tradition, often citing both Aristotle (384–322 BC) and Thomas Aquinas (1225–1274). Vitoria, however, used the sources that belonged to nominalist-voluntaristic subjectivism and was thus familiar with subjective rights theories. One of the most cited scholars within this tradition was the German theologian Conrad Summenhart (1458–1502) whose doctrine of dominion rights he further developed.[22] Vitoria also relied on classical philosophy, in particular on Roman Stoic philosophers Cicero (106–43 BC) and Seneca (*c.*4 BC–AD 65).[23]

Vitoria's position between two main philosophical traditions – *via antiqua* (the Aristotelian-Thomistic tradition) and *via moderna* (the nominalistic-voluntaristic tradition) – and his ability to compose material from both these traditions was essential also to his ideas on rights. It has been argued that the Aristotelian tradition provided a basis for the classical doctrine of objectively understood natural right that scholastic authors inherited and exemplified in their doctrine of the natural law.[24] Thomas Aquinas, for instance, is seen to represent this tradition. For him, *ius* was primarily a thing (*res*), something existing in external reality, as justice (*to dikaion*) also was for Aristotle and *ius* for Ulpian. Aquinas followed the ancient legal and philosophical traditions, and for him the most common definition of *ius* was that it is an objective entity. The ancient concept of objective right was reshaped into the modern language of subjectively understood rights when new insights of a human person were introduced. According to recent studies, subjectively understood rights require the supposition of a power inhering in an individual and thus late medieval voluntarist psychology seems like a necessary theoretical basis for subjective rights.[25] In this framework, a person was conceived as an autonomous individual and a member of a civic state that, on the basis of a social contract, protects the rights of the individual. However, the subjective and the objective interpretations together[26] and the objective perspective as employed by the Spanish scholastics in the sixteenth century also gave rise to new ways of articulating subjective rights – as Vitoria's theory will show.[27]

Most modern scholars have interpreted Vitoria as the inheritor of the subjective rights tradition. According to Brian Tierney, Vitoria's discussion in the first part of the *De indis* concerned individual natural rights because 'the subsequent discussion centered on the term *dominium* ... [which] was nothing else but a right'. Thus Vitoria's 'argument was essentially about rights and, insofar as he was considering natural dominion, about natural rights'.[28] Luis Cortest challenges Tierney and argues instead that 'the difference between the traditional notion of *dominium* as Vitoria understood it and a doctrine of "natural rights" is vast'. According to Cortest, Vitoria followed a traditional Thomistic teaching of *dominium* as a right that denotes the thing itself (i.e. an objective meaning of right) and his primary issue in the *De indis* concerned legal and civil jurisdiction, not natural rights. 'The only way that Tierney's claim can be true', Cortest added, 'is if we are convinced that Vitoria radically changed the doctrine defended by St. Thomas. In fact, this is precisely what Tierney tries to prove'.[29] Annabel Brett describes Vitoria's doctrine of *dominium* right as '*the* (unqualified) subjective right, or better, subjective right *simpliciter*'. According to her interpretation, Vitoria understood *dominium* right as a common idea, and not as something which belonged separately to each individual.[30] Thomas Williams sees Vitoria as a contributor to natural rights theory. His argument is based on the interpretation of both Aquinas's and Vitoria's contribution to individual rights. Considering Aquinas's theory, Williams argues that the notion of 'right' (*ius*) was often 'a static term with single application'. Aquinas also made 'note of the etymological development that the word had already undergone in the 13th century', that is to the subjectively understood notions of right.[31] Jörg Alejandro Tellkamp also sees Vitoria as a representative of the subjective rights tradition. His argument is based on careful comparison between Vitoria's and Conrad Summenhart's treatment of *dominium* rights.[32] Martti Koskenniemi points out Vitoria's importance both in the history of individual rights and in the early history of international law. According to Koskenniemi, Vitoria's re-evaluating of the conception of *ius gentium* and the way he related it to his notion of *dominium* rights (understood as individual rights) was crucial also for the development of international law.[33]

Qualities for possessing *dominium* right

In his *De indis*, Vitoria did not provide explicit definitions of *dominium*, although it is a central notion in his theory of rights. He did, however, refer to the discussion of restitution in his lectures on Lombard's *Sentences* (IV.15) and on Aquinas's *Summa theologiae* (2a 2ae, a. 62).[34] In his definition of *dominium* there, Vitoria referred to Conrad Summenhart's discussion of the several meanings of *dominium*. He begins by defining the notion of *ius*, citing Summenhart: 'It should be noted that Conrad ... posits in q. 1 a definition of that term "right" ... [which] is a power or faculty pertaining to a person according to the laws.'[35] This mode of definition of *ius* as a faculty (*facultas*) or power (*potestas*) within a person was common already from the late Middle Ages onwards. Summenhart himself referred to several sources, such as to Antonino and Jean Gerson.[36] After the definition of 'a right', Vitoria turned to discuss the equivalence between *dominium* and *ius*. This equivalence was a common notion among scholastics from the mid-thirteenth century onwards.[37] In this particular part, he distinguished between three modes of *dominium* with regard to the equivalence with *ius*. First, *dominium* could refer in its strict sense to a certain superiority, for instance, when rulers had dominion over their subjects, and were therefore called *domini*. According to Vitoria, this kind of dominion was not equivalent to *ius* because the notion of right was a broader category than *dominium* understood in this way. An inferior, for example, could have a right which contradicted a superior even though he had no dominion over him.[38] The second mode of *dominium* concerned its legal sense, as stated in *Corpus iuris civilis* and by the jurists, when it is understood as the ownership of property. In this meaning, too, *dominium* was not equivalent to *ius*. A person could, for instance, have a right to a piece of property, such as use or usufruct, without being its actual owner.[39] According to Vitoria, the largest mode of *dominium* concerned the faculty to use a thing in accordance with law. In this mode, *dominium* was equivalent to *ius*.[40] Thus we can call Vitoria's notion of the equivalence as *dominium ius*. This largest sense Vitoria also took from Summenhart.[41] As Annabel Brett notes, 'Vitoria thus appears to adopt from Summenhart the weak sense of *dominium* in which its peculiar senses of eminence or superiority, and of property, are lost in its equivalence with right'. Moreover, Vitoria did not treat 'his concept of *dominium–ius* as simply a juridical hold on other objects or persons' but understood it to cover 'the same sense of freedom and authority which it has in traditional mendicant theology and in Aquinas'.[42] Strictly speaking, *De justitia*, question 62, is, therefore, a theory of *dominium*, rather than of *ius* (a right).[43] According to Brett's interpretation, Vitoria did argue that natural right (in the sense of natural law) did conserve one's being 'but man is not said to have the "natural right" of conserving himself in being'. In spite of the importance of natural right, Vitoria is speaking here about dominion,[44] and this seems to be Vitoria's argumentation in his *De justitia*, question 62.

In *De indis*, the notion of *dominium* is also treated as equivalent to *ius* concerning both the juridical senses of superiority and property, as well as in the sense of freedom and authority. The first question of the *De indis* and its clarifications provide proof for this argument. Here, Vitoria asks: 'Whether these aboriginals, before the arrival of the Spaniards, had true dominion, public or private?' He clarified his question as follows: 'That is to say, whether they were true masters of their private chattels and possessions, and whether there existed among them any men who were true princes and masters of the others.'[45] The first part of the question concerned property rights, whereas the latter concerned superiority. Vitoria immediately gives his conclusion to these questions, stating that the Indians could be treated as having undisputed possession of their property, both publicly and privately. Therefore 'they must be held to be true masters (*domini*), and may not be dispossessed without due cause'.[46] His whole *relectiones* are concerned with providing arguments to prove this conclusion. I will especially focus on his arguments with regard to the property rights of aboriginal people.

In order to prove his arguments, Vitoria first discussed the qualifications for having *dominium* rights. He referred to four possible grounds for denying a status of true *domini* from the Indians. These were 'that they were either sinners (*peccatores*), unbelievers (*infideles*), madmen (*amentes*), or insensate (*insensati*)'.[47] Vitoria then discussed these grounds in greater depth. These qualifications provide the basis of Vitoria's idea of *dominium* rights as dominium of *human beings*, which is also the ground for his theory of political power founded on consent.

Concerning the first ground, whether sinners or those in a state of mortal sin can be true masters, Vitoria referred to some thinkers, especially to John Wycliff (*c.*1328–1384) and Richard FitzRalph (*c.*1300–1360), as well as to the Waldensians. He mentioned that the heresy of the Poor Men of Lyon (i.e. the Waldensians) and later of Wycliff was that they hold that 'the title to any dominion is grace, and consequently that "sinners, or at least those who are in a state of mortal sin, cannot exercise dominion over anything"'.[48] Vitoria further added that concerning the heresies condemned by the Council of Constance the opinion was raised that 'No one is a civil master while he is in a state of mortal sin'. He articulated the same heretical opinion to the Archbishop of Armagh, Richard FitzRalph, referring largely to his teaching on the subject. According to Vitoria, FitzRalph had, for instance, stated that 'dominion is formed in the image of God; but the image of God is not in the sinner, hence the sinner cannot have dominion' or 'the sinner commits the crime of lese-majesty, and therefore deserves to lose his dominion'.[49]

Vitoria replied to these arguments by stating that neither Wycliff nor FitzRalph made the necessary distinctions between natural (*dominium naturale*) and civil dominion (*dominium civile*), but referred solely to the dominion of sovereignty which belongs to princes (in another edition 'to the right of jurisdiction (*dominium jurisdictionis*) or lordship').[50] These kinds of arguments, Vitoria pointed out, were not applicable to all types of ownership (*dominium rerum*), both public and private, but were intended to apply to dominion in general.[51] As the Council of Constance (1414–1418) had already determined, 'mortal sin is no impediment to the civil right of ownership, not to true dominion'.[52] Vitoria, therefore, argued as follows:

> I prove the consequence; for natural dominion (*dominium naturale*) is a gift of God, just as a civil dominion [ownership] is, nay, more so, for civil dominion seems an institute of human law. Therefore, if for an offence against God a man loses civil dominion, he would for the same reason lose his natural dominion also. But the falsity of the consequent is demonstrated by the fact that the man in question [a sinner] does not lose dominion over his own acts and over his own limbs, for a sinner has a right to defend his own life.[53]

Vitoria states here a defence of self-dominion that every human being, as the image of God, had. He also added that since 'man is God's image by nature, that is, by his reasoning powers; therefore, dominion is not lost by mortal sin'. Vitoria spoke here natural dominion every human being had.[54]

For the second question, 'whether at any rate dominion may be lost by reason of unbelief', Vitoria first discussed the case of heretics and later of unbelievers.[55] His conclusion for the whole question concerning Indians is the following:

> the barbarians in question cannot be barred from being true owners, alike in public and in private law, by reason of the sin of unbelief or any other mortal sin, nor does such sin entitle Christians to seize their goods and lands.[56]

According to Vitoria, the third question, 'whether the Indians lacked ownership because of want of reason or unsoundness of mind', concerned the matter debated earlier among late medieval scholars of whether a human being requires the use of reason in order to have dominion.[57] Vitoria approached this question by discussing the case of non-rational beings, i.e. animals. He referred to certain authors who had concluded that non-rational creatures might have dominion. One of these authors was Conrad Summenhart, who had argued that both sensate and insensate non-rational creatures had dominion. According to Vitoria, Summenhart had defined dominion as 'the right to use a thing for one's own benefit' (*ius utendi re in usum suum*) and had stated that brute creatures have this sort of use from grasses and plants as well as the stars have the right to shed their light.[58]

Vitoria states the opposite: 'Irrational creatures cannot have any dominion. This is clear, because dominion is a right, as even Conrad admits'.[59] He presents several arguments to defend his idea. He begins by stating that dominion is a legal right (*dominium est ius*) and irrational creatures cannot have legal rights.[60] Interestingly, Vitoria again uses Summenhart's definition of *dominium*, but this time he provides his own arguments. Another proof is that irrational creatures cannot be victims of an injustice (*iniuria*). According to Vitoria, 'to deprive a wolf or a lion of its prey is no injustice against the beast in question, anymore than to shut out the sun's light by drawing the blinds is an injustice against the sun'.[61]

Vitoria's second argument is that wild animals have no rights over their own bodies (*dominium sui*) and, therefore, they cannot have rights over other things either. He confirms the argument by stating that it is lawful to kill them with impunity, even for pleasure.[62] The third argument is based on Aquinas's idea of self-mastery. According to this view, every rational creature has mastery over its own actions (*dominium sui actus*). Other animals act by necessity. 'If, then, brutes have no dominion over their own actions, they can have no dominion over other things', Vitoria concludes.[63] All the above arguments show how Vitoria stresses in his doctrine of dominion right the unique value and status of a *human* person.

In this connection, Vitoria also discussed the question of whether children before the age of reason can be true masters. According to him, children can have legal rights and, therefore, a right of ownership (*dominium rerum*) first, because they could suffer injustice (*iniuria*); second, because 'the possessions of an orphan minor in guardianship are not the property of the guardians'; third, because 'a child in guardianship may legally inherit property; but an heir is defined in law as the person who succeeds to the inheritance of the deceased, hence the child is the owner of the inheritance'; and fourth, since the foundation of dominion is based on the fact that every human being is already formed in the image of God, and the child is already formed in the image of God, thus he can be a true master. Last, Vitoria added that the child did not exist for another's use, like an animal, but for himself – which was also an important factor for being a rights-bearing person.[64]

Concerning the question whether madmen can be true masters, Vitoria first clarified that for madmen he meant 'the incurably mad, who can neither have nor expect ever to have the use of reason'.[65] In his reply he maintained that these madmen too might be true masters because they can also be the victims of injustice (*iniuria*) and therefore, have legal rights. However, Vitoria did not respond to the question whether they have civil dominion.[66] Considering the case of the Indians, Vitoria pointed out that they were 'not in point of fact madmen, but have, in their own way, the use of reason'.[67] He justified the argument as follows:

> This is clear, because there is a certain order (*ordo*) in their affairs, for they have polities which are orderly arranged and they have definite marriage and magistrates, overlords (*domini*), laws, and workshops, and a system of exchange, all of which require the use of reason; they also have a form (*species*) of religion. Further, they make no error in matters which are self-evident to others; this is evidence of the use of reason. Furthermore, God and nature never fail in the things necessary for the majority of the species. Now the special quality in man is reason, and potency which is not actualized is in vain.[68]

Vitoria's understanding of the qualities required for an ordered society are adapted from Aristotle's criteria for the civil life in *Politics*.[69] He also referred here to another of Aristotle's principles in accordance with 'nature does nothing in vain'.[70] With this principle Vitoria aimed to prove that the Indians as human beings potentially have the use of reason. Since they were able to have reason, they in fact did have it.[71] Vitoria ended with the notice that if the Indians 'seem to us insensate and slow-witted' it is mainly because of their evil and barbarous education. Sarcastically he added: 'Even amongst ourselves we see many peasants (*rustici*) who are little different from brute animals.'[72]

Vitoria concluded the first question in his *De indis*, where he had discussed the four kinds of qualities to possess dominion right as follows:

> the aborigines undoubtedly had true dominion in both public and private matters, just like Christians, and that neither their princes nor private persons could be despoiled deprived of their property on the ground of their not being true owners (*veri domini*). It would be harsh to deny to those, who have never done any wrong, what we grant to Saracens and Jews, who are the persistent enemies of Christianity. We do not deny that these latter peoples are true owners of their property (*dominium rerum*), if they have not seized lands elsewhere belonging to Christians.[73]

Arguments for common dominion rights

It was common to medieval as well as to early modern scholars that their theories of property rights considered the origins and division of property. As we have already seen, Vitoria understood that only human beings could have dominion rights and one sense of *dominium* was a property right. According to him, right and dominion (*ius et dominium*) were given to human beings over other creatures.[74] One reason was the natural law principle concerning the common possessions among all and the duty of self-preservation which involved the use of other creatures in order to survive. In accordance with this principle, every human had a right of using (*jus utendi*) other creatures.[75] Vitoria followed here other late medieval (e.g. William of Ockham) and early modern (e.g. Hugo Grotius) scholars who also maintained use rights where self-preservation was concerned. Henry of Ghent and Godfrey of Fontaines understood the duty of self-preservation even more strongly as a right to life.[76] It is interesting that Vitoria uses here the language that had been in use already in the long-lasting Franciscan poverty controversy (1250–1340). The notion of *ius utendi* was central for Ockham's theory of natural rights. He distinguished between the natural right of using (*ius utendi naturale*) and the positive right of using (*ius utendi positivum*). The latter form was 'common to all men, because it is had from nature, and not by some additional enactment', but it could be restricted by human law and by different kinds of permissions. The positive right of using was a juridical entity which was stated by human agreement.[77] Vitoria seems to use the notion of *ius utendi* in the same sense as Ockham.

Importantly, Vitoria maintained that this kind of right and dominion to use other creatures belonged to the human race not only universally or communally but also in the state of integral nature (*status naturae integrae*). With the notion of *status naturae integrae* Vitoria denotes to the state of man's original nature before the Fall. In this state, humans had God-given power to use and abuse (i.e. exploit/use up) all things provided for them as long as they did not harm other people or themselves.[78] He understood this power (i.e. right and dominion over other creatures) as a natural right (i.e. natural *dominium*).

The divisions of property

As we have seen, Vitoria argued that every individual human being was the *dominus* of all things with regard to use and abuse and this right and dominion was based on God's grant. How then can anyone deny a person this natural right to use and abuse (i.e. exploit) everything? Vitoria discussed this issue by referring to Summenhart, who had argued that 'natural law could be binding, recommendatory and permissive'.[79] The basic idea of this threefold division was that natural law was made of different kind of sentences that oblige to a different degree. Vitoria's solution was 'that the natural law ordaining community of property was not a precept binding for all time but only a kind of permissive law'.[80] This was a solution he derived from Summenhart who had it from the Franciscan theologian Alexander of Hales.[81] According to Vitoria, it was possible to divide up common dominion into private property in three ways: First, by Adam; second, by the elected ruler; or third, by the common consent of people. Here Vitoria again followed Summenhart.[82] In his discussion of the rights of the Indians over their lands, Vitoria focused primarily on the third point. He maintained that the majority could divide up the lands or decide to follow the principle of first occupant. He also pointed out that only virtual agreement (*consensus virtuali*), not formal consent among people or just one person starting to farm a piece of land, was enough to qualify as ownership.[83] Since this kind of division was valid everywhere, it could not be based on the civil law of any state. It was based on *ius gentium*.[84]

In his *De indis*, Vitoria also referred to the theory of first occupancy when defending the property rights of Indians to their lands before the coming of the Spaniards. According to the theory of first occupancy, which was drawn from Roman legal tradition, something which did not belong to anyone (*res nullius*) became the property of the first taker.[85] Referring to this theory, the Indians were legally the true owners of those lands as they were the first to occupy them.

In another context, however, Vitoria used the same theory to argue the Spanish rather than the Indian case. When speaking about trade he argued that the sea bed or the pearls in the sea, or anything else in the rivers that had not been appropriated, would belong by the law of nations (*ius gentium*) to the first taker, just as fish in the sea would belong to those who caught them first.[86] Dominion over the seas was naturally an important political matter for the Spaniards. Vitoria even added that the Spaniards might export the gold, silver, or other things which the Indians had in abundance since 'the law of nations (*ius gentium*) is clearly that travellers may carry on trade so long as they do not do harm to the citizens'. Also, if there were any things among the barbarians which were held in common both by their own people and by strangers, it was not lawful for the barbarians to prohibit the Spaniards from sharing and enjoying them. The Spaniards, however, were allowed to do this kind of thing only 'without causing offence to the native inhabitants and citizens'.[87]

The question of power and authority

The dominion rights of Indians over their territories also concerned the political question of imperial and papal power and especially divergent claims to *dominium* (in the sense of power and authority) of the whole world.[88] Vitoria thus asked whether the Indians had some superior temporal overlord, and also discussed the extent of the power of the Spanish emperor and the pope and their right to Indian lands. Question two of *De indis* considered seven 'unjust titles' for conquest, all of which depended either on spurious claims to world sovereignty by the pope and the emperor, or on the supposition that the Christian faith might be imposed by force.[89] I will only discuss the titles that are relevant to our subject.

Vitoria's conclusion was that 'even if the emperor were master of the world, he could not on that account occupy the lands of the barbarians, or depose their masters and set up new ones, or impose taxes on them'.[90] The proof for the argument was that even those who attributed dominion of the whole world to the emperor did not claim that he had it by property (*per proprietatem*), but only that he had it by jurisdiction (*per iurisdictionem*). Thus he concluded: 'Such a right does not include the licence to turn whole countries to his own use, or dispose at whim townships or even estates,' and 'from everything that has been said, therefore, it is clear that the Spaniards could not invade these lands using this first title'.[91] The same concerned the power of the pope. Vitoria distinguished the spiritual and temporal power stating that 'the pope is not the civil or temporal master of the world, in the proper meaning of "dominion" and "civil power"'.[92] The pope had temporal power only insofar as it concerned spiritual matters. Considering the Indians, Vitoria continued that the pope had no temporal power over the barbarians, or any other unbelievers, but he did not have even spiritual jurisdiction over infidels.[93]

Vitoria then turned to discuss the third unjust title, namely that the possession of these countries was by right of discovery (*in iure inventiones*). This law stated that 'all things which are unoccupied or deserted become the property of the occupier by natural law and the law of nations' (*ius gentium*).[94] Since the barbarians already possessed true public and private dominion before the arrival of the Spaniards, as Vitoria had shown earlier, and because the law of nations also stated that 'goods which belong to no owner pass to the occupier ... the goods in question here had an owner' – the Indians.[95] Here Vitoria also used the *ius gentium* in order to defend the case of the Indians.

Concerning the sixth unjust title, the voluntary choice of the barbarians, Vitoria referred again to Roman law. It has been stated in the *Institutiones* that 'nothing is so natural as that the will of an owner who wishes to transfer his property to another should be ratified'.[96] However, for Vitoria this title was inapplicable because the choice ought not to have been made in fear and ignorance. He pointed out that the 'barbarians do not realize what they are doing; perhaps, indeed, they do not even understand what it is the Spaniards are asking of them'. Vitoria concluded that on account of a lack of requisite conditions for a legitimate choice the occupation of countries overseas was neither appropriate nor legitimate.[97]

Dominion rights, justice and equality

In the introduction of *De indis*, entitled 'Whether this dispute is justified', Vitoria commented on the situation of the Indians as follows: 'But when we hear subsequently of bloody massacres and of innocent individuals pillaged of their possessions and dominions, there are grounds for doubting the justice of what has been done.'[98] Thus his defence of the case of the Indians and their dominion rights were closely related to justice. Vitoria dealt the notion of *dominium* in the context of commutative justice, 'that is relationships between subjects themselves, excluding the ideas about the intervention of public power'. He sees this just relationship between human beings – i.e. a commutative justice – as basis of his theory of dominion rights and its universal applicability.[99]

In this last section, I will sum up Vitoria's ideas on the dominion rights of Indians and argue that his doctrine of dominion rights in general and of property rights in particular represent the natural rights tradition, where rights were understood as subjectively belonging to each individual person.

It has been argued that the Aristotelian tradition provided a basis for the classical doctrine of objectively understood natural right that medieval scholastic authors like Thomas Aquinas inherited and exemplified in their doctrine of natural law.[100] In the Aristotelian–Thomistic tradition in general, a right was understood as 'the just portion which is due between persons, rather than something belonging to the person herself'; it was an object to justice (*ius est iustitia*); an objective entity.[101] In his treatment of dominion rights, Vitoria also uses this objectively understood definition of a right and blends it with his idea of individual rights in a novel way.

The subjective rights idea that a right was something which inherently belonged to a person on the grounds of humanity and individuality started to develop as early as the late Middle Ages. The importance of late medieval voluntarist psychology is seen as a necessary theoretical basis for this development. However, recent studies have also shown that the distinction between objective right and subjective rights was not clear among medieval and early modern thinkers. On the one hand, the whole vocabulary concerning *ius* and other similar terms such as *dominium* and *possessio* related to ownership varied from one author to another, and the terms were interpreted differently in different sources. What is more, even the same author could have different meanings for one term. For example, the term *dominium* could refer to private property rights, possession in general, or authority in a political sense. Some authors, Conrad Summenhart for instance, gave almost 20 different explanations of *dominium*.[102]

Thus late medieval and early modern authors operated in the language of subjective individual rights along with objectively understood right. These two interpretations (objective and subjective) developed together and the objective perspective, as employed by the School of Salamanca also gave rise to new ways of articulating subjective rights. This is evident in Vitoria's doctrine of dominion rights as well. Vitoria's interpretations both of Aristotle and Aquinas (the Aristotelian–Thomistic objective right tradition) and of Conrad Summenhart (the voluntarist-nominalistic subjective rights tradition) were often tendentious and did not always consider their discussions from a wider perspective. Some scholars have stated that objective rights in later medieval scholasticism cannot be seen as a direct opposite of subjective rights. All of these senses of right were available to Vitoria.[103] However, the way he connected these two traditions paved the way and provided important material for later interpretations of individual rights as the basis of moral, legal and political discussion among the other representatives of the School of Salamanca.[104]

Besides justice, Vitoria's idea of individual dominion rights also entailed the notion of the fundamental liberty of human beings. He considered human beings to have self-mastery and to be autonomous rights-bearing individuals and members of a civic state on the basis of a social contract that protects the individual's rights.[105] The very idea of possessing dominion rights (Vitoria used the notion *dominium sui*) indicated a rational human being who owned him- or herself, and was, therefore, *sui iuris*. This was an important factor in Vitoria's theory: the existence of rights was based on the possession of a rationality, not in the exercise of reason.[106] Thus the core of Vitoria's doctrine of dominion rights was that all human beings, whether they were sinners, infidels or mad men, could be right-holders in a legal and moral sense and, therefore, also masters (*domini*) in their own affairs (*sui iuris*). This explicates a fundamental equality between human beings.

Vitoria's main point regarding the aboriginal people's right of ownership over their lands was that they were the true owners (*veri domini*). They had *dominium* rights over the lands before the arrival of the Spaniards and thus the Castilian crown had no legal or moral reason to take them away. Vitoria's notion of *dominium* rights explicated that he understood it also as an exclusive right. This was not only based on the defence of dominion rights (including property rights) for the community but also individually. According to Vitoria, property implied a form of ownership, but for the most part, the ownership could only be of qualities inherent in the subject. Vitoria also thought that the Indians had full *dominium* which covered use rights as well as rights to dispose property as one likes, e.g. to sell, hire or exchange it. He did not explicate the right to inheritance but referred to the idea implicitly. Nevertheless, the idea of true *dominium* included a right to inheritance.

It is important to notice that Vitoria tried to develop a concept of expansive universal law which would solve the case of native inhabitants. For him, the Indians had *dominium* rights to their lands in accordance with the law of nations (*ius gentium*). These rights also included the right to inheritance. However, Vitoria explicated it only in one sentence. In this way, Vitoria was able to speak their rights as natural, human rights. Unfortunately, Vitoria's *De indis* was used for contrary policies.

Notes

1 Arnold (2011) which is mainly based on Folsom's (1996) larger study on the subject. Folsom's study is, however, problematic for my subject since his examples concern mainly the Pueblo tribes. In Vitoria's time, the Spanish conquistadores had hardly met these tribes. I thank Markku Henriksson, Professor of American Studies (University of Helsinki) for explaining Native American history to me, and especially the different kinds of 'Indian' tribes and nations. I have used here Andersson and Henriksson (2010); Valtonen (2002).

2 Ortiz (1996: 14–15) explains both systems in his introduction to Folsom's (1996) study.

3 Pagden (1991: xxiv).

4 Koskenniemi (2010: 48).

5 Pope Innocent IV (Pope from 1243–1254) defended the rights of infidels as early as the mid-thirteenth century. According to Williams (2004: 54), the Dominican friar Antón Montesino (*c.*1475–1540) was the first to make an appeal on behalf of the aboriginal peoples of the New World in Salamanca in 1511.

6 See Pagden and Lawrence (2010: xxiii).

7 Koskenniemi (2010: 44).

8 See Palacios Rubios (1954).

9 For Vitoria's participation in the debate, see Williams (2004: 54–55); Pagden and Lawrence (2010: xxiii–xxviii); Koskenniemi (2010: 47–49). For Vitoria's life, education and career, see Martín (1995). Williams (2004: 54) points out that Vitoria's first document concerning the subject was a letter to his religious superior, Miguel de Arcos, at the monastery of St. Gregory at Valladolid. In it, Vitoria condemned the Spanish colonists for their abusive treatment of the indigenous people. For the letter, see Vitoria (2010: 331–333).

10 Vitoria often used the notion of 'barbarians' when discussing the case of the Indians. Sometimes he also referred to them by the term 'Indians'. Pagden and Lawrence (2010) follow Vitoria in their translation. Bate (1995) prefers 'Indians' or the modern term 'aboriginals' in his translation. I mainly follow the translation by Pagden and Lawrence (2010).

11 The titles are added within the text by Pagden and Lawrence in their translation of *De indis*, see Vitoria (2010: 233–292). In the Latin edition, I have used (edited by Nys 1995) the titles are listed in the beginning of each part.

12 Vitoria did not publish anything himself. His pupils collected his writings into two categories: first, the *lectio* (lecture) on Aquinas's *Summa theologiae* and on Peter Lombard's *Sentences*; second, a series of *relectiones* (rereadings), formal public lectures which consider the particular topics related to the lectio. Tierney (1997: 265).

13 *De indis*, 222: '…quia cum illi barbari, ut statim dicam, non essent subiecti iure humano, res illorum non sunt examinandae per leges humanas, sed divinas, quarum iuristae non sunt satis periti, ut per se possint huiusmodi quaestiones diffinire.' Translation by Pagden and Lawrence in Vitoria (2010: 238).

14 Vitoria did not explicitly refer to it but another Dominican defender of the Indians and Vitoria's pupil, Bartolomé de Las Casas (*c.*1484–1566), called it 'a satanic invention' in his preface to *In Defense of the Indians* (Las Casas, 1967: 7).

15 See also Tierney (1997: 265).

16 For Vitoria's interpretation of the hierarchy of laws, see Niemelä (2008: 315–319).

17 Pagden and Lawrence in Vitoria (2010: 280, note 77).

18 Koskenniemi (2010: 51).

19 *De potestate civile* 3.4.

20 Pagden and Lawrence (2010: xv–xvi), where they also point out that Vitoria differs here from Aquinas's understanding of *ius gentium*. For Aquinas *ius gentium* was not essentially a part of the positive law as it was for Vitoria. According to Vitoria, *ius gentium* was 'that which is not equitable of itself, but [has been established] by human statute grounded in reason'. See *De potestate civile* 3.12.

21 Scott (1934); Tierney (1997: 265); Niemelä (2008), who speaks about Vitoria's inconsistent idea of international law; Koskenniemi (2010). Cf. Pagden and Lawrence (2010: xvi), where they state that to argue Vitoria as the father of international law 'is anachronistic, since the conception of an "international law" has its origins in the "modern" natural-law theorists, notably Hugo Grotius, Samuel Pufendorf, and John Selden, whose project was very different from Vitoria's, and wholly indifferent to the Thomist definition of *ius*'.

22 For Vitoria's teaching on rights, see Tierney (1997: 255–272); Brett (1997: 124–137); Koskenniemi (2010).

23 It is possible that also the Stoic ideas of *ius gentium* influenced Vitoria's thought.

24 Tierney (1997).

25 Mäkinen (2001); Varkemaa (2012).

26 Brett's main thesis in her study (1997) is that the distinction between objective and subjective right was not clear among medieval and early modern thinkers.

27 Tierney (1997); Brett (1997).

28 Tierney (1997: 265). See also Tierney (2009: 49) where he cites Vitoria's *De justitia*, 64.

29 Cortest (2008: 23), where he refers to Tierney (1997).

30 Brett (1997: 130–131), where she also criticizes Deckers's interpretation (Deckers 1991: 191–193, 220) who sees subjective rights and ideas on modernity in Vitoria's theory. Brett's interpretation is not very clearly stated. I will return to the difficulties with her interpretation later on in this chapter.

31 See Williams (2004: 50–52), where he also refers to Hering's (1939) study. Tierney (1997: 23) also lists similar terms in Aquinas's treatment of *ius* in a subjective sense,

but states that: 'Yet it remains true that he [Aquinas] developed no explicit doctrine of subjective rights or natural rights.' I prefer Tierney's position.

32 See Tellkamp (2009). I agree with Tellkamp that the influence of Summenhart is crucial to study in order to understand Vitoria's doctrine of *dominium* rights.

33 See Koskenniemi (2010). Koskenniemi's study is an important contribution of Vitoria's role in the development of international law. The relationship between dominion rights (understood as subjective rights) and *ius gentium* is clearly argued. However, the argument of the importance of virtue ethics and the idea of commutative justice in Vitoria's theory remains unclear to me.

34 *De indis*, 4, 223. As Pagden and Lawrence notice in Vitoria (2010: 240, note 14), the text concerning restitution in Peter Lombard's *Sentences* was the standard context where the scholastics considered the definition of *dominium*. For Vitoria's own treatment of *dominium* in his commentary on Aquinas, see Vitoria (1934: part III, qq. 62–67).

35 *De justitia* 2a 2ae, 62, 1, 5: 'Et ideo de diffinitione quid rei notandum est quod Conradus ... q. 1 ponit late diffinitionem illius nominis "jus" ... est facultas vel potestas conveniens alicui secundum leges.'

36 For late medieval definitions, see Tierney (1997). For Summenhart's sources, see Varkemaa (2011).

37 For Vitoria's discussion on *dominium ius*, see Brett (1997: 128–129). For the history of the equivalence in Roman legal sources and its impact on medieval discussions on rights, see Mäkinen (2001: 11–17).

38 *De justitia*, 2a 2ae, 62, 1, 5.

39 *De justitia*, 62, 1, 5, 7: 'Secundo modo dominium capitur, latius quidem, sed proprius, ut capitur in Corpus juris civilis et apud jurisconsultos prout tantum valet sicut proprietas, id est secundum quod distinguitir ab usu et usufructu et possessione.'

40 *De iustitia*, 67: 'Tertio modo capitur dominium largius prout dicit facultatem quamdam ad utendum re aliqua secundum jura, etc., sicut diffinit Conradus q. t De contractibus [tr. 1], ubi dicit quod dominium est facultas utendi re secundum jura vel leges rationabiliter institutas. Et isto modo, si sic diffiniatur large capiendo, idem erit just et dominium.' For Summenhart's treatment of *dominium*, see his *Opus septipartitum*, tr. 1, q. 1, 1a. The most recent study of Summenhart's theory of rights is Varkemaa (2012).

41 The notion *dominium-ius* and *dominium* rights is from Brett (1997); especially concerning Vitoria, see ibid., 129. For similarities between Vitoria's and Summenhart's theory of *dominium* as *ius*, see Tellkamp (2009).

42 Brett (1997: 129).

43 Cf. Pagden and Lawrence (2010: xvi) and Cortest (2008: 23) who argue that Vitoria's theory was mainly based on the Thomistic notion of *ius* and do not see the importance of the notion of *dominium* in the subject.

44 See Brett (1997: 129–130), where she refers to Deckers' (1991: 282–283) study. Deckers argues that Vitoria speaks about natural subjective rights.

45 *De indis*, 222: 'Redeundo ergo ad quaestionem, ut ex ordine procedamus, quaeritur primo, utrum barbari isti essent veri domini ante adventum Hispanorum, et privatim et publice, i.e. utrum essent veri domini privatarum rerum et possessionum et utrum essent inter eos alios veri principes et domini aliorum.' Translation by Pagden and Lawrence in Vitoria (2010: 239).

46 *De indis*, I, 4, 223: 'In contrarium est, quia illi erant in pacifica possessione rerum, et publice et privatim. Ergo omnino, nisi contrarium constet, habendi sunt pro dominis, neque, indicta causa, possessione deturbandi.'

47 *De indis*, I, 4, 223: 'Et ideo ... notandum quod, si barbari non haberent dominium, non videtur quod posset praetendi alia causa, nisi vel quia sunt peccatores vel quia infideles vel quia amentes vel insensati.' Vitoria has discussed these four qualifications already in his commentary on Thomas Aquinas's *Secunda secundae*, see

De justitia, part III, qq. 63–67. Later on John Locke made similar qualifications in *The Reasonableness of Christianity as Delivered in the Scriptures*. I thank Dr. Tim Stanton (University of York) for this reference.

48 *De indis*, I, 5, 223. These heresies were condemned in the Council of Constance in 1414–1418.

49 *De indis*, I, 5, 223–224: '…cuius unus error damnatus in Concilio Constantiensi fuit: "Nullus est dominus civilis, dum est in peccato mortali." Eadem fuit sententia Armachani, lib. 10, *De quaestionibus Armenorum*, cap. 4, et in Dialogo, *Defensorium pacis*…. Apparet ergo quod dominium fundetur in imagine Dei. Sed haec non est in peccatore. Ergo non est dominus. Item talis committit crimen laesae maiestatis. Ergo meretur perdere dominium.' Richard FitzRalph's discussion on *dominium* is very briefly noted by Tierney (1997: 229, 238, 266). Varkemaa (2012: 37–44) offers a more precise picture of FitzRalph's theory and its context.

50 The Latin edition (1557) which Pagden and Lawrence (2010) use in their translation includes here the words *dominium jurisdictionis*. For the edition, see Francisco de Vitoria, *Relectiones XII in duos tomos diuisae, quarum seriem uersa pagella indicabit, summariis suis ubique locis adeictis una cum indice omnium copiosissimo.* 2 vols. (in one), Jacobus Boyeris: Lyon 1557.

51 *De indis*, I, 5, 224. According to Vitoria, Summenhart also adopted their conclusion in his *Septipertitum opus de contractibus* I, 7.

52 *De indis*, I, 6, 224: 'Sed contra hanc sententiam ponitur propositio: Peccatum mortale non impedit dominium civile et verum dominium. Haec propositio licet sit determinata in Concilio Constantiae…'

53 *De indis*, I, 6, 225: 'Probo consequentiam, quia etiam dominium naturale est ex dono Dei, sicut civile, immo plus, quia civile videtur esse de iure humano. Ergo, si propter offensam Dei homo perderet dominium civile, eadem ratione perderet etiam dominium naturale. Falsitas autem consequentis probatur, quia non perdit dominium super proprios actus et super propria membra; habet enim peccator ius defendendi proriam vitam.' Translation by Bate in Vitoria (1995: 122).

54 *De indis*, I, 6, 225: '…sed homo est imago Dei per naturam, scilicet per potentias rationales; ergo non perditur per peccatum mortale.' Translation by Bate in Vitoria (1995: 122). Tierney (2009: 45–47) notices that when speaking about self-ownership in his commentary on Thomas Aquinas's *Secunda secundae*, and the question on *De justitia*, Vitoria even added that as the owner (*dominium proprietarius*) of one's own body, a human being could use it as he pleased, otherwise he would be a slave. Tierney refers only generally to Vitoria's work without giving specific references.

55 *De indis*, I, 6, 226: 'Utrum saltem ratione infidelitatis perdatur dominium.' Translation by Bate in Vitoria (1995: 123).

56 *De indis*, I, 19, 229: 'Ex omnibus his sequitur conclusio quod barbari, nec propter peccata alia mortalia nec propter peccatum infidelitatis, impediuntur quin sint veri domini; tam publice quam privatim, nec hoc titulo possunt a Christianis occupari bona et terrae illorum…' Translation by Bate in Vitoria (1995: 125).

57 *De indis*, I, 20, 229: 'Restat, an ideo essent domini, quia sunt insensati vel amentes. Et circa hoc dubium est an ad hoc, ut aliquis sit capax dominii, requiratur usus rationis.'

58 *De indis*, I, 20, 229–230. See Conrad Summenhart, *Septipertitum opus de contractibus*, I, 6. Summenhart follows here Jean Gerson.

59 *De indis*, I, 20, 230: 'Creaturae irrationales non possunt habere dominium.' Translation by Bate in Vitoria (1995: 126).

60 *De indis*, I, 20, 230: 'Patet, quia dominium est ius, ut fatetur etiam Conradus. Sed creaturae irrationales possunt habere ius. Ergo nec dominium.'

61 Op. cit. Translation by Pagden and Lawrence in Vitoria (2010: 248).

62 *De indis*, I, 20, 230: 'Item, ferae non habent dominium sui. Ergo multo minus aliarum rerum. Assumptum probatur, quia licet eas impune interficere etiam animi

gratia.' The words 'etiam animi gratia' are translated by Pagden and Lawrence (Vitoria, 2010: 248) as 'even by sport'. Vitoria refers here to Aristotle's *Politics* (1256b9–25), where it is stated that hunting wild animals is naturally just.

63   *De indis*, I, 20, 230: 'Sola creatura rationalis habet dominium sui actus … per hoc aliquis est dominus suorum actuum, ergo nec aliarum rerum.' Vitoria refers here to Aquinas *Summa theologiae, Prima secundae*, q. 82, a. 1, ad. 3.

64   *De indis*, I, 21, 231. Vitoria referred here to Roman law sources, see *Digest* XLIV, 3.11. and *Institutiones* 2.19.7. Translation by Pagden and Lawrence in Vitoria (2010: 249).

65   *De indis*, I, 22, 231: 'Sed de amentibus quid? Dico de perpetuo amentibus, qui nec habent nec spes habituros usum rationis.' Translation by Pagden and Lawrence in Vitoria (2010: 249).

66   *De indis*, I, 22, 231: 'Sitque tertia propositio: Videtur adhuc quod possint esse domini, quia possunt pati iniuriam, ergo habent ius. Sed hoc remitto ad iurisconsultos, utrum possint habere dominium civile.'

67   *De indis*, I, 23, 231: 'Probatur, quia secundum rei veritatem non sunt amentes, sed habent pro suo modo usum rationis.'

68   *De indis*, I, 23, 231: 'Patet, quia habent ordinem aliquem in suis rebus, postquam habent civitates, quae ordine constant, et habent matrimonia distincta, magistratus, dominos, leges, opificia, communitationes, quae omnia requirunt usum rationis; item religionis speciem. Item non errant in rebus, quae aliis sunt evidentes, quod est indicium usus rationis. Item Deus et natura non deficiunt in necessariis pro magna parte speciei. Praecipuum autem in homine est ratio, et frustra est potentia, quae non reducitur ad actum.' Tierney (1997: 270) notes that Anthony Pagden in *The Fall of Natural Man* (1982: 94) 'has misunderstood this passage as meaning that the Indians' rationality was still *in potentia*, not actualized, and their minds "frozen in a state of becoming"'. I have used both the translations of Pagden and Lawrence (in Vitoria, 2010: 250) and of Bade (in Vitoria, 1995: 127) and made modifications to them, especially concerning the last sentence which I have translated in accordance with Tierney's notion and translation in Tierney (1997: 269–270).

69   See Aristotle, *Politics* 1328b6–22. As Pagden (1986: 68–79) has noted, Vitoria also used in his treatment articles 74 to 93 on barbarians as natural slaves from Aquinas's commentary on the *Secunda secundae*.

70   See Aristotle, *De anima* 432b22–23, where he states that 'nature never makes anything without a purpose and never leaves out what is necessary'. In his *Politics* 1253a8, 1256b20–21, Aristotle stated that 'nature makes nothing incomplete and nothing in vain'.

71   See Pagden and Lawrence in Vitoria (2010: 250, note 36). For the discussion of the use of the passages from Aristotle's principle that 'nature does nothing in vain' in the defence of Indians by other Spanish neo-scholastics, see Pagden (1986: 49–50, 93–97).

72   *De indis*, I, 23, 231–232: 'Unde, quod videantur tam insensati et hebetes, puto maxima ex parte venire ax mala et barbara educatione, cum etiam apud nos videamus multos rusticorum parum differentes a brutis animantibus.' Translation by Pagden and Lawrence in Vitoria (2010: 250).

73   *De indis*, I, 24, 232: 'Restat ergo ex omnibus, dictis quod sine dubio barbari erant et publice et privatim ita veri domini, sicut Christiani; nec hoc titulo potuerunt spoliari aut principes aut privati rebus suis, quod non essent veri domini. Et grave esset negare illis, qui nihil iniuriae unquam fecerunt, quod concedimus Saracenis et Iudaeis, perpetuis hostibus religionis Christianae, quod non negamus habere vera dominia rerum suarum, si alias non occupaverunt terras Christianorum.' Translation by Bate in Vitoria (1995: 128).

74   *De justitia*, 2a 2ae, 62.1, 71: '…homo est omnibus perfectior: ergo omnia alia ordinantur propter illum … ergo habent jus et dominium super omnes illas.' See also Gen. 1:29–30.

75 *De justitia*, 2a 2ae, 62.1, 73: 'Item, de jure naturali est quod homo conservet se in esse. Sed hoc non potest sine aliis creaturis ... Ergo habet jus utendi omnibus illis.' For the history and development of the principle of extreme necessity, see Swanson (1997).

76 For Ockham, see Kilcullen (1995); Mäkinen (2012); for Grotius, see Horne (1990, 10–28); for Henry of Ghent and Godfrey of Fontaines, see Mäkinen (2001: 105–139).

77 William of Ockham, *Opus nonaginta dierum*, ch. 60, 556 (93–94). For Ockham's theory of natural rights, see Mäkinen (2012).

78 *De justitia*, 2a 2ae, 62.1, 74: 'Non solum universitas et communitas ... sed quilibet homo in statu naturae integrae, id est, stando in solo jure naturali, erat dominus omnium rerum creatarum et poterat uti et abuti omnibus illi ... dummodo non noceret aliis hominibus vel sibi.' Abuse (*abuti*) means here 'to use up' or exploit, not to misuse. See Tierney (1997: 263).

79 *De justitia*, 76: 'Sed arquit Conradus ... lex potest esse praeceptiva, et alia potest esse consultiva, et alia permissiva.'

80 Cited in Tierney (1997: 263–264).

81 See Varkemaa (2009: 191–195).

82 *De justitia*, 78: 'Primus est quod Adam fecit illam ... Secundo modo ... homines ex consensu omnium potuerunt eligere principem ... qui dividere et appropriare potuit illis res omnes ... Tertio modo potuit fieri per communem consensum.'

83 Ibid., 79. For Vitoria's ideas, see also Tierney (1997: 263–265).

84 *De justitia*, 79.

85 See *Institutiones* II, 1, 12.

86 *De indis*, III, 4, 259.

87 *De indis*, III, 3, 258–259.

88 According to Cortest (2008: 23–25), these questions of legal and civil jurisdiction were the primary issues in Vitoria's *De indis*, not the issue of personal human rights. Thus Vitoria and other scholars of the School of Salamanca defended 'the legitimacy of Native American communities ... "the right" of these peoples to govern themselves in human societies'. Vitoria's main point was that the Indians were the legitimate rulers of their lands. According to Cortest, all the questions posed by Vitoria, including the first question of *De indis* (whether the barbarians had public and private dominion before the arrival of the Spaniards) were intended to defend this policy. I do not find Cortest's argument that Vitoria defended only the legitimacy of communities plausible, because in the large first question he especially discussed the basis of dominion rights also as individual rights.

89 *De indis*, II, 233: 'De titulis non legitimis, quibus barbari Novi Orbis venire potuerint in dicionem Hispanorum', where Vitoria also listed all the titles he would discuss under this question.

90 *De indis*, II, 2, 238: 'Dato quod Imperator esset dominus mundi, non ideo posset occupare provincias barbarorum et constituere novos dominos et veteres deponere vel vectigalia capere.' Translation by Pagden and Lawrence in Vitoria (2010: 258).

91 *De indis*, II, 2, 238: 'Proba, quia etiam qui Imperatori tribuunt dominium orbis, non dicunt eum esse dominum per proprietatem, sed solum per iurisdictionem, quod ius non se extendit ad hoc, ut convertat provincias in suos usus aut donet pro suo arbitrio oppida, aut etiam praedia. Ex dictis ergo patet quod hoc titulo non possunt Hispani occupare illas provincias.'

92 *De indis*, II, 2, 240: 'Papa non est dominus civilis aut temporalis totius orbis, loquendo proprie de dominio et potestati civili.'

93 Vitoria discussed the power of the pope at length in his *De indis*, II, 2–7, 238–244.

94 *De indis*, II, 7, 244 where he referred to the *Institutiones* 2.1.12 (*Ferae bestiae*).

95 Op. cit.

96 *De indis*, II, 16, 254 where he referred to the *Instititiones* 2.1.40 (*Per traditionem*):

'Et "nihil tam naturale est, quam voluntatem domini, volentis rem suam in alium transferri, ratam haberi".'

97 Op. cit.
98 *De indis*, I, 221: 'Deinde cum audiamus tot hominum caedes, tot spolia hominum alioqui innoxiorum, deturbatos tot dominos possessionibus et dicionibus suis privatos, dubutari merito potest iure an iniuria haec facta sint.'
99 Cited in Koskenniemi (2010: 59). For Vitoria's understanding of commutative justice, see also ibid., 51–52.
100 Tierney (1997).
101 Brett (1997: 3). Cf. Miller (1995), who argued that even ancient authors such as Aristotle and especially Plato operated with a subjectively understood notion of rights.
102 See e.g. Brett (1997); Mäkinen (2001); Varkemaa (2012).
103 Brett (1997: 124). See also Tierney (1997: 265–272, 286–287). Cf. Deckers (1991).
104 Brett (1997: 136–137) sees Vitoria's *œuvre* as a whole as a 'split between two senses of right: not between "objective right" and "subjective right", but between two different senses of the latter'. According to Brett, this distinction is necessary in order to understand Vitoria's work and position in the tradition of rights. According to Brett's interpretation, the first sense involves the notion of obligation and law; i.e. it was a natural right associated with a politics of nature and necessity. The second sense wherein a right is equivalent to dominion 'bears the sense of liberty and freedom of obligation, [and] is at the base of the politics of free consent and of independent personal authority within the *civitas*'. Brett's analysis of Vitoria's doctrine of rights based only on his commentary on Aquinas's *Summa theologiae* and on the *Relectio De potestate civili*. She does not refer to the *Relectio De indis* at all. Vitoria's treatment of dominion rights seems to be slightly different in *De indis*. In it, Vitoria gives several arguments to prove who were capable of dominion rights and then applies these arguments to the case of the American Indians. I see all these arguments as necessary in order to understand the real nature of dominion rights in Vitoria's theory.
105 I have not discussed political notions of *civitas* in Vitoria's *De indis* in this chapter. However, he deals with them in question III.
106 Tierney (1997: 271–272) sees Vitoria's idea that 'natural rights were rooted in human nature, not in the nature of the external world' as an important humanistic factor for the further development of a right as a part of political theories.

References

Primary sources

Aristotle (1957) *Politica*, Ed. by W.D. Ross, Oxford: Clarendon.
Las Casas, Bartolomé de (1967) *In Defense of the Indians*, Transl. by S. Poole, Foreword by M.E. Marty, Illinois: Northern Illinois University Press.
Palacios Rubios, Juan López de (1954) *De las Islas del Mar Océano*, México: Fondo de cultura económica.
Summenhart, Conrad (1515) *Septipartitum opus de contractibus pro foro conscientie atque theologico*, Hagenau.
Vitoria, Francisco de (1934) *De justitia*, in V. Beltrán de Heredia (ed.) *Francisco de Vitoria: Commentarios a la secunda secundae de Santo Tomás*, Vol. 3, Salamanca.
Vitoria, Francisco de (1995) *De indis et de iure belli relectiones*, Ed. by E. Nys, Transl. by J.P. Bate, Buffalo, New York: William S. Hein & Co.

Vitoria, Francisco de (2010 [1991]) 'On the American Indians', in *Political Writings*, Ed. and Transl. by A. Pagden and J. Lawrence, Cambridge Texts in the History of Political Thought (eleventh printing), Cambridge: Cambridge University Press, 233–292.

William of Ockham (1963) 'Opus Nonaginta Dierum, Caps. 7–124', in *Opera Politica*, Ed. by J. Sikes and H.S. Offler, Manchester: University Press, Vol. 2, 375–858.

Secondary sources

Andersson, R. and Henriksson, M. (2010) *Intiaanit: Pohjois-Amerikan alkuperäiskansojen historia*, Helsinki: Gaudeamus.

Arnold, M. (2011) 'Land tenure and use in native American culture', Available http:// matriarchy.info/index.php?option=com_context&task=view&id=146&Itemid=29 (accessed 16 November 2011).

Beltrán de Heredia, V. (1939) *Francisco de Vitoria*, Barcelona, Madrid.

Brett, A. (1997) *Liberty, Right and Nature: Individual Rights in Later Scholastic Thought*, Cambridge: Cambridge University Press.

Cortest, L. (2008) *The Disfigured Face: Traditional Natural Law and Its Encounter with Modernity*, New York: Fordam University Press.

Deckers, D. (1991) *Gerechtigkeit und Recht: Eine historisch-kritische Untersuchung der Gerechtiskeitslehre des Francisco de Vitoria (1483–1546)*, Freiburg: Universitätsverlag.

Folsom, F. (1996) *Indian Uprising on the Rio Grande: The Pueblo Revolt of 1680*, 15th ed., Albuquerque: University of Mexico Press.

Garnsey, P. (2007) *Thinking about Property: From Antiquity to the Age of Revolution*, Cambridge: Cambridge University Press.

Horne, T.A. (1990) *Property Rights and Poverty: Political Argument in Britain, 1605–1834*, Chapel Hill and London: University of North Carolina Press.

Hurtado, A., Iverson, P. and Paterson, T. (eds) (2001) *Major Problems in American Indian History: Documents and Essays*, 2nd ed., Boston: Wadsworth.

Kilcullen, J. (1995) 'Medieval theories of natural rights.' Available www.humanities.mq. edu.au/Ockham/NaturalRights.html (accessed 7 November 2011).

Koskenniemi, M. (2010) 'Colonization of the "Indies": The origin of international law?', in Y. Gamarra (ed.) *La idea de la América en el pensamiento ius internacionalista del siglo XXI*, Zaragoza: Institución Fernando el Católico, 43–63.

Mäkinen, V. (2001) *Property Rights in the Late Medieval Discussion on Franciscan Poverty*, Recherches de Philosophie et Theologié Médiévales. Bibliotheca 3, Leuven: Peeters.

Mäkinen, V. (2012) 'Moral psychological basis of William of Ockham's theory of natural rights', *American Catholic Philosophical Quarterly*, 86:3, 507–525.

Martín, R.H. (1995) *Francisco de Vitoria: Vida y pensamiento internacionalista*, Madrid: BAC.

Miller, F. (1995) Nature, Justice, and Rights in Aristotle's Politics, Oxford: Oxford University Press.

Muldoon, J. (1979) *Popes, Lawyers, and Infidels: The Church and the Non-Christian World*, Philadelphia: University of Pennsylvania Press.

Niemelä, P. (2008) 'A cosmopolitan world order? Perspectives on Francisco de Vitoria and the United Nations', in A. von Bogdandy and R. Wolfrum (eds) *Max Planck Yearbook of United Nations Law*, E.J. Brill: Leiden, 12. 301–344. Available www.mpil.de/ shared/data/pdf/pdfmpuny/08_niemelae_12.pdf (accessed 14 November 2011).

Pagden, A. (1982) *The Fall of Natural Man*, Cambridge: Cambridge University Press.

Pagden, A. and Lawrence, J. (2010), 'Introduction', in Francisco de Vitoria, *Political Writings*, Cambridge: Cambridge University Press, xiii–xxviii.

Scott, J.B. (1934) *The Catholic Conception of International Law: Francisco de Vitoria & Francisco Suárez*, Washington: Carnegie Endowment for Peace.

Swanson, S.G. (1997) 'The medieval foundation of John Locke's theory of natural rights: Rights of subsistence and the principle of extreme necessity', *History of Political Thought*, 18, 399–456.

Syse, H. (2007) *Natural Law, Religion, and Rights: An Exploration of the Relationship between Natural Law and Natural Rights, with Special Emphasis on the Teachings of Thomas Hobbes and John Locke*, South Bend, Ind.: St. Augustine's Press.

Tellkamp, J.A. (2009) "Ius est idem quod dominium: Conrado Summenhart, Francisco de Vitoria y la conquista de América", Veritas, 54(3), 34–51.

Tierney, B. (1991) 'Aristotle and the American Indians – Again. Two critical discussions', *Christianesimo nella Storia*, 12, 295–322.

Tierney, B. (1997) *The Idea of Natural Rights: Studies on Natural Rights, Natural Law and Church Law 1150–1625*, Atlanta, Georgia: Scholars Press.

Tierney, B. (2009) 'Historical roots of modern rights: Before Locke and after', in P. Frohnen and K.L. Grasso (eds) *Rethinking Rights: Historical, Political, and Philosophical Perspectives*, Columbia and London: University of Missouri Press, 34–57.

Tuck, R. (1997) *Natural Rights Theories: Their Origin and Development*, Cambridge: Cambridge University Press.

Valtonen, Pekka (2008) *Latinalaisen Amerikan historia*, Helsinki: Gaudeamus.

Varkemaa, J. (2012) *Conrad Summenhart's Theory of Individual Rights*, Studies in Medieval and Reformation Tradition, 159, Leiden: E.J. Brill.

Williams, T.D. (2004) 'Francisco de Vitoria and the pre-Hobbesian roots of natural rights theory', *Alpha Omega*, 7(1), 47–59.

3 Inheritance and bequest in Lockean rights theory

Robert Lamb

Introduction

In his book *Property and Political Theory*, published in 1984, Alan Ryan suggests that 'students of theories of property rightly spend a lot of time in the company of Locke' (Ryan, 1984: 14). Over 25 years later, this situation is unchanged: among political theorists, the perennial interest in and use of Locke's theory of ownership shows no signs of dwindling. Within political theory, work on this subject can be separated into two different scholarly spheres. First, there has been the interpretive sphere: the large number of extremely detailed, intricate analyses of Locke's arguments. Here the aim has usually been to precisely and rigorously locate the arguments of the *Two Treatises* within the broader context of Locke's other philosophical and theological writings.[1] Second, there has been the normative sphere: the various attempts made by libertarian political philosophers to generate comprehensive normative theories from Locke's key moral premises. Here the aim has been to construct a 'Lockean' political theory with the concept of property at its centre that is at once defensible, coherent and attractive on its own terms.[2]

It is remarkably strange that these contemporaneous scholarly spheres have been almost entirely disconnected.[3] The nature of the strangeness concerns the way in which the increasingly sophisticated interpretive accounts of Locke's political thought have completely transformed our understanding of the moral premises that are customarily invoked by the normative theorists as 'Lockean'. This transformation stems from the increasing recognition by Locke scholars of the deeply religious character of his moral and political philosophy.[4] A broad consensus has emerged in the interpretive sphere that it is very difficult, if not impossible, to 'bracket off' Locke's religious commitments and consider particular parts of his thought – such as his justification of property rights – as independent, discrete arguments that can be comprehended and assessed on secular grounds.[5] This is because the role of Locke's theology is not merely as the provider of detachable axiomatic principles; it rather functions as a network of beliefs, one that 'shapes and informs' his political theory 'through and through' (Waldron, 2003: 82). As John Dunn puts it, the *Two Treatises* are 'saturated with Christian assumptions' and to ignore this runs a high risk of misunderstanding the ideas expressed therein (Dunn, 1969: 99).

In spite of this fairly well-established interpretive consensus, self-styled Lockean political philosophers like Robert Nozick and Michael Otsuka have ignored the religious foundations of his thought and have instead treated him as the defender of a comprehensive, rights-based liberalism.[6] When advancing his stark 'minimal state' libertarianism in *Anarchy, State, and Utopia*, Nozick begins theorizing from Locke's state of nature without proper acknowledgment that the moral principles contained therein are fundamentally theological (1974: 9). He is aware of this omission but attempts to justify his selective reading of the *Two Treatises* on the grounds that the 'the moral background' of Locke's thought is not wholly relevant to his political philosophy and, in any case, there is not 'anything remotely resembling a satisfactory explanation of the status and basis of the law of nature in his *Second Treatise*' (Nozick, 1974: 9). The vast amount that Locke wrote throughout his life about natural law and the morality it implies renders Nozick's assertion slightly breathtaking, but his attitude is also mirrored by that of Otsuka in *Libertarianism without Inequality*. Herein, Otsuka describes his 'left-libertarian' theory as based on the 'system of truths of political morality that Locke first sketched in his *Second Treatise*' again without any mention of the theological commitments that inform those 'truths' in myriad ways (Otsuka, 2003: 2). He adds that Locke was not 'always able to grasp these truths' and suggests further that 'often he did not fully understand how they were true in detail or why they were true'. It is because of such failures of understanding by Locke that Otsuka characterizes his aim as being to provide a Lockean theory that is 'unblinded by the ideology and prejudice of his day' (2003: 1). It is likely that the prejudice and ideology that Otsuka is mindful of are Locke's religious commitments, since they are completely absent from his analysis, which presents the *Two Treatises* as housing a 'natural rights' theory that can provide the basis for an account of left-libertarianism.

The bracketing strategy employed by contemporary political philosophers in their uses of Locke is not the main theme of this chapter, but it does provide an important backdrop for it. My central aims are to show how an appreciation of the theological commitments that structure Locke's moral theory reveals his theory of property to be radically and problematically different to his libertarian followers and that these differences emerge when the issue of posthumous transmissibility is considered. In order to reveal the nature of the problems with Locke's account of posthumous transfer, I separate his understanding of inheritance from that of bequest. Though inheritance and bequest are frequently conflated both philosophically and colloquially, it is nevertheless possible to draw an important, meaningful conceptual distinction between them that makes a real difference to the moral justification for each. When understood narrowly, a right of inheritance is the right to own the private property that was owned by a parent or family member after that person dies. By contrast, the term bequest can be understood to denote a quite different, more capacious concept: expressed in Hohfeldian terms, bequest refers to the power to alter legal relations of ownership such that one's property can be posthumously transferred to *any* person or institution of choice, regardless of a family connection.

Inheritance, on this understanding, refers to a practice that pays *no* attention whatsoever to the wishes of the owner (and eventual testator) of the property in question and places moral emphasis or relevance on the entitlements held by the familial recipient and the interests such entitlements are supposed to serve. Bequest, on this understanding, places *all* moral emphasis or relevance on the wishes of the testator, to the apparent exclusion of any concern with the interests of the intended recipient. Through a discussion of Locke's account of posthumous property transfers, I suggest that whilst the right to inherit is firmly woven into the framework of his moral theory, the power to bequeath is not and that attempts to fit it into that framework appear unconvincing. I then conclude by suggesting that Locke's failure to adequately justify bequest alongside his reliance on a thickly religious understanding of natural law in order to justify inheritance might explain the consistent failure of modern libertarianism to provide a compelling account of what should happen to a property holding upon the death of its owner.

Natural law and the problem of posthumous property transfer

One the main reasons for the enduring interest in Locke's theory of property seems to be the crucial role played by acts of individual labour in the justification of ownership rights and the continuing intuitive resonance the labour-ownership connection seems to have.[7] Another reason is that his labour theory of just acquisition is resolutely non-consequentialist, which marks it out as rather unique within the modern, canonical accounts of property ownership. Taken together, these two aspects of his theory of private property raise questions about the grounds for the posthumous transfer of ownership rights. Locke's well-known argument – leaving aside its various complications and provisos – is that God bequeathed the earth to all humanity equally, but that this situation of original communism can be (and was) legitimately disrupted by acts of individual labour, which privatize ownership of the object upon which such acts are directed. Of individuals, Locke writes, 'The *Labour* of his Body, and the *Work* of his Hands, we may say, are properly his' and therefore the deployment of this labour on initially commonly owned objects establishes an individual ownership right 'that excludes the common right of other men' (Locke, 1988: II: 27). Although God did bequeath the world to mankind 'in common', he 'hath also given them reason to make use of it to the best advantage of Life' and thus 'there must of necessity be a means to appropriate' and that means is the application of labour (ibid.: II: 25, emphasis suppressed). An apple that falls into your hands as you sit beneath a tree does not belong to you, even if possession of it would make you happier than anyone else or if you shook the branch from which it fell: it rather belongs to the person that *first* laboured to cultivate the tree in question.

The significance of labour stems from the most important part of Locke's account of natural law: the paramount obligation we owe to God to preserve ourselves. Human beings are 'all the Workmanship of one Omnipotent, and infinitely wise Maker' and thus each person is '*bound to preserve himself*' (ibid.: II: 6), a duty that Locke cites when explaining the purpose of private property (ibid.: II: 26). Labour is an activity that individuals have been 'commanded' (ibid.: II: 32) to undertake, but there are two things worth emphasizing about it. First, although it is a moral duty, it is an imperfect one that individuals can legitimately shirk.[8] Second, although labour is an imperfect moral duty and thus in some sense praiseworthy when fulfilled, it does not represent a desert-base that is subject to universal recognition or reward. Indeed, after legitimate initial acquisition individuals need not labour *any further* to protect or maintain their ownership: provided they do not violate the various provisos Locke details (such as allowing their perishable holdings to spoil (ibid.: II: 31), property rights survive regardless of the owner's propensity to labour and regardless of the propensity of any other person.[9] The key point though is that labour generates property rights because of its connection to the preservation of human life: the 'Fundamental Law of Nature and Government', which states that 'as much as may be, *all* the Members of the Society are to be *preserved*' (ibid.: II: 159).

As sketched so far, Locke's account comprises an ostensibly coherent justification for the original acquisition of private property: it tells us why individuals can (and should) come to own things. It is, however, thus far silent about any possible justification for the individual features associated with that institution, the conventional legal relations that ownership implies. When sketching what he dubs the 'full ownership' account of property Anthony Maurice Honoré (1961) identifies a number of fundamental components that characterize the concept and can, he claims, be found in all 'mature' legal systems. Such components include the rights and powers of use, possession, security and most relevantly for our discussion, posthumous transmissibility. But what justifies these features of ownership? Why does a right of private ownership imply posthumous transmissibility? One response to these questions would simply be to deny their force. It could thus be argued that the concept of property ownership has some essential characteristics and we therefore do not need to seek a *separate* or *independent* justification for posthumous transmissibility (or any other legal right, power or immunity) because it is simply part of the meaning of the concept itself. On inspection, however, this seems an unsatisfactory philosophical strategy, since it would seem to suggest that there is an over-arching, stable concept of property ownership, rather than a number of competing conceptions. In the same way as we can conceive of marriages without churches or football matches without the offside rule, we can conceive of the institution of property ownership functioning in a different way than it does in Honoré's sense. We can clearly imagine a world where ownership does not imply posthumous transmissibility. It thus seems strange to deny the question of justifying the conventional aspects of property ownership on the grounds that they form part of the meaning of the concept. But even were the strategy a sound one, it would be of little use when considering Locke's theory. This is because Locke's account of property is quite plainly *not* the modern, full ownership account described by Honoré. The modern understanding of ownership does not, to take just a couple of examples, incorporate a spoilage proviso or a duty of charity to those in danger of death, as Locke's does.[10] We can then probe Locke's theory of property not only for justifications of legitimate *acquisition* but also for the rights that such ownership subsequently entails.

As noted above, for Locke ownership rights survive when a proprietor ceases to labour. But what happens to rights of private ownership when a proprietor actually ceases *to live*? Who comes then to own the property that has been acquired? Posthumous transmissibility is not an issue that poses any significant questions of internal coherence for the arguments of Locke's natural law predecessors. Samuel Pufendorf, for example, also justifies the move from original communism to private property with reference to divinely-sanctioned natural law, but does not grant acts of labour any intrinsic moral significance and in doing so is able to embed his account of inheritance within his broader account of ownership. For Pufendorf, property ownership as a social institution comes into being because God commands it; this general command does not, however, privilege any specific means of acquisition. Rather than being obliged to labour, individuals were under the far vaguer obligation to 'make such arrangements about them as seemed to be required by the condition of the human race and by the need to preserve peace, tranquillity and good order' and, because of this, 'to avoid conflict … property in things … was introduced by the will of God with consent among men' (Pufendorf, 1991: 84–85).

Such a consequentialist justification for the general existence of property ownership effectively obviates any questions about the distribution of its particular parts and about the various legal relations that come with it. Indeed, the theoretical strategy Pufendorf usually employs is to trace the legitimacy of conventional legal relations surrounding private ownership back to the original argument for property itself. Thus, when he attends to the issue of posthumous property transfer, he simply repeats the general justificatory principle based on a peace-seeking convention for cases of both inheritance and bequest. The power to bequeath a holding is defended as part of the conventional package that comes with property ownership: though the precise details of the practice vary between societies, Pufendorf maintains that it is nevertheless the case that 'most peoples have adopted the custom which is itself a kind of consolation for mortality, that a man may make arrangements during his lifetime for the transfer of his property in the event of his death to the person he most loves' (ibid.: 88). On those occasions when there is no such will in evidence, this does not mean that the property in question now has no owner. Pufendorf instead insists that

> it is contrary to common human feeling and *scarcely conducive to the peace of mankind* that the goods which a man has acquired with such labour through his life be regarded as abandoned on the death of the owner and available to anyone to occupy.
>
> (ibid.: 87, emphasis added)

Although he does gesture in this passage towards a connection between labour and ownership, this connection is justified instrumentally, as a means of attaining the prized goal of peace, which is what is doing the work in the argument. The maintenance of peace prohibits any notion that ownership rights are simply 'abandoned' if an owner dies intestate. In the absence of a written will, Pufendorf defends the practice of familial inheritance: according to him, the children of a proprietor (or the parents if there are no children) have 'rights of blood' (ibid.: 87). The familial right to inherit necessarily trumps any rival claims – even if there are owners 'who may love certain outsiders more than those of their own blood' – on the grounds that it is 'in the interests of peace', because it is 'most obvious and not liable to complex disputes' (ibid.: 87). The demands of peace and harmony can thus be seen not only to justify property ownership as an institution, but also the conventional features that have developed with it, including a power to bequeath and – when this is not enacted – a right to inherit.

Locke on the right to inherit

Unlike Pufendorf, Locke does face a problem when explaining the legitimacy of posthumous transmissibility. This problem arises because of the non-consequentialist nature of Locke's argument, because he rejects the notion that property ownership can be justified conventionally (Locke, 1988: I: 88) and because posthumous transmissibility appears inconsistent with the morality of the labour theory of legitimate acquisition. As explicated thus far, his theory would seem to imply that upon the death of an owner no living individual could have any morally significant relationship with the once owned object. No other individual but the owner can have laboured on the object because it is the fact that he was the sole, first labourer that generates the ownership right in the first place.[11] So to whom, if anyone, does the ownership right transfer in the event of the death of a proprietor? It might be supposed that the logic of Locke's overall argument entails that upon the death of a proprietor, any once-appropriated object return from whence it came, 'the common'. If God initially bequeathed the earth to all individuals, it seems plausible that those portions of it acquired through acts of labour could then legitimately return to an 'unowned' state, at least until another person 'mixes' her labour with it and then acquires subsequent rights of private ownership. Locke does in fact acknowledge the potential reasonableness of this suggestion, yet nevertheless resists such a conclusion (ibid.: I: 88).

The question of what happens to ownership rights over an object after the death of the relevant proprietor is, perhaps curiously, absent from Chapter 5 ('of property') of Locke's *Second Treatise*. It is, however, discussed on several occasions in the *First Treatise*, where he articulates and defends a right of children to inherit the property of their parents on their death. The main point of the *First Treatise* is to provide a robust case against inheritance as a comprehensive *political* principle as defended by Sir Robert Filmer. Nevertheless, despite this and the effort taken to undermine Filmer's claim that Adam (by virtue of being God's creation) had a right to inherit ownership of the entire world, Locke asserts quite unequivocally – and explicitly against the thought that once-owned property could 'return again to the common stock of mankind' – that children always have 'a Title, to share in the *Property* of their Parents, and a Right to Inherit their Possessions'. By way of defence of this, he explains that:

> Men are not Proprietors of what they have meerly for themselves, their Children have a Title to part of it, and have their Kind of Right joyn'd with their Parents, in the Possession which comes to be wholly theirs, when death having put an end to their Parents use of it, hath taken them from their Possessions, and this we call Inheritance. Men being by a like Obligation bound to preserve what they have begotten, as to preserve themselves, their issue come to have a Right in the Goods they are possessed of.

> (ibid.: I: 88)[12]

In this and surrounding passages, Locke is quite clear about the posthumous transfer of ownership rights: children 'have a Title to part' of the property owned by their parents and have the 'Right to Inherit' this part when those parents die (ibid.: I: 90–93).[13] The explanation for this relates to Locke's understanding of morality itself, the aforementioned cornerstone of which is the duty to preserve life. The importance of human preservation explains why whenever individuals become parents, they not only have a general obligation to God to maintain their own lives and those of others, but they also now incur an additional, particular obligation to preserve the lives of their children. For Locke, what this duty to preserve then implies is a right for the children to inherit the property of parents.

In fact, the way in which Locke phrases the right of inheritance, such that children have a Title to *part*' of owned property, one that they then become 'wholly' possessive of in the event of parental death, actually means they are in some sense owners even before this event takes place, which would, in turn, suggest a significant curtailment of parental behaviour whilst alive. It would seem that a certain quantity or a certain proportion must be reserved for children under all circumstances. The implicit claim is that this right held by children to inherit a certain portion of property requires parents to *protect* and *preserve* that property: in becoming parents, their freedom to legitimately use or transfer the objects they own is immediately restricted.[14] One can thus easily imagine a Lockean government taking measures to prohibit actions that threaten the part of the property that the children share a title in, such as the creation of laws that outlaw certain types of high-stakes gambling or any other behaviour that would put the inheritance at risk. The obligation of posthumous property transfer is part of a wider catalogue of duties owed by parents to children including education and love.[15] The property covered by the obligation goes beyond mere subsistence, extending to the 'conveniences and comforts of Life' and it also varies according to the relative wealth of the parents in question. Parents are bound to provide for the children they beget, partly because *they* do in fact beget them (and therefore owe them some particular duties that no other agents do) and partly because of the unique needs that children themselves face (ibid.: I: 89).

Locke's account of parental obligations is thus firmly embedded within his moral theory as a whole, an appreciation of which resolve the apparent tension between grounding property ownership in morally significant acts of labour on the one hand and validating its posthumous transfer to those who have *not* laboured on the other. The centrality of Locke's understanding of normatively prior obligations within his teleological moral theory explains why the 'right' to inherit held by children correlates with a *perfect* duty on the part of the parents. He insists that ownership rights over property transfer to children even if 'the dying Parents, by express Words, declare nothing about them'; it is rather that 'nature appoints the descent of their Property to their Children, who thus come to have a Title, and natural Right of Inheritance to their Father's Goods, which the rest of Mankind cannot pretend to' (ibid.: I: 89). The posthumous transfer of property from parent to child is thus not optional and any legitimate government – which is one bound by the law of nature – must act to enforce and protect it.

Locke and the power to bequeath

Attention to Locke's understanding of parental duties in the *Two Treatises* should dissolve the apparent inconsistency between the moral justification for ownership based on initial acts of labour and the claim that such ownership can posthumously transfer to certain specific individuals regardless of the fact that they have not laboured. The inconsistency vanishes once it is acknowledged that it is not labour as such that is doing the real justificatory work in Locke's argument, but rather the normatively prior duty to preserve one's life laid down in natural law. Once this central premise is taken seriously, the justification for inheritance looks like a fairly plausible extension: children, by virtue of their very existence, are entitled to preservation and the particular duty to ensure this preservation falls on the particular parents involved in their creation, which in turn places restrictions on the way in which they treat their property, part of which must be safeguarded for their inheritance.

There remains, however, a problem. As noted, Locke explains and justifies inheritance via the same account of morality that explains and justifies ownership in the first place: it is part of the human duty to God to preserve children, whom they bring into the world and whom need assistance in various aspects of life. Children hold a right to inherit parental property, a right that does not require (and can trump) any written will. But the placement of all emphasis on the moral rights of children to inherit raises questions about the power to bequeath, which, as noted earlier, is a completely different moral right. Does Locke include bequest in his theory of ownership and, if so, on what grounds? Unlike Pufendorf who tied both inheritance and bequest to conventions and consequences, Locke's theory would appear to have no obvious room to explain non-familial posthumous transfer.

As Jeremy Waldron has observed, at one key point in the *First Treatise*, Locke does appear to signal his commitment to bequest. He writes

if any one had began, and made himself a Property in any particular thing
... that thing, that possession, *if he dispos'd not otherwise of it by his positive Grant*, descended Naturally to his Children and they had a right to
succeed to it, and possess it.

(ibid.: I: 87, emphasis added)

What would otherwise be merely a restatement of the right to inherit is transformed by the proviso concerning the possible existence of a 'positive Grant' to
direct the transfer of property after death: what Locke appears to be saying here
is that children have a perfect right to inherit property *when there is no existing
written will that states otherwise*. This of course implies the possibility that a
written will could direct the transfer of property to other non-familial agents.
The obvious problem with this is that it completely contradicts the view outlined
above wherein the right held by children over a 'part' of parental property is a
perfect one. The claim that children are part-owners in the property of their
parents cannot be true if those parents can direct the property elsewhere through
a 'positive Grant'. The power to bequeath surely undermines the right to inherit.

It is worth noting that Waldron might actually be misconstruing the passage
in question: the relevant absence of a 'positive Grant' might merely refer to the
decision of the deceased proprietor not to transfer certain holdings to others
while alive. But let us assume for the moment that Waldron is onto something
here. After noting the apparent conceptual tension, he suggests a way in which
the right to inherit and the power to bequeath can be rendered coherent within
Locke's theory of property. In order to do so, he draws attention to a passage in
the *Second Treatise* where Locke asserts that 'A Father may dispose of his own
Possessions as he pleases, when his Children are out of danger of perishing for
want' (ibid.: II: 65; Waldron, 1988: 246). Waldron argues that, given this statement, the most consistent position that can be constructed from Locke's overall
account is that the 'priority as between bequest and inheritance is exactly the
opposite to that asserted in [the 'positive Grant' passage in] the *First Treatise*',
which had suggested bequest trumped inheritance. Waldron's claim is that it is
possible to separate the right to inherit from the power to bequeath within
Locke's theory by pointing to the different portions of property to which they
apply (Waldron, 1988: 246). To understand this, recall the idea of a minimum
threshold for inheritance that was noted earlier, the portion of property that must
be reserved for the children who are part-owners of it and for the sake of which
parental behaviour must be curtailed, such that what is to be transferred is always
maintained. Waldron's suggestion is that such a minimum threshold must always
be protected by the right to inherit, but that any surplus beyond this then falls
under the purview of a power to bequeath held by the parents, who also hold
rights to other forms of discretionary disposal of it (subject to the other various
provisos that bind ownership).

The coherent vision of Locke's theory is very neatly presented by Waldron
and there appears no other way of making sense of the relationship between
inheritance and bequest within the theory of property ownership articulated in

the *Two Treatises*. But although he shows how the two concepts can cohere, Waldron admits (ibid.: 247) that the original problem identified above – the apparent lack of any independent justification for bequest within Locke's theory – remains. Why does (and how can) Locke argue that private property ownership includes the power to posthumously transfer our goods to whomever we please, when such a power is unidentified in his account of natural law, conflicts with the emphasis on the moral significance both of labour and of need and cannot seemingly be propped up by the duties involved with familial bonds? This is an especially pressing question since Locke is quite comfortable, as Waldron points out, with 'the idea of a usable surplus reverting to common ownership' under certain circumstances, notably in accordance with his proviso that property cannot be permitted to spoil (ibid.: 247). Locke also allows that when a property owner dies intestate and there are not any children (nor parents) to claim an inheritance, property can legitimately either recede to the common (in the state of nature) or be appropriated by government (in political society).[16] So why does the surplus property of parents or *all* of the property owned by those without dependents not likewise revert to the common or become owned by the state in the event of death? Both of these options seem in line with the fundamental law of nature of human preservation. In fact, there would seem to be a much stronger case for a redistribution of such property according to a principle of need than for an indefeasible power of bequest to whomever the original proprietor prefers, regardless of the relative wealth of the recipient. What moral difference can the existence of a will make for Locke?

Waldron does attempt to offer a possible defence for bequest within Locke's theory. He imagines a scenario in which a wealthy merchant dies and leaves behind an estate with enough resources to comfortably sustain his widow and a number of children who happen also to have become wealthy merchants in their own right. Prior to his death, the merchant made a will that expressed his desire to leave the remaining surplus of property to a close friend. Before, however, the bequest 'can be put into effect', Waldron imagines that 'a fortune hunter (who has read the first few sections of Chapter 5 of the *Second Treatise*) comes along to the dead man's house, mixes his labour with the goods in the estate (digging the garden or whatever), and calls the property his own' (ibid.: 248). What, he asks, does Locke's theory prescribe in such a situation?

The answer Waldron gives is that there is nothing in Locke's theory that precludes the establishment of legal conventions within positive law to regulate property ownership, provided that such conventions to do not run contrary to the law of nature. He further provides seemingly sound consequentialist reasons for a Lockean society to support the practice of bequest, such as the avoidance of the considerable chaos that would ensue when individuals scramble around to acquire things after the deaths of proprietors. Waldron's conclusion is that a Lockean government 'deprives no one of any natural right by preventing surplus property from falling back into the common stock of mankind' (ibid.: 250). Such a solution does not seem wholly convincing. It is true that Locke does defend some autonomy for positive law, with regard to the regulation of rules of ownership within political societies (Locke, 1988: II: 50, II: 120). However, he is nonetheless adamant that the status of the Law of Nature is such that it 'stands as an Eternal Rule to all Men, *Legislators* as well as others' (ibid.: II: 135). Furthermore, legislative power is '*limited to the publick good* of the Society', a power that he explicitly states 'hath *no other end* but preservation' (ibid.: II: 135, second emphasis added). This would seem to suggest both that the autonomy of positive law is severely restricted and that the precise form that it takes should be guided by the end specified in natural law. So, since Locke so doggedly emphasizes the crucial importance of human preservation, it will not really do to identify any, otherwise intuitively attractive, consequentialist case for conventions such as bequest. The specified consequences need either to be tied to or at the very least not conflict with the end required by the law of nature.

Waldron might be right to think that Locke would be ultimately rather unsympathetic to the fortune hunter in his example. But he is surely wrong to suggest that this example can provide Locke with an independent justification for bequest. Were the individual in question not a 'fortune hunter' but instead a person in a position of severe poverty, such that her life were in danger but could be saved by appropriation of the property in question, Locke would clearly defend a claim to charity over any concern with bequest. In situations where the person in question is in a position of severe, but *non-life-threatening* indigence or a person with an uncomfortable disability, then the case becomes less clear cut, but there are no good arguments in Locke's thought as to why the wishes of a testator should trump the claims of the (non-desperately) needy. The unavoidable conclusion is that whilst the right to inherit is firmly embedded within Locke's overall theory of property, there is not even an implicit justification available for the power to bequeath.

The Lockean legacy on inheritance and bequest

What should we make of Locke's failure to offer an account of bequest? What does it mean for the legacy of his theory of property? On the one hand, it does not mean very much at all: compelling defences of bequest are notably absent from the writings of the canonical political thinkers who advanced influential theories of property. Although Locke fails to address bequest, others (such as Hume, Mill as well as the aforementioned Pufendorf) have tried to give it a consequentialist justification, while others still (such as Hegel) have sought to undermine the legitimacy of the concept. The absence of a defence of bequest does not make Locke's theory of property any less interesting. On the other hand, however, we might think that his omission of bequest has implications for contemporary political theory. At the beginning of this chapter, I observed that influential 'Lockean' political philosophers have constructed comprehensive normative theories from premises or arguments they claim to find in the *Two Treatises*. As noted, libertarian and left-libertarian theorists such as Nozick and Otsuka make no mention of the fundamental religious commitments that directly inform so many of Locke's arguments. They seem to believe that such commitments are merely axioms that can be removed to reveal philosophical arguments that are nevertheless interesting for a secular, liberal audience.

The temptation to adopt this position stems from what would be entailed by any rejection of it. Consider the conclusions reached by the two scholars who have done most to emphasis the all-encompassing role of religion in Locke's thought: on the one hand, John Dunn who has said that to the extent that it is theologically grounded, Locke's political thought is irrelevant to modern political philosophy (Dunn, 1990: 13) and on the other, Jeremy Waldron (2003), who has said that Locke remains relevant precisely because of the important religious voice that he brings to contemporary debates. Both of these conclusions – that Locke is irrelevant to the concerns of political theory or that his relevance lies in his theology – would seem to be unpalatable. There is thus naturally a huge appeal in believing that we can mine the *Two Treatises* for arguments and ideas that we can use in contemporary debates. Nevertheless, the analysis of inheritance and bequest in Locke's theory of property would seem to illustrate some of the dangers of using him to ground any form of libertarianism. As shown, Locke provides a robust defence of inheritance that is embedded within his account of natural law, whereby we owe duties to preserve ourselves and those beings that we create. At the same time, he fails to provide any independent justification of the power to bequeath and attempts to construct one look unconvincing.

By the late eighteenth century, Lockean political theories, such as those advanced by Thomas Paine, drop the thick account of natural law and along with it the right to inherit, collapsing consideration of all posthumous transfers into the power to bequeath (Paine, 1969). Modern libertarianism does the same thing. Nozick and Otsuka treat the power to bequeath as self-evident: both treat it as part of the libertarian understanding of property ownership, though Otsuka presents its exercise as morally impermissible by appealing to an egalitarian proviso, which – ironically enough – is also described as 'Lockean' (Otsuka, 2003: 24–25, 38). Neither Nozick nor Otsuka include any discussion of the right to inherit, presumably because such a right rests on assumptions about normatively prior duties. Inclusion of such duties would of course prompt questions about their origins and metaphysical status, but, more importantly, their existence would violate the foundational commitment to self-justifiable rights of 'self-ownership' that animates their theories but is actually absent from Locke's. This does not mean that some form of libertarianism is indefensible without Locke. It does, however, mean that its advocates need to come up with some comprehensive justifications for their foundational claims rather than continually cite a misguided view of spirit of the *Two Treatises*. It also makes it no surprise that libertarians have been unable to explain or justify why property ownership implies the power to direct the destiny of a holding after death, a problem that still receives scant attention within contemporary theories of property and justice.[17]

Notes

1 Examples include Tully (1980); Tully (1993); Andrew (1988); Waldron (1988); Simmons (1992); Sreenivasan (1995); Cohen (1995: 165–194); Kramer (1997).
2 See, most memorably, Nozick (1974) and also the recent development of an explicitly Lockean left-libertarianism, outlined in Steiner (1994) and Otsuka (2003). See also Steiner and Vallentyne (2000).
3 It is *almost* entirely, as there are important exceptions, such as Simmons (1992) and Waldron (2002).
4 See Dunn (1969); Waldron (2003). For discussion, see Sigmund (2005).
5 The notable exceptions to this consensus are the scholars influenced by Leo Strauss's reading of Locke's religious beliefs as insincere. See Strauss (1953).
6 He is also regarded as the original philosophical advocate of 'self-ownership', which is extremely problematic. For critical discussions of this theme in Locke, see Lamb (2010) and Coleman (2005).
7 For a balanced philosophical discussion of the strengths and weaknesses of a labour-based justification of property ownership, see Munzer (1990: 254–291). See also Becker (1977: 32–56).
8 We know this, because Locke expects individuals not to labour and not to be punished for this. Those who fail to labour *and* claim to be unjustly affected by the property acquisition of others are merely 'Quarrelsom and Contentious' (Locke, 1988: II: 34) and it is likely and legitimate for those who labour less to acquire less resources (ibid.: II: 48). If individuals fail to labour and become a 'social nuisance', then they will be punished by, ironically enough, being forced to labour (Locke, 1997).
9 This is what then facilitates an economy of wage-labour and why 'the tufts my servant' (Locke, 1988: II:28) has cut belong to me as original labourer rather than my servant as current labourer.
10 The duty to provide charity to those whose poverty is life-threatening is spelled out in somewhat ambiguous terms by Locke in paragraph 42 of the 'First Treatise'. For discussion of its implications and status within Locke's thought, see Lamb and Thompson (2009).
11 This lack of a morally significant relationship through labour would also be true for someone who receives the holding through gift or market exchange. Nevertheless, this observation does not undermine the need for a justification for posthumous transmissibility; indeed, if anything it broadens the need to justify the conventions tied to ownership within Locke's theory to all forms of transmissibility.
12 He goes on to argue: 'For Children being by the course of Nature, born weak, and unable to provide for themselves, they have by the appointment of God himself, who hath thus ordered the course of nature, a Right to be nourish'd and maintained by their Parents, nay a right not only to a bare Subsistence but to the conveniences and comforts of Life, as far as the conditions of their Parents can afford it. Hence it comes, that when their Parents leave the World, and so the care due to their Children ceases, the effects of it are to extend as far as possibly they can, and the Provisions they have made in their Life time, are understood to be intended as nature requires they should, for their Children, whom after themselves, they are bound to provide for' (Locke, 1988: I: 89).
13 The only proviso on the right to inherit is the material condition of the proprietor's parents, who can claim subsistence ownership if they are in dire need. (Locke, 1988: I: 90).
14 I should acknowledge here that I elsewhere mistakenly ascribe the opposite view to Locke (that parents hold full ownership rights over property regardless of the claims of their children) (Lamb, 2010: 139, n. 11).
15 For a comprehensive analysis of the moral relationship between parents and children in Locke's thought, see Simmons (1992: 177–221).

16   But where no such are to be found, *i.e.* no Kindred, there we see the Possessions of a Private Man revert to the Community, and so in Politic Societies come into the Hands of the Public Magistrate: but in the State of Nature become again perfectly common, no body having a right to Inherit them: nor can any one have a Property in them.

(Locke, 1988: I:90)

17 Steiner (1994) argues that anyone who accepts the 'will theory' account of rights – which libertarians would seem implicitly committed to – must also accept that bequest is a 'legal fiction' defensible only on consequentialist rather than rights-based grounds. This is because the necessary condition for a change in relations of ownership (a person's active choice) is absent. Even those unconvinced by Steiner's argument are likely to admit that it puts further pressure on libertarians to offer an account of the legitimacy of bequest.

References

Andrew, E. (1988) *Shylock's Rights: A Grammar of Lockian Claims*, Toronto: University of Toronto Press.

Becker, L. (1977) *Property Rights: Philosophic Foundations*, London: Routledge and Kegan Paul.

Cohen, G.A. (1995) *Self-Ownership, Freedom and Equality*, Cambridge: Cambridge University Press.

Coleman, J. (2005) 'Pre-modern property and self-ownership before and after Locke', *European Journal of Political Theory*, 4: 125–145.

Dunn, J. (1969) *The Political Thought of John Locke: An Historical Account of the 'Two Treatises of Government'*, Cambridge: Cambridge University Press.

Dunn, J. (1990) 'What is living and what is dead in the political theory of John Locke', in J. Dunn, *Interpreting Political Responsibility*, Princeton, NJ: Princeton University Press.

Honoré, A.M. (1961) 'Ownership', in A.C. Guest (ed.), *Oxford Essays in Jurisprudence*, Oxford: Clarendon Press.

Kramer, M. (1997) *John Locke and the Origins of Private Property*, Cambridge: Cambridge University Press.

Lamb, R. (2010) 'Locke on ownership, imperfect duties and the "art of governing"', *British Journal of Politics and International Relations* 12: 126–141.

Lamb, R. and Thompson, B. (2009) 'The meaning of charity in Locke's political thought', *European Journal of Political Theory*, 8: 229–252.

Locke, J. (1988) *Two Treatises of Government*, Ed. by P. Laslett, Cambridge: Cambridge University Press.

Locke, J. (1997) 'An essay on the Poor Law', in M. Goldie (ed.) *Locke: Political Essays*, Cambridge: Cambridge University Press.

Munzer, S. (1990) *A Theory of Property*, Cambridge: Cambridge University Press.

Nozick, R. (1974) *Anarchy, State, and Utopia*, Oxford: Basil Blackwell.

Otsuka, M. (2003) *Libertarianism without Inequality*, Oxford: Clarendon Press.

Paine, T. (1969) 'Agrarian Justice' in P.S. Foner (ed.), *The Complete Writings of Thomas Paine, Volume I*, New York: Citadel Press.

Pufendorf, S. (1991) *On the Duty of Man and Citizen*, Ed. by J. Tully, Cambridge: Cambridge University Press.

Ryan, A. (1984) *Property and Political Theory*, Oxford: Basil Blackwell.

Sigmund, P. (2005) 'Jeremy Waldron and the religious turn in Locke scholarship', *The Review of Politics*, 67: 407–418.

Simmons, A. John (1992) *The Lockean Theory of Rights*, Princeton, NJ: Princeton University Press.

Steiner, H. (1994) *An Essay on Rights*, Oxford: Blackwell.

Sreenivasan, G. (1995) The Limits of Lockean Rights in Property, Oxford: Oxford University Press.

Steiner, H. and Vallentyne, P. (eds) *Left-Libertarianism and Its Critics*, Basingstoke: Palgrave.

Strauss, L. (1953) *Natural Right and History*, Chicago: University of Chicago Press.

Tully, J. (1980) *A Discourse on Property: John Locke and His Adversaries*, Cambridge: Cambridge University Press.

Tully, J. (1993) *An Approach to Political Philosophy: Locke in Contexts*, Cambridge: Cambridge University Press.

Waldron, J. (1988) *The Right to Private Property*, Oxford: Clarendon Press.

Waldron, J. (2002) *God, Locke, and Equality: Christian Foundations in Locke's Political Thought*, Cambridge: Cambridge University Press.

4 Equal inheritance and equal shares

A reconsideration of some nineteenth-century reform proposals

John Cunliffe and Guido Erreygers

In this chapter, we examine three sets of proposals advanced independently in the mid-nineteenth century for a radical reform of existing inheritance practices. The contributions we concentrate on are:

i   The 'Rational Socialists' in Belgium, whose core argument was that individuals owned any material wealth they produced only provided that inheritance taxation secured an egalitarian title in the 'patrimony of humanity' to be realized through an equal capital grant to each maturing adult.
ii The proposal advanced initially by the Catholic theorist, François Huet, at the time of the 1848 Revolutions, that inheritance taxation should be graduated according to the number of intergenerational transfers, with the proceeds being used to provide equal financial endowments to all young adults.
iii The idea advanced by various American writers in the same period that individual inheritance should be subject to confiscatory taxation, with the receipts again being disbursed to secure equal starting points for maturing adults.

These normative commitments to equal opportunity, and the policy proposals for a type of socialized inheritance, reveal particular affinities to present-day calls for individualized 'stakeholding' in the form of capital grants to all young adults.[1] In advancing their schemes, these earlier theorists directly addressed and astutely responded to a range of issues that still figure prominently in debates over this version of stakeholding. Their reform proposals sought to integrate coherently three contested principles. The first, the equality of opportunity principle, was concerned to reduce the *ex ante* inequalities in assets held by young individuals, especially as they assumed the adult responsibility for securing their own subsistence by their own labour. The second, the family principle, took the view that the individual transmission of property was integral both to the traditional family unit and a private property regime. The third, the justice principle, was concerned rather with correcting the *ex post* outcomes of the exercise of those equal opportunities.[2] Whereas the family principle endorsed private transmission, the other principles favoured its abolition or moderation through inheritance taxation and the appropriate disbursement of the proceeds. Although these proposals were designed principally to secure equal opportunities, there was also some limited concern with unequal outcomes, especially if they resulted in destitution. Above all, however, the objective was to prevent these intra-generational outcomes developing into cumulative inter-generational advantages or disadvantages.

This chapter examines these earlier basic capital schemes in the light of the issues raised in the present-day literature on similar projects. Since this provenance is largely unknown to present-day advocates of the idea, they are vulnerable to the charge advanced in André Gide's aphorism that: 'Everything has been said before, but since nobody listens we have to keep going back and beginning all over again.'[3]

In the first three sections, we present the views of the mid-nineteenth century authors. Our presentation of their views is followed by a comparison of some striking differences and similarities between the proposals. The conclusion indicates some of the resonances with present-day debates along with continuing and unresolved issues.

The rational socialists

'Rational socialism' is the brainchild of the idiosyncratic Belgian baron Hippolyte de Colins (1783–1859), who advanced it in numerous repetitive (and increasingly dogmatic and turgid) works. The temptation is to dismiss the doctrine 'as mere nonsense' being nothing more than 'vast pseudo-scientific construction' erected by 'the last of the French-inspired utopian system makers' in the manner of Saint-Simon and Comte. But, it must be conceded that Colins and his followers 'built a considerable superstructure of practical proposals' (supposedly) on its basis.[4] The doctrine was subsequently promoted in a more accessible form by a group of disciples who were mainly Belgian, until it was cast into almost complete oblivion by the outbreak of the First World War. The core argument was that individuals fully owned any artifactual wealth they produced only provided that inheritance taxation secured an egalitarian title in the 'patrimony of humanity' which included natural resources and produced assets received from previous generations.

In his very first work (1835) Colins endorsed the significance attached to individual inheritance by the Saint-Simonians but vehemently rejected their proposal for its abolition. With some exaggeration, he condemned this type of inheritance as 'the sole cause of social injustice' (Colins, 1835: 11, 246). Nonetheless, its abolition would have two disastrous consequences. In the first place, production would cease because the transmission of property within families was the crucial incentive to labour, and secondly, the 'traditional' family itself would disappear to be replaced by 'a universal family owning everything in common.' The problem for 'social justice' was to reconcile two conflicting principles: that the transmission of mobile property within families was 'necessary for social existence'; but also that the stock of natural resources and produced assets received from previous generations constituted a general patrimony to which each individual was entitled to an equal share.

The conflicting demands of efficiency and equity could be reconciled for Colins only through a taxation system which equalized inherited shares in both fixed and mobile property by balancing the privilege of those who received more than that share by a counter-privilege to those who received less. Taxation would penalize the former and compensate the latter, at least insofar as the redistribution was compatible with the incentive effect. The funding mechanism would consist in the socialization of rent on fixed property and taxation of intergenerational wealth transfers of mobile property at the highest level compatible with sustaining economic efficiency. The equivalent to an equal share in the inherited stock of fixed and mobile property would be provided through the collective provision of education and maintenance for all children, provided by the receipts from the fixed property tax. This collective provision would be complemented by a more individualistic measure in the form of a capital grant available to each young adult, funded from the proceeds of inheritance taxation.

These central aspects of Colins's property theory were further developed in a sustained and cogent analysis by Agathon De Potter (1827–1906), arguably the leading intellectual publicist of the doctrine.[5] De Potter painted an unremittingly bleak picture of the inequalities generated or exacerbated by existing practices of individual transmission: 'everything, absolutely everything, conspired against' the proletarian (De Potter, 1912: 22). In what amounted to an hereditary class or indeed a caste system, the life prospects of the proletarian were shaped from the outset by vastly unequal access to educational opportunities and accumulated wealth. The system was one of social predestination according to the privileges of birth in which classes were ossified into castes by the hereditary transmission of advantages or disadvantages. Despite that bleak picture, the appropriate response could not be the suppression of transmission within 'the family properly speaking (...) the domestic family' (De Potter, 1874: II, 37). So long as provision for children was considered as the more or less exclusive responsibility of the family, those two elements were linked 'indissolubly' (ibid.: 30). The 'necessary [infallible] result' of any attempt to suppress the right of individual transmission would be an immense reduction in productive activity (ibid.: 27). Given that private property had to be accepted as the crucial incentive to labour, and that the essential feature of such property was the right of free disposal, it was impossible to eliminate individual transmission without destroying production and the domestic family. Whether that disposal took place *inter vivos* or *causa mortis* made no difference: in both cases, transfers of property titles were based on the will of the owner. Admittedly, bequests expressed the final will, but if that were not implemented, then why should previous transfers be respected? (ibid: 27).

The tension between individual transmission and the realization of equal shares could be resolved only through an inheritance regime which reversed completely the balance between private and social inheritance. Under the existing regime, private inheritance was maximized through unequal individual transmission, and social inheritance minimized; under a rational socialist regime, private inheritance would be reduced to the minimum extent necessary to sustain the incentive effect of individual transmission, and social inheritance maximized by securing equal individual shares in the general patrimony.

Were the state to assume responsibility for the maintenance and education of all children, the connection with their family in this respect could be based on the principle of a discretionary bequest, which permitted rather than required the transmission of property to them. From that viewpoint, the legal priority currently accorded to inheritance rather than bequest constrained free disposal and might constitute a disincentive in cases where one's own children were not the preferred beneficiary. By contrast, under a bequest regime, the discretion allowed the possibility of excluding one's own children altogether, or of discriminating between them, on the ground of varying degrees of devotion to their parents. It remains, of course, a contested point as to which of these modes of transmission best promotes family solidarity. But, even if one's own children were the preferred beneficiaries, the resultant inequalities would not be significant in comparison with the equal shares entitlement.

Given these *ex ante* measures, De Potter endorsed a meritocratic view that readily accepted unequal outcomes provided these reflected choices about the exercise of different natural abilities, rather than different social backgrounds. The central concern was that these unequal lifetime outcomes should not be perpetuated between generations. Even so, since the state was a mutual assurance system against both bad luck and personal folly, some provision would be made to ensure that none became destitute.

Those incapable of working, on any ground, would be provided for as matter of right not charity, and more than adequately. To that extent, the initial capital grant, following free public education and maintenance, would be the central but not exclusive form of state welfare provision. That said, although those incapable of working would be covered, there was no suggestion that this would hold for those able but unwilling to sustain themselves by their own labour. Given the background condition of equal opportunities, all those capable of making a contribution would be expected to live from their own labour: there would be no-one who could live without working, or without having worked, if able to do so.

In relation to mobile property, the balance between the incentive effect of individual transmission and the equal shares entitlement was to be realized through a number of practical measures. Only bequests within the immediate family would be exempt from taxation; and collateral transfers along with all others would be subject to a 25 per cent tax rate. In cases of intestacy, the whole estate would pass to the state, unless there were direct family heirs. The proceeds from this inheritance taxation would fund the *ex ante* equal capital endowment to all young adults as well as the other *ex post* welfare measures to prevent destitution. The capital endowment would follow extensive state provision for the education and maintenance of all children financed by receipts from the socialization of rent on fixed property.

François Huet

The next reform scheme we consider is that advanced by the French philosopher François Huet (1814–1869), who taught for some time at the University of Ghent, where he animated a group of students and colleagues known as the Huet society. Following the February 1848 Revolution in France, Huet was accused of 'socialism' and of 'republican propaganda' by some Belgian newspapers. In 1850 he was forced to resign from his professorship (officially for reasons of health), and Huet returned to Paris. He wrote his main work in social theory, *Le Règne Social du Christianisme*, in 1850/1851 and published it in 1853. Huet developed his social philosophy further in books published in 1864 and 1868, but without changing the 'fundamental idea' of *Le Règne*, 'a guarantee of property to all'.[6] His general intellectual ambition was to reconcile the principles of Christianity with those of the French Revolution. Liberty would be expressed through ownership of self-produced wealth; equality by a uniform capital grant (*dotation*) to all maturing adults; and fraternity by public welfare restricted to instances of involuntary misfortune.

In determining the 'rational law of succession' (Huet, 2000[1853]: 106) Huet introduced the distinctive thought that inheritance taxation should be graduated according to the number of intergenerational transfers. This thought rested on a distinction between the 'general patrimony' of mankind, on the one side, and 'acquired goods', on the other. The 'general patrimony' consisted in natural resources (the 'primitive and divine patrimony') and produced goods (the 'hereditary capital') (ibid.: 106–8). Everyone had the right to receive an equal share of the general patrimony, but this was not an unrestricted right; it was limited by the rights of future generations. The right to inherit an equal share of that patrimony was balanced by the obligation to pass it on intact to the next generation. Individuals were entitled accordingly to use their share, but not to abuse it: it was neither to be squandered nor consumed. The share was not to be disposed of by gifts *inter vivos* or by bequest, and at death, it returned to the general patrimony. These were, in the first place, moral obligations, but if necessary, they would be enforced legally.

The acquired goods were those regarded as the personal creations of their possessors as a result of their own efforts, be it by labour or frugality. The persons who created such goods had a right of free disposal over them, including gifts *inter vivos* or bequest. This unimpeded transfer could occur only once: after that, these gifts of property would be incorporated in the general patrimony, through inheritance taxation at 100 per cent.

The right to a share in the general patrimony would be realized by a system of annual dividends. These would divide the value of the property left by those who died in a given year equally between all those who reached adulthood in that year. This share would be given in two instalments: one-third at the age of 14, two-thirds at the age of 25. The earlier share would enable further education, and the later share would provide the possibility of independent self-employment. Although 'the right to (basic) education' was crucial, the responsibility for providing it along with the maintenance of children lay with parents, as the pro-creators. That responsibility devolved to others only in exceptional circumstances. The equal share in the general patrimony could be supplemented by gifts and bequests, depending upon the 'liberality' of parents and others.

Before publishing his particular version of the *dotation* scheme, the general idea had been discussed in the Huet Society, a group of colleagues and students who met regularly to consider social issues. It seems that two possible objections were raised: that it would disrupt 'family relations' and substitute 'dissipation' for 'thrift' (Voituron, 2004[1848]: 54–5).[7] In his published writings Huet addressed both objections. The rejoinder to the first objection was that family relations would be improved not harmed by the scheme. The current system of individual transmission was a major source of family disputes. That problem would be solved under equal division and the family purified and strengthened by the increased security provided by the scheme. Against the second charge, the response was that allowing one unimpeded transfer would still retain 'the noble incentives' which motivated labour, but that even the children of poor families would now receive an inheritance. (Huet, 2000[1853]: 113)

Huet nevertheless realized that the system could have some disadvantages. The suspicion was that the confiscatory tax rate of 100 per cent on a second intergenerational transfer constituted an incentive to the consumption or dispersal of inherited property so that nothing remained on the death of the first time recipient. Regardless of the precise jurisprudential status of the right of bequest, Huet acknowledged the point that so long as gifts *inter vivos* were permitted they could be used to bypass transmission *causa mortis*. In response to this admitted difficulty, Huet appealed to the influences of religion, ethics and honour, but also suggested legal measures, such as giving wide publicity to transactions and putting the property dealings of older people under surveillance. The initial discussion of the scheme raised an additional and persuasive argument to the effect that some property would remain liable to inheritance duty even if unintentionally: excessive consumption by the elderly (and by implication wholesale dispersal *inter vivos*) would be limited by the uncertain time of death and the concern to secure a comfortable and financially independent old age.

Once the *dotation* scheme was in place, individuals were expected to assume the adult responsibility of meeting their own needs by their own labour. The legal right to further public assistance would be severely restricted to victims of involuntary disasters which could neither be foreseen nor prevented: disasters which rendered an individual incapable of work or deprived of the means of subsistence. As examples of these, Huet mentioned disability, incurable or prolonged illness, and unemployment – when its scale reached the level of a public catastrophe. In contrast, the consequences of improvidence or negligence, and everyday risks, would have to be borne by the individual, or by recourse to charity. The restricted public welfare measures would be funded by proportional wealth taxes.

Huet's core idea of inheritance taxation being graduated through time was adopted knowingly or otherwise by later theorists, but with different intellectual aims.[8] In some cases, the aim was again to prevent an initial inheritance cascading through generations, with the proceeds of taxation being disbursed as private property. In others, the proceeds would be used for the quite distinct purpose of gradually socializing the means of production.

Brownson and Skidmore

The final set of reform proposals we consider is drawn from two American authors in the early nineteenth century. The first and more comprehensive case was presented by the New York labour activist Thomas Skidmore (1790–1832) in his only major book, *The Rights of Man to Property!*, published at the end of 1829. Its long and significant subtitle aptly summarized his ideas: 'Being a Proposition to Make it Equal among the Adults of the Present Generation: and to Provide for its Equal Transmission to Every Individual of Each Succeeding Generation, on Arriving at the Age of Maturity'. The second, and perhaps more intriguing case, was presented by the prolific writer Orestes Brownson (1803–1876) in 1840 when he published two articles in his own journal, the *Boston Quarterly Review*, which sparked a controversy that may have played a role in the Presidential election of that year. The July issue carried his 'The Laboring Classes' and the October issue a much longer article with the same title which later became known as 'Brownson's Defence of the Article on the Laboring Classes' In the first article on the Laboring Classes, Brownson argued that hereditary property was a form of unearned privilege that should be abolished in the American system. It should be replaced by a procedure through which the property of the deceased reverted to the state for equitable allocation to a new generation. In the second article, Brownson argued that the allocation should be in the form of an equal cash endowment. This would confirm the American spirit of equal chances by providing equal starting points. After his conversion to Catholicism in 1844, Brownson published many works typified by religious and political conservatism.[9]

Both writers endorsed unreservedly an already familiar view in American jurisprudence that established conventions of individual transmission were a creature only of municipal law and nothing more than a matter of convenience (especially for current property holders). In their view, those conventions rested on the absurd legal fiction of testamentary bequest, and should be abandoned in favour of natural law requirements. These were interpreted as calling not only for the reversion of the property of the deceased to the common stock, but also for its redistribution through equal shares to each maturing adult. On that basis, they independently formulated very similar proposals for equal starting positions for all young adults to be secured by universal cash endowments funded by 100 per cent inheritance taxation. A mechanism of annual dividends would divide the value of the property left by those who died in a given year equally between all those who reached adulthood in that year. The endowments would be provided in conjunction with publicly funded education and maintenance for all children.

The distinctive and highly controversial feature of Skidmore's programme was that the introduction of this annual redistributive mechanism had to be preceded by a sweeping *tabula rasa* in which *all* existing property would be reallocated equally to all adult individuals. The essence of Skidmore's revolutionary programme was laid down in an ambitious plan which consisted, on the one hand, of a proposed 'General Division of Property', aimed at the equalization of property amongst all living adults, and on the other, of a scheme for an 'Annual Dividend', meant to preserve equality over time. In his view, it was not sufficient to postpone the realization of equal initial shares to some future when the annual dividend mechanism had been realized: the dispossessed had already waited far too long.

In defending their proposals to secure equal opportunities through confiscatory inheritance taxation, both Skidmore and Brownson challenged the received opinion that transforming property rights into a 'life lease' would have adverse effects on the economy and family structures. Skidmore rejected the view that 'a man works for his posterity and not for himself' (Skidmore, 1829: 221) on a number of grounds. To begin with, if parents were so concerned for their own offspring, why was it that in most cases the transmission of property to them occurred only *causa mortis*, when they were already mature adults? And, why was it so rarely the case that parents provided a 'full and sufficient patrimony' (ibid.: 223) to their offspring when they were young adults, at a time when they most needed it and would benefit most from it? Second, there was simply no evidence whatsoever that the desire for the accumulation of wealth differed systematically between those who had children and those who neither had nor expected to have them. Third, if it were claimed that the incentive was provided by the right of bequest rather than inheritance, then most property transfers *causa mortis* were not strategic but 'accidental'. They arose not from dynastic ambition, but from a precautionary concern to secure one's own welfare against the uncertainties of life and the certainty of death only 'at some uncertain and unknown period' (ibid.: 224). Finally, to the extent that indolence presently existed, it was caused either by 'despair and discouragement' on the part of the poor, or by 'ease and indulgence' on the part of the rich (ibid.: 231). Given this scepticism about the claimed effect of individual transmission, Skidmore rejected as fundamentally erroneous the widespread opinion that its abolition would 'thereby destroy all incentive to exertion, or industry' (ibid.: 221). On the contrary, he was confident that the 'equal system' would have little effect on the propensity to accumulate property; just as at present, most individuals would do so to secure their own current and future welfare, rather than with the strategic intention of passing assets on to their chosen successors.

In contrast, Brownson readily conceded that his scheme would indeed reduce but not destroy 'the propensity to accumulate' (Brownson, 2004[1840]: 44). Even so, he regarded this not as an 'objection' to it, but on the contrary as a 'recommendation' (ibid.). Instead of an all pervasive concern for the accumulation of wealth, more time would be available for 'mental and moral culture' (ibid.: 44–5). Within limits, there was nothing wrong with the desire for wealth, which had the positive advantage of enabling individuals to gather objects enabling a comfortable life. The level of the initial capital grant would not be sufficient to sustain a long period of voluntary unemployment; sooner, rather than later, the alternative would be to work or starve, and since 'activity' was natural to man, it could be expressed through work, especially if it came to be regarded as attractive labour rather than being associated with 'servitude and dependence' (ibid.: 45).

As for family structures and values, Skidmore argued that the abolition of discretionary bequests would have beneficial consequences: avoiding on the one side the 'flattery, fraud and cunning' displayed by expectant heirs, culminating in harrowing death-bed scenes as they circled like 'carrion crows' waiting for their spoils, and on the other, the 'revolting tyranny' exercised by fathers as they sought to control the lives of their offspring (Skidmore, 1829: 234–5). But, in a singularly uncompromising manner, Skidmore further asserted that 'gifts in any and every form whatever' (ibid.: 267) should be prohibited and subject to draconian punishment; not only because *inter vivos* dispersal would frustrate the objective of the reform scheme, but also because even within families they expressed inequality. For the recipient, the offer created feelings of resentment at being treated like a menial dependent, and for the donor, it was a symbol of a superior position: everyone knew that 'gifts did not prevail between equals', even between parents and children (ibid.: 347). More cautiously, Brownson accepted that gifts *inter vivos* should be respected, with the exception of those evidently designed as a surrogate for a bequest *causa mortis*, an exception already recognized in existing law. With that reservation, he suggested that gifts *inter vivos* would not frustrate the reform scheme: given that there were no guarantees, parents were justifiably cautious about rendering themselves wholly dependent on their children for support as old age approached. He also acknowledged directly the objection that his proposal might destroy 'the family relation' but only offered by way of a rejoinder some rather incoherent and irrelevant arguments about the geographical dispersal of family members under the present system of private transmission.

Once the capital grant scheme was in place, Brownson and Skidmore readily accepted unequal outcomes related to differences in ambition or talent. If Brownson saw no role for any further state support, Skidmore favoured generous state provision for those reduced to necessity by calamities which were neither foreseeable nor preventable. But, no specific tax base for that provision was suggested.

A comparative analysis

Although developed independently, these equal share schemes identified and rebutted common objections to their proposals. The first was that equal socialized inheritance would threaten family structures and values, whereas existing practices of individual transmission strengthened them. The second was that socialized inheritance would have adverse effects on incentives to work and save, with the consequence that the funds available for redistribution would amount to zero.

In response to the first objection, those who favoured existing practices were accused of conveniently overlooking the extent to which individual transmission encouraged mercenary attitudes threatening family unity. Under bequest regimes, the donor could act capriciously, having the choice of unequal dispersal within the family, or going beyond it. In that knowledge, donors might use their testamentary freedom as a means of control, with potential beneficiaries responding as they saw fit, doing whatever they thought necessary to enhance their prospects of securing a legacy. Whereas the right of bequest was considered as potentially weakening the family unit, the right of inheritance was seen as strengthening it, through constraining testamentary freedom. This was especially the case when equal division was compulsory and restricted to the direct line. But, because wealth could be lost as well as gained, expectations might be thwarted, and most inheritances were actually received when heirs were already established adults in their own right. Even if these inheritance practices promoted equality within families, by the same token they perpetuated inequalities between them, concentrating wealth within dynasties to the exclusion of others. When the locus of responsibility for providing inherited shares to children lay with their parents, only some benefited, and even then, rarely as young children. Were equal shares to be given to each maturing adult through inheritance taxation, then all would benefit at a more appropriate stage in their life cycle. Family values would be unsullied by the mercenary considerations of a bequest regime or the dynastic ambition of an inheritance regime. Instead, the family would become what it should be, infused with equal respect and an absence of corrupting dependence. Since each partner would enter marriage with an equal endowment, over which each retained independent control, that institution would become a meeting of persons rather than estates; and, in their turn, children would no longer have to rely on their parents for any inheritance.

This reform involved a decisive change in the locus of responsibility for providing inherited shares. The duty was no longer parental but devolved to everyone through the agency of the state. With the notable exception of Huet's, the other schemes agreed that the education and maintenance of all children was a collective responsibility of every citizen. The point was emphasized particularly by Skidmore. The equal share entitlement held at birth, but until the shares were allocated to young adults, all citizens benefited from them. This benefit should be recognized in the form of a proportional property tax, with the proceeds being used to fund a system of child allowances and education. This placed special duties on parents to use the allowances in support of their children, but those duties were held not in their capacity as parents but in their role as citizens acting as agents for the state. In marked contrast, Huet retained the more conventional view that whenever possible the responsibility for providing maintenance and education lay with parents, as the procreators. These differences accord with Alstott's view, drawing on Beckert's comparative historical study, that far from reflecting 'a simple or unitary ideal of the family' (Alstott, 2008: 4), debates over inheritance law incorporate multiple and sometimes conflicting conceptions of that institution. Three such conceptions are identified: 'the liberal family, the conventional family, and the functional family' (ibid.). The liberal family accords priority to bequest and testamentary freedom; the conventional family constrains that freedom, regarding property as a joint asset, subject to a right of inheritance and particularly equal inheritance within the direct line, or preferential tax status for bequests within that domain; and the functional family emphasizes its role as an insurance agency providing some measure of economic security for its members, and transmission according to the extent of economic insecurity experienced.

Since the level of the equal shares was a function of the annual ratio between deaths and maturing adults, demographic changes and the locus of procreative responsibility were significant but largely neglected factors in all of the reform schemes. Apart from suggesting minor adjustments to accommodate exceptional mortality rates, or an extraordinarily large number of maturing adults in a particular year, none of the schemes fully addressed demographic factors. Huet alone acknowledged the concern of others that population increase might result in individual shares becoming so small that they would entail only 'a community of suffering' (Huet, 1853: 367). Against that concern, he offered four counter arguments: the first disputed its arithmetical basis; the second claimed that it rested on confusion between necessities and luxuries; the third maintained that it underestimated the total stock of resources; and finally, if more tentatively, Huet considered the possibility that the Malthusian prospect could be averted, or its onset delayed, if equal shares were calculated globally rather than on a national basis.

The second common objection identified in the reform schemes was that changes in the locus of responsibility for providing an inheritance from the family to society would have adverse effects on incentives to work and save. At one extreme, Skidmore made no concession whatsoever to that objection: in his view, even confiscatory taxation at 100 per cent would leave existing incentives unchanged. Individuals worked and saved to secure their own current and future welfare, not for posterity: if any property remained when they passed away, this was not due to strategic intention, but the 'accidental' consequence of what turned out to be over-provision against the contingencies of old age including the uncertain time of death. In his plan, the likelihood of some property still being held at death might be increased, due to the prohibition against dispersal by *inter vivos* gifts (which were only 'wills by anticipation').

Brownson accepted that there might be some disincentive effect but still advocated a 100 per cent tax rate. In similar vein to Skidmore, he argued that the probability of property remaining at death even if accidentally still held. Although not all forms of dispersal *inter vivos* were to become illegal, those clearly designed to evade inheritance duty were to be made so. Dispersal would also be constrained by the desire to secure a comfortable and financially independent retirement, with an associated reluctance to leave oneself overly reliant on the uncertain reciprocity of family members to whom one might have gifted assets. In both schemes, these prudential concerns would be strengthened by the absence of any state provision for old-age retirement, which would have to be funded out of personal savings or by family support. In marked contrast, the other schemes acknowledged that the incentive argument had some purchase, and retained a moderated form of individual transmission. For the rational socialists, it was essential that this form of transmission continued precisely because of the incentive effect, but even so it was to be subject to two restrictions: it was to hold exclusively for mobile property, and only bequests within the direct family line would be tax exempt. Although the incentive was provided by the right of bequest rather than that of inheritance, this arrangement privileged transmission within the family, but left open the possibility of dispersal beyond it subject to a tax liability.

Huet's scheme also retained a moderated right of individual bequest, again subject to two distinctive qualifications: that right held only for the 'acquired goods': and it could be exercised on a tax exempt basis only through one intergenerational transfer, with the next such transfer being subject to a 100 per cent tax rate, returning the value of those goods to the general patrimony. Given Huet's uncompromising view of individual responsibility for all but exceptionally bad 'brute luck', the first unimpeded transfer posed no incentive problem. The inducement to work would be retained as before, with 'normal' unemployment along with the typical contingencies of life not being covered by state assistance, and responsibility for young children still resting with their parents. The encouragement to savings would remain, with old-age retirement having to be funded individually or by charity, and bequest whether within the family or beyond it being permitted and indeed welcomed. Against this, the confiscatory tax rate of 100 per cent on a second intergenerational transfer was recognized as being an incentive to the consumption or dispersal of inherited property. Apart from the financial surveillance measures suggested by Huet himself, another consideration was that any temptation to excessive consumption or premature dispersal by the elderly would be restricted by the uncertain time of death and the necessity to secure financial security in the absence of state pensions.

Conclusion

The three reform schemes discussed in this chapter directly anticipated present-day schemes for a basic capital grant as a type of 'citizen endowment'. The core idea is that there is a set of external resources which are properly regarded as a social inheritance: that this set of resources includes natural resources and produced resources resulting from the labour of previous generations; that each individual has a right to an equal share of them; that the value of those equal shares should be realized by taxing the holders of those external resources; and that the proceeds should be distributed unconditionally and equally to each maturing adult through a one off cash lump sum.[10] In the particular schemes examined in this chapter, before the development of modern tax and welfare systems, inherited wealth was an obvious source of state revenue. This proposed change from the practice of individual to social inheritance was acknowledged as raising a set of controversial issues, which still figure prominently in present-day debates.

The first of these issues was that this social inheritance fund should have a substantial positive value, allowing the individual payments to be substantial enough to affect opportunities decisively. Despite addressing this issue, none of the schemes offered a convincing response. Some of them readily conceded that transmission within families might have to remain as an incentive to the creation and conservation of property through time; and that it would have to be retained even though in an attenuated form. Others vehemently opposed any concessions to familial inheritance and argued for its complete abolition. The schemes all recognized that *inter vivos* dispersal would probably be used to avoid inheritance taxation but the responses were different; some sought to establish modest restrictions on such transfers, while others again argued more uncompromisingly for total proscription. Some of the schemes admitted that inheritance taxation might provide a temptation to increased consumption as old age set in and sought to counter it, whilst others thought that there would be no such danger. Very different views on the optimal tax rate necessary to maximize the yield were presented, ranging from total confiscation to a more moderate 25 per cent. These wide differences reflected sharply contrasting views on the motivations for bequests and whether they were mainly 'accidental' or based on strategic dynastic ambition. Despite all of these uncertainties, the proposals (implausibly) maintained that the social inheritance fund would be sufficient to yield equal shares large enough to decisively affect opportunities at a crucial stage in the life cycle of young adults.

The second and related area of controversy concerns the unconditional nature of the proposed grants. Although the relevant set of external resources was considered a social inheritance, the equal shares were to be distributed in the form of private property. As such, the grants could not be made conditional on any particular form of use. Despite that formal unconditionality, the very strong presumption was in favour of productive use. The sustainability of the schemes depended on there still being sufficient incentives to the creation and conservation of property through time; otherwise the inheritance fund would diminish across generations. The level of the equal shares would vary not only according to the annual ratio between deaths and adulthood but also to the size of the taxable estates. The prospect of stake losing would be reduced insofar as the initial capital grant would be provided only on completion of an education designed in part to provide young adults with the skills required for work and necessary to manage the grant, together with a general culture of responsible stakeholding. Even so, whether through bad luck or personal folly, the opportunities provided by the capital grant might be lost.

This raises the third issue of the extent to which the capital grant was integrated with or considered a substitute for other welfare reforms. To begin with, the most radical schemes saw the grant as complementing state funded education and maintenance for all children. The funding mechanism for this would consist in either a property tax or inheritance taxation. In this latter case, there was a clear tension in the allocation of resources between funding education or capital grants. Even though the proposals emphasized that the general patrimony should secure equal opportunities, they were not entirely indifferent to outcomes. Again, however, quite different views were presented on the degree to which those outcomes were to be addressed by state welfare, and the extent to which inheritance taxation was seen as funding the twin aims of reducing *ex ante* as well as *ex post* inequalities. Insofar as it was, this placed additional restrictions on the scale of the capital grants. Despite these differences, the general presumption was quite clear: all adults capable of working should secure their own livelihood by their own labour. The objection was neither to wage labour as such nor to meritocratic outcomes over a lifetime. It was above all that these intra-generational outcomes should not give rise to cumulative inter-generational advantages or disadvantages.

All this said, these doubts and uncertainties indicate the continuing and unresolved difficulties still confronting similar proposals even now. In this chapter, we have demonstrated that controversies over 'equal shares' entitlements in a general patrimony have a long and often neglected pedigree, from which all of us might still benefit.

Acknowledgements

We are very grateful to Andrew Reeve and Matthew Clayton for their comments on an earlier draft.

Notes

1 White (2003: Chapter 8, 'Basic Capital') presents a cogent analysis of these present-day proposals.
2 These principles are developed in Beckert's (2008) sustained and incisive study.
3 'Toutes choses sont dites déjà; mais comme personne n'écoute, il faut toujours recommencer.' (Gide, 1892: 20).
4 The assessment is offered in Cole (1957: 62). Many other analyses argue that the property theory stands independently of the curious general system. An anthology of writings by Colins and his main disciples has been edited by Ivo Rens (1970); extracts of Colins (1835) can be found in the anthology edited by Peter Vallentyne and Hillel Steiner (2000). On Colins and the rational socialists, see Rens (1968), Rens and Ossipow (1979) and Angenot (1999).
5 Translated extracts of his main work, De Potter (1874), can be found in the anthology edited by Cunliffe and Erreygers (2004).
6 On Huet and his circle in Ghent, see: Cunliffe (1997) and Cunliffe and Erreygers (1999). Translated extracts from Huet (1853) can be found in the anthology edited by Vallentyne and Steiner (2000).
7 We are referring here to the translated extracts of Voituron (1848) which can be found in the anthology edited by Cunliffe and Erreygers (2004).
8 The main examples are the proposals by Ernest Solvay and Eugenio Rignano; for more details, see: Erreygers (1998) and Erreygers and Di Bartolomeo (2007).
9 On Skidmore, see Pessen (1967); on Brownson, see Doudna (1978). Extracts of their work can be found in the anthology edited by Cunliffe and Erreygers (2004).
10 This summary of the core position is drawn from White (2011: 69).

References

Alstott, A.L. (2008) *Family Values, Inheritance Law, and Inheritance Taxation*, Harvard Public Law Working Paper No. 08–49.

Angenot, M. (1999) *Colins et le Socialisme Rationnel*, Québec: Presses de l'Université de Montréal.

Beckert, J. (2008a) 'Inherited wealth. Why is the estate tax so controversial?', *Society*, 45(6): 521–8.

Beckert, J. (2008b) *Inherited Wealth*, Princeton: Princeton University Press.

Brownson, O. (1840) *The Laboring Classes (1840) with Brownson's Defence of the Article on the Laboring Classes*, Delmar, NY: Scholar's Facsimiles and Reprints, 1978. Extracts in Cunliffe and Erreygers, 2004, pp. 32–47.

Cole, G.D.H. (1957) *A History of Socialist Thought, Vol. 11, Marxism and Anarchism*, London: Macmillan.

Colins, J.-G.-C.-A.-H. de Ham (1835) *Du Pacte Social et de la Liberté Politique Considérée comme Complément Moral de l'Homme*, 2 Vols., Paris: Moutardier. Translated extracts in Vallentyne and Steiner (2000), pp. 125–32.

Cunliffe, J. (1997) 'The liberal case for a socialist property regime: The contribution of François Huet', *History of Political Thought*, 18(4): 707–29.

Cunliffe, J. and Erreygers, G. (1999) 'Moral philosophy and economics: the formation of François Huet's doctrine of property rights', *European Journal of the History of Economic Thought*, 6(4): 581–605.

Cunliffe, J. and Erreygers, G. (2000) 'Colins and Huet: Two examples of a French–Belgian tradition of "basic entitlements"', in: P. Dockès, L. Frobert, G. Klotz, J.-P. Potier and A. Tiran (eds) *Les Traditions Economiques Françaises. 1848–1939*, Paris: Editions du CNRS, pp. 785–96.

Cunliffe, J. and Erreygers, G. (2003) '"Basic income? Basic capital!" – Origins and issues of a debate', *Journal of Political Philosophy*, 11(1): 89–110.

Cunliffe, J. and Erreygers, G. (eds) (2004), *The Origins of Universal Grants. An Anthology of Historical Writings on Basic Capital and Basic Income*, London: Palgrave Macmillan.

Cunliffe, J. and Erreygers, G. (2005) 'Inheritance and equal shares: Early American views', in: Karl Widerquist, Michael Anthony Lewis and Steven Pressman (eds) *The Ethics and Economics of the Basic Income Guarantee*, Aldershot: Ashgate, pp. 55–76.

Cunliffe, J. and Erreygers, G. (2008) 'The archaeology of stakeholding and social justice: The foundations in mid 19th century Belgium', *European Journal of Political Theory*, 7(2): 183–201.

De Potter, A. (1874) *Économie Sociale*, 2 vols., Bruxelles: Chez Les Principaux Libraires. Translated extracts in Cunliffe and Erreygers (2004), pp. 73–8.

De Potter, A. (1912) *Résumé de l'Économie Sociale*, 2nd ed., Bruxelles: Monnom.

Doudna, M.K. (1978) 'Introduction', in Orestes Brownson, *The Laboring Classes (1840) with Brownson's Defence of the Article on the Laboring Classes*, Delmar, NY: Scholar's Facsimiles and Reprints, pp. v–xx.

Erreygers, G. (1998) 'The economic theories and social reform proposals of Ernest Solvay (1838–1922)', in W.J. Samuels (ed.) *European Economists of the Early 20th Century, Volume 1*, Cheltenham: Edward Elgar, pp. 220–62.

Erreygers, G. and Di Bartolomeo, G. (2007) 'The debates on Eugenio Rignano's inheritance tax proposals', *History of Political Economy*, 39(4): 605–38.

Gide, A. (1892) 'Le traité du Narcisse', *Entretiens Politiques et Littéraires*, 4(22): 20–8.

Huet, F. (1853) *Le Règne Social du Christianisme*, Paris: Firmin Didot Frères, Bruxelles: Librairie Polytechnique. Translated extracts in Vallentyne and Steiner (2000), pp. 99–123.

Pessen, E. (1967) *Most Uncommon Jacksonians. The Radical Leaders of the Early Labor Movement*, Albany: State University of New York Press.

Rens, I. (1968) *Introduction au Socialisme Rationnel de Colins*, Neuchatel: La Baconnière.

Rens, I. (ed.) (1970) *Anthologie Socialiste Colinsienne*, Neuchatel: La Baconnière.

Rens, I. and Ossipow, W. (1979) *Histoire d'un Autre Socialisme. L'École Colinsienne 1840–1940*, Neuchatel: La Baconnière.

Skidmore, T. (1829) *The Rights of Man to Property*, New York: Burt Franklin, facsimile reprint, 1964. Extracts in Cunliffe and Erreygers (2004), pp. 23–31.

Vallentyne, P. (2000) 'Introduction: Left-libertarianism – A primer', in P. Vallentyne and H. Steiner (eds) *Left Libertarianism and Its Critics: The Contemporary Debate*, Houndmills and New York: Palgrave Macmillan, pp. 1–20.

Vallentyne, P. and Steiner, H. (eds) (2000) *The Origins of Left Libertarianism. An Anthology of Historical Writings*, Basingstoke and New York: Palgrave Macmillan.

Voituron, P. (1848) *Le Droit au Travail et la Propriété*, unpublished manuscript (Central Library of the University of Ghent, Cat. N° Hs. 1795). Translated extracts in Cunliffe and Erreygers (2004), pp. 48–55.

White, S. (2003) *The Civic Minimum; On the Rights and Obligations of Economic Citizenship*, Oxford: Oxford University Press.

White, S. (2011) 'Basic income versus basic capital', *Policy and Politics*, 39(1): 67–81.

5 Are we still modern?

Inheritance law and the broken promise of the Enlightenment

Jens Beckert

The regulation of the transfer of property *mortis causa* has been a major concern of social reformers for more than 200 years. Reform of the laws on inheritance became a pressing topic in the eighteenth and nineteenth centuries for thinkers and politicians such as Montesquieu, Rousseau, Mirabeau, Jefferson, Alexis de Tocqueville, Blackstone, Hegel, Fichte, and John Stuart Mill. All of these thinkers agreed on the importance of inheritance law for the transformation of the social and family order, based on principles of individuality, social justice, democracy, and equality before the law. In fact, reform of inheritance law was seen as a key instrument of social reform, undoing the feudal order of the past and realizing the bourgeois order. The centrality of inheritance law reform is very aptly described by two quotes from Alexis de Tocqueville and John Stuart Mill. Tocqueville wrote that the question of inheritance was so important to a society's development that when 'the legislator has once regulated the law of inheritance, he may rest from his labor' (1980[1835]: I, 48). And John Stuart Mill (1976[1848]: 202–203) saw inheritance law as the most critical area of law, equaled in significance only by contract law and the status of workers.

For social reformers, the bequest of property was often deeply problematic. It was associated with a system of privileges of birth characteristic of aristocratic societies and stood in conflict with crucial bourgeois values of equality and meritocracy. These values are intimately linked to modernity. In his pattern variables, the American sociologist Talcott Parsons (1951) distinguished modern societies from traditional societies in terms of five pairs of categories that pattern social relationships and institutions. While social relationships in traditional societies are characterized by affectivity, collectivity orientation, particularism, diffuseness, and ascription, relationships in modern societies are, by contrast, characterized by affective-neutrality, self-orientation, universalism, specificity, and achievement.

It is just one of these categorical juxtapositions that I will discuss: The distinction between ascription and achievement. Ascription means that social status is institutionally allocated based on characteristics ascribed to people by birth. Certain rights, obligations, roles, or privileges are conferred upon a person, based on the social position of his or her parents or based on gender, age, ethnicity, or nationality. Achievement, by contrast, means that the distribution of wealth and social status is based on the actual contribution or performance of the individual.

From this perspective, the bequest of wealth from generation to generation is deeply problematic in the context of modernity (Beckert 1999). Inherited property comes to the heir 'effortlessly', through the death of another person. The institution of inheritance thus runs counter to the justification of unequal distribution of wealth based on individual merit and achievement and perpetuates social privileges. It also violates the principle of equality of opportunity, which asserts that the starting conditions should be as equal as possible for all, so that differences in wealth can reflect the actual accomplishments of individuals. How can the 'unearned' acquisition of wealth be justified within the context of a social order that legitimizes social inequalities as the product of the different contributions its members make through personal achievement?

But are our societies today really still concerned with the issue of the bequest of wealth from generation to generation? I will argue that the topic of inheritance has concerned social reformers from the age of the Enlightenment onwards, up until the mid-twentieth century. Thereafter, however, the topic lost its significance in public debates. Today, it is a marginalized issue that pops up here and there without creating the social controversy it once did. This is not an interesting observation in itself. It may be, one might suspect, that after 150 years of reform the law has finally become 'modern', and therefore social discourse can shift its attention to other subjects. However, as I will argue, this is not the whole story. Instead, what we can observe over the past 40 years is a backlash in crucial areas of inheritance law which breaks with the Enlightenment promise of moving from ascription to achievement. Hence the question: 'Are we still modern?'

I will first describe three fields of reform of inheritance law which have been of crucial importance to liberal reformers since the late eighteenth century. These are: changes in statutory law, the abolition of entail, and the introduction of progressive estate taxation. I will show how changes in these legal fields can be understood as the recognition of values of equality, meritocracy, and social justice. Following this, I will argue that at least in two of these areas the past 40 years have seen a backlash which breaks in important ways with previous achievements.

But is this really problematic? Do we still have to bother about debates conducted 200 years ago, however passionately? Are the normative principles of the eighteenth and nineteenth centuries still of any relevance today? In the last part I will discuss the question of what the diagnosed backlash means for society and what it means for the concept of modernity.

Inheritance law and the family

Let me start with reforms of statutory inheritance law and their implications for family relations.

Historical analysis reveals how crucial reforms of inheritance law were believed to be for political and social modernization (Beckert, 2008). One of the aims of reforms in inheritance law in the late eighteenth and early nineteenth centuries was changing the structure of family relations. These changes to the family were seen, at the same time, as part of reforms of the political order. This finds clear expression in reforms of inheritance law in France during the Revolution. The reforms were aimed at altering family structures by establishing equality among the children, abolishing the father's arbitrary license in making decisions relating to inheritance, and breaking the dynastic continuity of noble families. The change in family structures brought about by changes in inheritance law was also a *means* of creating the social conditions for new political structures. In France, family relationships based on greater equality were seen to be the foundation stones on which the social structures of the new political community were to be erected. In a constantly recurring metaphor, the family was described as the cell of the nation, whose structure would have a decisive influence on the nature of the political order. Family affairs were thus an '*affaire d'État*'.

These normative and political convictions found expression in several reform projects. The first of these was the abolition of primogeniture. This is a measure introduced in most European countries at about this time, with the remarkable exception of England, where primogeniture was abolished only in 1925. Primogeniture was an important part of intergenerational preservation of economic and political power in feudal societies. Its abolition was a means of breaking with this order.

Other reform projects in statutory inheritance law referred to the equality of brothers and sisters and the rights of the surviving spouse to parts of the property of the deceased. While children achieved equality before the law independent of their gender with the abolition of primogeniture, the strengthening of inheritance rights of the surviving spouse was a long-drawn-out process that was completed only in the second part of the twentieth century.

The issue here is largely one of gender equality. Property law privileged men over women. This was most pronounced in common law. Common law stipulated that, upon marriage, disposition over the wife's property passed to the husband. The wife's moveable property was transferred to the husband, which meant that he also passed it on by will. In the case of real property, while it remained formally in the wife's possession, its economic benefit belonged to the husband. In short, the wife became a *femme covert*. The legal background to this was the principle of marital unity in common law. The 'executor' of this unity was the husband. 'The husband and wife are one person in law', according to William Blackstone's famous dictum (2002[1771]: I, 339).

Reforms to strengthen the legal position of the surviving spouse started in the first half of the nineteenth century. Over a period of 150 years one can observe a steady process of increasing equality between men and women in property law and in inheritance law. These trends demonstrate a growing assertion of the principle of equality. They also demonstrate the declining role of dynastic bequest of wealth within the family blood line.

Gender equality was not the only way in which reforms of inheritance law interfered in traditional family relations aiming at equality in the family.

Especially in France, but also in Germany, the normative principle of equality should also be asserted through the limitation of testamentary freedom. At one point during the Revolution testamentary freedom was completely abolished and even today the stipulations of the Code Civil contain strong restrictions on testamentary freedom. The normative motivation behind this can be seen in a quote taken from a speech by Mirabeau in the Assemblée Nationale in 1791:

> I do not know, gentlemen, how it should be possible to reconcile the new French constitution, in which everything is traced back to the great and admirable principle of political equality, with a law that allows a father, a mother to forget these sacred principles of natural equality when it comes to their children, with a law that favors differences that are universally condemned, and thus further increases the disparities brought forth in society by differences in talent and industry, instead of correcting them through the equal division of the domestic goods.
>
> (Mirabeau, 2 April 1791, in Lettke, 2003: 24)

Entails

A second field in which the reform of inheritance law was meant to transform the social order on the basis of Enlightenment ideas was the abolition of entails. Entails were an important and highly controversial instrument for preserving the concentrated distributions of landownership of feudal societies by placing restrictions on heirs' rights of disposition. If property is entailed it cannot be sold; instead, it is passed on from generation to generation according to the succession determined by the founder. As a rule, the landed property was bequeathed to the eldest son and had to be passed on in all subsequent successions to the eldest son in the next generation. Entails are a legal institution of dynastic bequest through which the testator can control the use of his property across generations, thereby exerting influence on the property relationships of the succeeding generations. The wealth is directed by the 'dead hand' of the person who established the entail.

Fierce criticism developed against entails as early as the eighteenth century. It was aimed at the special privileges granted to one class of property owners, as well as at the political structures propped up by these privileges. Preferential treatment of one social class in property law runs counter to the principle of civic equality, which serves as the normative foundation of the liberal concept of social order. Liberal social theory rejected entail as an instrument for the dynastic perpetuation of the nobility's privileged social status. In the liberal worldview, entail goes against civic equality, individual rights of freedom, the concept of meritocracy, and political democratization. This criticism was combined with economic arguments concerning the negative economic effects of restrictions on the mobility of property. John Stuart Mill (1976[1848]), for instance, denounced entails as an aristocratic institution which promoted an economic culture that ran counter to the acquisitive desire: the 'heir of entail, being assured of succeeding to the family property, however undeserving of it, and being aware of this from his earliest years, has much more than the ordinary chance of growing up idle, dissipated, and profligate' (Mill, 1976[1848], 895).

Two quotes show how much the abolition of entail was considered central to social modernization by contemporaries. A report to the Assemblée Nationale from 1792 reads: '(E)ntails are odious. ... their preservation is incompatible with the sacred principles of liberty and equality...' (Arch. Parl. 1. Série, t. 49, p. 55, quoted in Eckert, 1992: 183). In the United States, Thomas Jefferson formulated his rejection of entails in the famous formula: 'the earth belongs in usufruct to the living' (Jefferson). Even conservative legal scholars – at least in the United States – were outspoken critics of this institution. James Kent, for instance, wrote in the early nineteenth century that entails have

> no application to republican establishments, where wealth does not form a permanent distinction, and under which every individual of every family has his equal rights, and is equally invited, by the genius of the institutions, to depend upon his own merit and exertions.
>
> (Kent, 1971[1827]: 20)

Hence, one of the crucial reforms in inheritance law in the nineteenth century was the abolition of entail. This took place in the United States during the Revolution. The same holds true for France, with the exception, however, that entails were reintroduced in the period of restoration and finally abolished only in the Second Republic in 1848. In Germany, abolition had to wait until the Revolution of 1919.

Estate taxation

Finally, the third field in which the new regulations on inheritance were meant to be an important element of social reform was estate taxation. The early nineteenth century already saw the emergence of a debate among liberal and early socialist social reformers in which inheritance taxation was advocated as an important instrument for making good on the promise of equality and for solving the 'social question'. Within the framework of liberal social theory, inheritance taxation appeared to be an especially suitable tool for achieving equality of opportunity *within* a system based on private property (Beckert, 1999). Since inheritance taxation falls upon property that passes to heirs without any effort of their own, taxing this wealth is in line with the meritocratic principle. In normative terms, inheritance taxation seems far less problematic than an income or consumption tax.

The justification for the introduction of an inheritance tax referred to four different arguments:

1   The first of these was a direct reference to the principle of achievement. Many liberal thinkers argued that 'accidents of birth' have no normative

place in a liberal social order. Social inequality could be justified only by the different individual contributions of members of society, not by the luck of being born into a wealthy family. As a consequence, property needs to be redistributed with each generation. In the 1840s, the American social reformer Orestes Brownson, for instance, advocated confiscatory inheritance taxes. They alone were compatible with the principle of equality of opportunity and individual entrepreneurship: 'A man shall have all he honestly acquires, as long as he himself belongs to the world in which he acquires it. But his power over his property must cease with his life, and his property must then become the property of the state, to be disposed of by some equitable law for the use of the generation which takes his place.' (Brownson, 1978a[1840]: 24) Brownson's intention was to endow individuals with equal resources at the start of life. To that end, ascriptive material privileges were to be abolished (ibid.: 60ff.). Property rights terminated upon death and property thus reverted to society (ibid.: 71). If property became 'free', 'one man can rightfully appropriate to himself no more than, in an equal division of the whole among all the members of the new generation, would be his share' (ibid.: 75). Brownson's goal was to implement equal opportunities and with it an achievement-based distribution of social wealth.

2   The second argument in favour of estate taxation referred to changing family structures in the process of modernization. John Stuart Mill (1976[1848]), for instance, pointed to the change in the structure of property in bourgeois societies. Speaking of earlier societies, the family was the owner of property. For that reason, when a family member died there was no succession, because one share of the family wealth simply passed to the other members of the family. Death and birth merely changed the identity of those who participated in property jointly owned by the clan. Modern society, however, was characterized by a fundamental change in family structures, according to Mill. That change made it meaningful to speak of individual property in the first place, but at the same time it delegitimized inheritance: 'The unit of society is not now the family or clan, composed of all the reputed descendants of a common ancestor, but the individual; or at most a pair of individuals with their unemancipated children.' (ibid.: 222)

3   A third argument justifying inheritance taxes referred to the changing role of the state, which takes on more and more obligations and needs to secure the financial means to fulfill them. This was an argument that was advocated in particular by representatives of the historical school in Germany. In his *Rede über die soziale Frage* (Speech on the Social Question, 1872), Adolf Wagner advocated a progressive inheritance tax because, in the process of modernization, tasks of the family would increasingly shift to the state: 'The more individualism takes hold in the life of the people in place of the strict family and gender order, the more justified in principle, and the more necessary and just in practice, does the participation of the public body, especially the state, in inheritance become, and therefore the more justified is a system of expansive inheritance taxes.' (Wagner, 1880: 477f.)

4   Finally, the fourth argument referred to the consequences of wealth concentration through inheritances for the democratic political order. This argument was especially prominent in the American debate in the early twentieth century. It reflects mistrust of 'big business' and its role in the Gilded Age. The populist and progressive movements in particular pointed to the threat to the democratic political process stemming from wealth concentration. President Roosevelt applied this argument, for instance, in a speech to Congress in 1935: 'Such inherited economic power is as inconsistent with the ideals of this generation as inherited political power was inconsistent with the ideals of the generation which established our Government.' (Roosevelt, C.R., No. 79, vol. 9, p. 9712, 19 June 1935)

The introduction of progressive inheritance taxes took place in France in 1901, in Germany in 1906 and in the United States in 1916. The conflict over the taxation of inheritance was the most important theme in inheritance law in the twentieth century. Inheritance taxation was a highly contested political issue. This came about also because the taxation of inheritances introduced a new regulatory quality compared to the questions of inheritance law examined previously. Through inheritance taxes *the state* does not interfere with the distribution of property *within the family*, but *appropriates for itself* a part of the property left behind by the deceased. Questions of individual property rights, equality, justice, and the economic and familial consequences of the rules of inheritance law are related to the distribution of wealth *within society.*

Inheritance law as social reform

The discussion of the three legal fields in which inheritance law has been most controversial shows the extent to which this legal realm had been considered crucial for social reform. While most of the arguments brought forward can be identified already in the first half of the nineteenth century, the political controversy continued until about the 1930s. In the first part of the twentieth century, many of the reforms discussed in the nineteenth century were finally institutionalized. Entails were also abolished in Germany (1919), Great Britain ended primogeniture (1925), legal reforms in statutory law led to more gender equality and almost all Western European countries and the United States introduced progressive inheritance taxes. Hence we can observe how inheritance law, in accordance with the principles of achievement and equality of opportunity, changes along with the development of modernity.

This is not to say that the reforms that were implemented did not meet fierce opposition. It took until 1919 for entail to be abolished in Germany. The introduction of progressive inheritance taxes was met with furious opposition by conservatives and in the United States the federal estate tax was almost abolished again in the 1920s. But despite this opposition there was an understanding that the regulation of the transfer of property from generation to generation is an important topic which has important implications for the type of society we live in. The topic of inheritance law reform entered the political discourse from various social fields: from social movements that emanated from the lower social classes, as well as the middle class; from property owners themselves; and from scholarly discourse. While the reforms did not meet with universal approval, there was a climate of public opinion in which reform was perceived as necessary to enhance equality of opportunity, as a counterweight to the existing concentration of wealth, and as a contribution to tax equity. In the United States, a new understanding of the role of the state in social reform articulated itself in the late nineteenth century, one that would shape large parts of the history of Western countries in the twentieth century.

The backlash against inheritance law in the late twentieth century

Popular support for inheritance taxation can be observed in the United States, for instance, in populist movements such as Senator Huey Long's *Share Our Wealth* movement in the 1930s. Long's demand was to impose a confiscatory tax on fortunes over one million dollars (Fried, 1999: 65ff.). By 1935, the *Share Our Wealth* movement had grown to 7 million members, all over the United States. However, this popular support of estate taxation was not sustained throughout the twentieth century.

It is this change to which I now turn. To understand the change in the dominant perception of bequeathed wealth in the last quarter of the twentieth century, two other populist movements in the United States are indicative. One is the failed presidential campaign of George McGovern in 1972. McGovern had called for a progressive inheritance tax, which would reach 100 percent for inheritances above half a million dollars (Weil, 1973: 74). McGovern assumed that the vast majority of voters had strong reservations about the existing concentration of wealth in American society and would therefore support his plan. But the political mood in the United States had changed by that time and the broad American middle class now turned its back on such demands. By the 1990s, opposition to estate taxation had become even more influential. In the context of debates in the United States on abolishing the federal estate tax, the advocacy group *nodeathtax.com* lobbied for the abolition of the estate tax, exerting a strong political influence on public attitudes towards the tax. The vast majority of American voters supported the tax reforms of the Bush administration in 2001, which included the phasing out of the estate tax in 2010.

The lack of support for McGovern's plan in 1972 can be seen as a symbolic turning point in applying inheritance law and inheritance taxes as instruments of social reform. Since the early 1970s, a process of restoration in inheritance law has taken place against the backdrop of vanishing public support for using inheritance law as a reform instrument and an increasing public ignorance with regard to the topic.

1   Estate taxes have been abolished or severely reduced in many OECD countries, starting in 1972 with New Zealand. Opinion polls regularly show that

the tax finds very little support among the electorate, even among the majority of voters who would never be personally affected by this tax because
they lack taxable assets. It is puzzling that this is the case. Is it because
voters lack accurate information, as the American political scientist Larry
Bartels (2005) argues in his analysis of the Bush tax reforms? Is it because
the taxation of bequests is seen as an undue interference in family relations?
Is it because many people dream of being an heir to a large fortune themselves one day? Is it because (small) countries seek advantages in international tax competition?

2   The discussion of entails showed that Enlightenment reformers were especially suspect of forms of dynastic wealth transfer which tie up wealth
according to the will of the testator over many generations or infinitely. In
common law, the rule against perpetuities prevents wealth from being
locked for more than about 100 years. In recent years, this rule has been
abolished or significantly modified by almost half the American States. It
has also been abolished in Ireland (Röthel, 2010: 75; Moshman, 2006). Also
in other jurisdictions wealthy testators seek increasingly to control the living
through their 'dead hand', whether through trusts or by donating their
wealth to foundations. What does this imply for the possibility of social
mobility in a society? What does it mean for the living to have their lives
partly controlled by decisions taken by a preceding generation? What does it
mean with regard to Thomas Jefferson's dictum: 'the earth belongs in usufruct to the living'?

3   It is only in the field of statutory inheritance law that we can observe a continuation of modernization processes that started in the early nineteenth
century. Husband and wife are treated equally by inheritance law today; the
horizontal relationship between husband and wife has been strengthened at
the expense of the inheritance rights of the blood line; increasingly, homo-
sexual couples enjoy inheritance rights from their partners; and children
born out of wedlock were granted the same inheritance rights as legitimate
offspring. Many of these developments are very recent. Some of them have
not been completed. But there is no reversal in direction observable, as in
the realms of estate taxation and the control of the 'dead hand'.

Conclusion

'Are we still modern?' It is, I believe, a helpful exercise to go back in history
and try to understand the normative concerns of the time in which the foundations of our political and social orders were formed. This provides a yardstick
against which current discourses and institutional changes can be measured.
Inheritance has been seen as an important instrument of social and democratic
reform. Indeed, it has been an instrument of social modernization. Concerns
about equal opportunities, individual freedom, social justice, and the viability of
the democratic order stood front and center in these debates. Today, interest in
the topic has largely vanished and when the taxation of inheritances is debated,

issues of efficient taxation dominate. This is but a small part of the issues involved in the regulation of transfers *mortis causa*.

It is certainly not easy to explain this change. I believe it is part of the great transformation (Blyth, 2002) that has taken place since the 1970s in all Western countries. Support for a strong state as an instrument of social reform has declined dramatically since the years of the postwar consensus. Taxation is seen as inhibiting economic growth within the context of the dominant supply-side economics. Globalization allows mobile capital to choose among legal jurisdictions on a global scale, providing incentives, especially to small states, to offer low taxation regimes to wealthy individuals.

The change, however, is not just economic, but social and cultural as well. The increasing social pressures on the middle class, combined with processes of individualization observed by sociologists since the 1960s, contribute to desolidarization. Attempting to protect one's offspring from the vagaries of the market through inheritance is an individualized reaction to social conditions which expose actors to more and more insecurity. The taxation of inheritances is not perceived as a means of securing the provision of opportunities socially, but as a further threat.

Culturally, there seems to be a tendency for the distribution of wealth to find legitimation even if it is not based on achievement resulting from individual performance. Instead, 'success' – as the German sociologist Sighard Neckel (2008) argues – is the category according to which wealth and social status are allocated, whether it concerns the incomes of top managers which have increased to levels which bear no relationship to their work performance, the income celebrities receive from their popularity, the promise of riches from lotteries, or inheritances. Societies seem once again willing to allow the disconnection of life chances from individual performance. Nevertheless, if one is to believe sociological studies on attitudes towards inequality, it seems to be that structures that reproduce social inequality are much less a normative problem for the average person than they are for the social scientist (Sachweh, 2010).

'Are we still modern?' What it means to be modern must be defined ever anew. If judged by the normative standards defined in the era of the Enlightenment and informing political controversies through much of the nineteenth and twentieth century, we are observing a profound shift in social organization. The way inheritance law and debates on this law change are informative indicators for this shift.

References

Bartels, L.M. (2005) 'Homer gets a tax cut: Inequality and public policy in the American mind', *Perspectives on Politics*, 3: 15–31.

Beckert, J. (1999) 'Erbschaft und Leistungsprinzip. Dilemmata liberalen Denkens', *Kursbuch*, 135: 41–63.

Beckert, J. (2008) *Inherited Wealth*, Princeton: Princeton University Press.

Blackstone, W. (2001[1771]) *Commentaries on the Laws of England*, Four volumes, London and Sydney: Cavendish Publishing.

Blyth, M. (2002) *Great Transformations. Economic Ideas and Institutional Change in the Twentieth Century*, Cambridge: Cambridge University Press.

Brownson, O. (1978a[1840]) 'The Laboring Classes', in O. Brownson, *The Laboring Classes*, Delmar: Scholars' Facsimiles Reprints, pp. 5–24.

Eckert, J. (1992) *Der Kampf um die Familienfideikommisse in Deutschland*, Frankfurt a.M.: Peter Lang.

Fried, A. (1999) *FDR and His Enemies*, New York: St. Martin's Press.

Kent, J. (1971[1826–1830]) *Commentaries on American Law*, Four volumes, New York: DaCapo.

Mill, J.S. (1976[1848]) *Principles of Political Economy*, Fairfield, NJ: Augustus M. Kelley.

Mirabeau, H.-G. Riquetti (2003[1791]) 'Rede über die Gleichheit der Teilung bei Erbfolge in direkter Linie', in F. Lettke (ed.) *Erben und Vererben. Gestaltung und Regulation von Generationenbeziehungen*, Konstanz: Universitätsverlag, pp. 11–22.

Moshman, R.L. (2006) 'Dynastic trusts today. An interview with Steven J. Oshins', in *The Estate Analyst*, Available www.oshins.com/images/Bob_Moshman_s_Article.pdf (accessed 29 July 2010).

Neckel, S. (2008) *Flucht nach vorn: Die Erfolgskultur der Marktgesellschaft*, Frankfurt a.M.: Campus.

Röthel, A. (2010) *Ist unser Erbrecht noch zeitgemäß?*, Gutachten A zum 68. Deutschen Juristentag, München: Verlag C.H. Beck.

Sachweh, Patrick (2010) *Deutungsmuster sozialer Ungleichheit. Wahrnehmung und Legitimation gesellschaftlicher Privilegierung und Benachteiligung*, Frankfurt a.M./ New York: Campus.

Parsons, T. (1951) *The Social System*, New York: Free Press.

Tocqueville, A. de (1980[1835]) *Democracy in America*, 2 volumes, New York: Knopf.

Wagner, A. (1872) *Rede über die soziale Frage*, Berlin: Wiegandt und Grieben.

Weil, G.L. (1973) *The Long Shot. George McGovern Runs for President*, New York: W.W. Norton.

6 Entailed citizenship

Ayelet Shachar and Ran Hirschl

Citizenship theory has long been dominated by concepts such as nationhood, membership and identity. In this chapter, we draw on several key concepts in property and inheritance theory to suggest that birthright citizenship laws, and the inter-generational transmission of political membership more generally, may be conceptualized as a form of inherited property. Such fresh conceptualization may help us understand the 'worth' of citizenship in an unequal world, as well as open the door to new and innovative ideas for mitigating the profound distributive consequences that attach to relying on circumstances of birth in allotting political membership.[1]

Consider this stunning fact. The vast majority of today's global population – 97 out of every 100 people – have acquired their political membership by virtue of birthplace or 'pedigree'.[2] There is little doubt that securing membership status in a given state or region – with its specific level of wealth, degree of stability, and human rights record – is, even in the current age of increased globalization and privatization, a crucial factor in the determination of life chances. However, birthright entitlements still dominate both our imagination and our laws in the allotment of political membership to a given state. In fact, material wealth and political membership (which are for many the two most important distributable goods) are the only meaningful resources whose intergenerational transfer is still largely governed by principles of heredity. And whereas the normative foundations of these principles have been thoroughly discussed in terms of the intergenerational transfer of property, they have seldom been considered in terms of citizenship.

This lacuna is especially disturbing in light of recent and vibrant debates in political and legal theory concerning the claims of cultural and religious minorities, the narratives of collective-identity formation, and the ethics of political boundaries. These debates engage with what can be referred to as the 'identity-bonding' dimension of citizenship. What remains conspicuously absent from these discussions, however, is a serious analysis of what we might call the 'opportunity-enhancing' implications of the entrenched norm and legal practice associated with automatically allocating political membership according to parentage (*jus sanguinis*) and territoriality (*jus soli*) principles.

In today's world, one's place of birth and one's parentage are – by law – relevant to, and often conclusive of, one's access to membership in a particular political community.³ As a result, access to affluent countries in our unequal world is still reserved primarily to those born in a particular territory or to a particular ancestry; those born on the 'wrong side' of the border of security and prosperity are shut out. A recent report solemnly captures this last point: 'Even in today's mobile and globalized world, most people die in the same country in which not only they are born, but their parents as well.'⁴

It is undisputed that birthright citizenship largely shapes the allocation of membership entitlement itself. But it does more than that: it also distributes opportunity in a vastly unequal manner. Upholding the legal connection between birth and political membership renders citizenship in a well-off society beyond the reach of the vast majority of the world's population. It is in this way that birthright citizenship may be thought of as the quintessential inherited entitlement of our time. In a world where membership in different political communities translates into very different starting points in life, the implications of this citizenship-transmission regime are profound.

Under the present allocation system of birthright citizenship, 'some are born to sweet delight' as William Blake memorably put it in *Auguries of Innocence*, while others (through no fault or responsibility of their own) are 'born to endless night'. The reality of our world is that the endless night is more prevalent than the sweet delight. As a regime of 'entailed' transmission, our birthright citizenship laws effectively become intertwined with distributing shares in human survival on a global scale. This raises the moral disdain against acquisition and transfer rules that systemically exclude prospective members on the basis of ascriptive criteria. It also highlights the urgent need to place the discussion of bounded membership within a broader framework of debate, exploring the distributional effects of birthright citizenship, which often translate into dramatically different life prospects for the individuals involved. And whereas we find vibrant debates about the legitimacy of citizenship's *demos*-demarcation function (or 'gate-keeping'), the perpetuation of unequal starting points through the intergenerational transmission of membership has largely escaped scrutiny. It remains conveniently concealed under the current system of entailed citizenship transmission.

We begin our discussion of birthright citizenship transfers as conceptually analogous to opportunity-enhancing structures of inheritance transmission by highlighting the disparities in the living conditions and opportunities offered to citizens born into different political communities in an unequal world. In the second section, we show how this new framework helps explain the two core functions of bounded membership in the world today: 'gate-keeping' and 'opportunity-enhancing'. In the third part we venture into an exploration of the early common-law mechanisms of entailed estates, showing the surprising commonalities in both form and function between these antiquated forms of property transmission in perpetuity and present-day birthright principles that regulate access to prized membership. Both these mechanisms serve to preserve and legitimize immensely advantageous starting points in life to the beneficiaries of the entailed transmission. In the concluding part, we suggest that the analogy between birthright citizenship and the fixed intergenerational transfers allows us to draw upon ideas and institutions found in the realm of inheritance as a model for imposing restrictions on the currently unburdoned and perpetual transmission of membership – with the aim of ameliorating the current system's most glaring opportunity inequalities.

What is the 'worth' of citizenship?

Much has been written about global inequality. Everybody knows that the living conditions of a child born in Swaziland are *ceteris paribus*, far worse than those of a child born in Switzerland. Publications such as the UNDP's *Human Development Report* or the World Bank's *World Development Report* reveal just how tremendous global disparities in life opportunities, chances and choices actually are.[5] Consider, for example, measurements reflecting absolute deprivation: that is, the number of people falling below a threshold of decent human functioning, such that the possibility of autonomous human agency is severely restricted if not outright removed.[6] According to recent World Bank statistics, approximately 1.1 billion people live in extreme poverty with an income of $1 per day per person, measured at purchasing power parity.[7] Another 1.6 billion live in moderate poverty, defined as living on between $1 and $2 per day. In other words, over 2.7 billion people – approximately 45 per cent of the world's population survive on less than $2 a day. Virtually all of the world's extreme and moderate poor live in Asia, Africa, and Latin America. The overwhelming share of the extremely poor live in South-East Asia and sub-Saharan Africa – at least 25 per cent of the households in almost all sub-Saharan Africa or East Asian countries subsist on less than $1 per day per person in real purchasing power. As of the early 2000s, the average annual per capita income in the United States exceeded $30,000, with an average annual growth of 1.7 per cent over the last two centuries. In contrast, the per capita annual income in Africa is just over $1,300 (far below that in sub-Saharan Africa), with an average annual growth of 0.7 per cent over the last 200 years. Global inequalities in terms of income are even more striking when gender is factored in. Whereas in most industrialized polities, significant strides have been made toward the elimination of at least formal gender inequality, women in most developing countries continue to lag far behind their fellow countrymen in terms of income and the ability to make meaningful life choices.

But global inequalities in opportunity go far beyond income and expenditure. The mean years of educational attainment for the world have almost doubled from 3.4 in 1960 to 6.3 in 2000. However, disparities in educational attainment and achievement between students in developing and OECD countries remain strikingly large. In many developing countries, literacy rates are still unacceptably low. According to the 2006 World Development Report, developing countries constitute the lower tail of the learning distribution. Students in these countries fare on average far worse than students in even the poorest-performing OECD countries. A recent study found that among children in Argentina and Chile, average performance is two standard deviations below that of children in Greece – one of the poorest performing countries in the OECD. Another recent study found that the reading ability of an average Indonesian student is equivalent to that of a French student at the seventh percentile.

Whereas in 2008 the health expenditure per capita in Switzerland and Norway was roughly $5,000 (PPP US$), the health expenditure per capita in Mongolia in the same year was $131, and a meagre $18 in Eritrea.[8] Or take the crucial indicator of access to clean water. In 2002, 100 per cent of Australia's population had permanent access to safe water source. But only 70 per cent of Australia's neighbouring Solomon Islands' population, and approximately 39 per cent of neighbouring Papua New Guinea's population had sustainable access to safe water sources. Another revealing disparity is found in health care provisions. Even health outcomes of the rich citizens in poor countries remain well below OECD average – for all countries with average per capita GDP below $2 a day, the infant mortality rate of the richest quintile of the population is more than 10 times higher than the OECD average. Basic sanitation standards seem to be a long way off throughout the developing world. The availability of appropriate medical services and drugs is sporadic. And we have not yet taken into account the developing HIV/AIDS pandemic, with its clear regional concentration and impact on infant mortality.

A baby born in 2001 in Mali – one of the world's poorest countries – had a 13 per cent chance of dying before reaching the tender age of one year, with his or her chances improving a mere 4 per cent, to 9 per cent, if the baby was born to a family in the top quintile of Mali's asset distribution. It is further estimated that approximately one in five children (18 per cent) born in Mali in 2010 will not reach age five.[9] By contrast, a baby born in United States the same year had less than a 1 per cent chance of dying in its first year or first five years. The probability at birth of not surviving to age 40 (percentage of cohort 2000–2005) in Mali was 37.3 per cent. In other words, at least one in every three people born in Mali between 2000 and 2005 will die before reaching the age of 40. As of 2003, only 48 per cent of Mali's population had sustainable access to an improved water source (100 per cent had such access in the US). That year, over 70 per cent of Mali's population lived on less than $1 a day, and over 90 per cent of Mali's population on less than $2 a day. While the average American born between 1975 and 1979 has completed more than 14 years of schooling (roughly the same for men and women, and in urban and rural areas), the average attainment of the same cohort in Mali is less than two years, with women's attainment less than half that of men, and virtually zero in rural areas. Not surprisingly, the illiteracy rate in Mali (percentage of ages 15 and above as of 2003) was 81 per cent. Taking into account the actual quality of education in the two countries is likely to yield far greater differences.

In short, the general well-being, quality of services, safety, and scope of freedoms and life-prospects enjoyed by those born in affluent polities are all far greater, *ceteris paribus*, than the opportunities of those born in poor countries. Ours is a world in which disparities of opportunity between citizens of different countries are so great that about half of the population of the world, according to the World Bank, lives 'without freedom of action and choice that the better-off take for granted'.[10] While extant citizenship laws do not create these disparities, they perpetuate and reify dramatically differentiated life prospects by reliance on morally arbitrary circumstances of birth, while at the same time camouflaging the crucial distributive consequences of this human-made legal system by appealing to the presumed 'naturalness' of birth-based membership.

These dramatically differentiated life prospects should disturb not only egalitarians, but also free-marketers who believe in rewarding effort and distributing opportunity according to merit, rather than station of birth.[11] This problem of unequal allocation, which has gained plenty of attention in the realm of property, is, as the data provided here documents, far more extreme in the realm of hereditary citizenship. Remarkably, in spite of the conceptual affinity between the intergenerational transfer of property and birthright citizenship, and irrespective of the thousands of pages devoted to debating the justifications for inheritance in property theory, there have been few, if any, scholarly attempts to scrutinize the justifications for automatic inheritance of citizenship by birth. Political theory's silence with respect to the intergenerational transfer of citizenship by the random location or station of birth becomes all the more astonishing considering that the incredible gaps in life opportunities created and perpetuated by birthright citizenship regimes are far deeper and infinitely more multifaceted than the material inequalities perpetuated through intergenerational transfer of fungible wealth. By proposing a new way of thinking about the intergenerational transfer of citizenship as a special kind of property inheritance, a new space is opened up for the development of just such debate.

Property and citizenship: several analogous functions

Bounded membership regimes share several important characteristics with 'property', broadly conceived.[12] To begin with, citizenship provides a textbook example of the *combination* of a right to exclude *and* the right not to be excluded. Where citizenship is concerned, we will call the right to exclude 'gate keeping' and the right not to be excluded 'opportunity-enhancing'. We analyse each in turn.

The gate-keeping function of citizenship

Citizenship crafts, to borrow from Jeremy Waldron's definition of property, a system of rules governing access to and control of a scarce resource; in this case, the precious good of membership in our human communities.[13] It demarcates who is included in the body politic and who is excluded from it. States in the real world tend to be stringent, if not outright unyielding, in terms of drawing and enforcing the boundaries that distinguish those who 'belong' from those who do not.[14] Every state currently limits access to its citizenship, typically by granting automatic entitlement only to a select group of beneficiaries according to ascriptive principles of birthplace and bloodline (*jus soli* and *jus sanguinis* respectively).[15] Focusing on gate-keeping, it is notable that '[c]itizenship is not only an instrument of closure, a prerequisite for the enjoyment of certain rights, or for participation in certain types of interaction. It is also an object of closure, a status to which access is restricted.'[16] In other words, polities follow through on their *right to exclude*. This is in part based on the rationale that in a liberal-democratic country, once a person is included in the membership, that person is entitled (or will eventually be entitled) to the complementary *right not to be excluded* from any additional attendant rights and privileges. This simultaneous quality of (external) exclusion and (internal) inclusion matches the twin properties we earlier identified as central to the broad conception.

Despite much academic fanfare about the 'demise of borders', in practice, entry into a foreign land is still restrictive for most of the world's population, especially for those arriving from low-income or politically unstable countries. Only members have an unconditional right to enter and stay in the state; strangers do not. Their cross-border mobility is anxiously guarded by border agencies whose main task is to monitor and regulate admission. Such regulation is carefully enforced at the external perimeter, though it increasingly bleeds into the interior as well.[17] It typically involves a legal checkpoint, a passport, and the discretion of the official gatekeeper of the state as to whether or not to grant admission to a non-member, and under what conditions.

Just as with property, citizenship creates a set of obligations on the admitting state – the right to exclude is never unlimited in practice – but it also specifies the types of sanctions that can be imposed against a person who seeks to 'trespass' or enter its territory without permission. The ultimate sanction for such breach, whether in property or citizenship law, involves physical removal from the estate/territory. Both systems create legal boundaries that are backed up by force. These boundaries generally protect the interests of designated legitimate owners, while imposing severe legal sanctions against those who are perceived (by these very same laws) as illegal entrants who breach them.

Both systems of exclusion share another important characteristic: they typically preserve unequal structures of holdings that tend to concentrate control over power, means and opportunities. In the context of property, we find volumes of competing arguments that attempt to justify this unequal system of accumulation and transmission. No similar elaborations or theoretical justifications are found with respect to citizenship. There are also no convincing explanations for why a draconian system of legal exclusion can legitimately be perpetuated by reliance on the 'natural' event of birth in the conferral of membership rights. Thinking through this analogy yields yet another surprising revelation: whereas the principle of automatic and irrevocable birthright has been roundly criticized as a basis for the intergenerational transfer of property, the birthright transmission of citizenship has largely escaped similar scrutiny. That is the case despite the fact that such transmission is relied upon by governments (rather than a select class of estate owners) – thus inviting more rigorous, rather than lenient, standards of review and accountability. More important still, citizenship as a form of inherited property affects a far greater number of individuals in the world, making it quantitatively and qualitatively far more crucial today to discussions of global justice and equality, than any antiquated – and in most countries now prohibited – form of perpetual transfer of landed estates.

The opportunity-enhancing function of citizenship

So far, we have emphasized citizenship's gate-keeping function, or the 'right to exclude'. Fortunately, citizenship does more than delimit access and preserve unequal accumulation of wealth and power in the hands of birthright heirs. It also entails the 'right not to be excluded'. Just as fiercely as it externally excludes non-members, citizenship can also internally level opportunity and provide the basic enabling conditions for each member to fulfil her potential. The argument for such inclusion is simple yet powerful: citizens enjoy these entitlements – which are of right – on the basis of a fundamental equality of status, which is their membership in the community.[18] This we label citizenship's *opportunity-enhancing* (or 'enabling') function.

Like other types of property, citizenship allows its possessor to exercise freedom and autonomy through what is legally hers and to protect her rights *in rem*: as against the world. But the right *not to be excluded* goes beyond this negative liberty. It involves a positive dimension as well. This positive component entails, just like property, a 'bundle of rights', which in this context translates, at the most minimal account, into the security of holding an irrevocable membership status.[19] This security of status cannot, save exceptional circumstances, be denied by one's government or fellow citizens. This stands in sharp contrast to the vulnerable situation of non-members, who remain potentially subject to deportation by the admitting polity, lacking precisely the property-like protections that attach to citizenship.

But the enabling function of citizenship guarantees more than just protection from deportation. For each member, it bestows the right to participate in the governance of the polity. It further provides, at least in its ideal type, the threshold condition of freedom-from-want as a classic expression of the 'right not to be excluded'.[20] Rather than merely operating to restrict access (through its gate-keeping function), citizenship on this broader account is seen as an *enabling* condition that offers members benefits and entitlements on an equal basis, and in the process assist in securing their well-being.[21]

In many respects, the opportunity-enhancing function is far more powerful in the context of citizenship than it is for most other types of property, material or abstract. Such entitlement guarantees that each member will enjoy 'a share in the protection conferred on the group as a whole over some asset and its wealth-potential'.[22] Such a protection implies (even on the narrow reading) that each individual will gain a fair share of equal liberties, access to public goods, and non-discriminatory participation in economic and labour markets.[23] The broader account may, however, endorse more robust conceptions of enabling: those that rise above the abolition of absolute deprivation to the fulfilment of relative prosperity as part of the prescription of shared citizenship; it could further suggest that part of the state's role as creator and enforcer of membership entails the obligation to mitigate inequalities among social actors; or that membership in a common polity entails an expectation of generosity by those citizens with greater authority and wealth towards those without it as part of their joint responsibility to the larger community; or, it might lend support to an interpretation of full membership as entailing that the political community owes to each member the provision of those basic living conditions and infrastructure services (clean water, police protection, health, education, shelter and the like) that are seen as preconditions for a decent life.[24]

None of these interpretations of opportunity, which offer different manifestations of the content that can be given to the right-not-to-be-excluded, are premised on an idea of flat equalization of results. Instead, citizenship's opportunity-enhancing function is better understood as emphasizing the goal of levelling starting points among those within the polity. As such, it is fully compatible with the moral intuition that people can justifiably claim the rewards of their enterprise as a result of relevant efforts. However, unlike the narrow conception of property – which emphasizes the self-interest of individual 'traders' at the expense of losing sight of the existence of a community – the broad account of citizenship treats success by such individuals as itself predicated, to some degree, on larger *societal* conditions.[25] This may include conditions such as effective government, the rule of law, protection against foreign invasion, domestic peace and security, and stable markets, as well as additional supporting conditions such as public investment in infrastructure, higher education, and various social services.[26] While the precise definition of what is included in the 'basket' of citizenship's benefits may vary (even among OECD countries), a societal commitment to providing these preconditions differs sharply from the narrow, fend-for-oneself conception of civil society. The latter focuses on negative liberty as a way to restrict the encroaching state, while the former treats citizenship's opportunity-enhancing function as corresponding with positive liberty as well as creating an environment that is conducive to best fulfilling the capacities of those fortunate enough to belong to the body politic.

Undoubtedly, meeting these requirements imposes a heavy burden that is not fully borne out even by the world's most affluent and generous polities – let alone by resource-strapped or corrupt governments. But it serves as a normative yardstick against which to measure how countries fare in their enabling commitment. There's another message, though, to be drawn here, which is crucial for our argument: automatic entitlement to political membership as encoded in today's birthright citizenship laws has *itself* become a valuable property-like claim, which generates for its holders secure access to certain common goods and the enjoyment of the basic infrastructures that permit human flourishing, in addition to establishing for those who count as members an enforceable right to participate in the governance of their shared polity.

We can now see membership boundaries that extend across generational lines in a more complex light: not only are these boundaries sustained for cultivating bonds of identity and belonging (as the conventional argument holds), they also serve a crucial role in preserving restricted access to the community's accumulated wealth and power. The latter is jealously guarded at the juncture of transfer of 'ownership' from the present generation of citizens to its progeny. In other words, birthright transmission mechanisms provide cover through their presumed

'naturalness' for what is essentially a major (and currently untaxed) property/
estate transmission from one generation to another. Ours is a world of scarcity;
when an affluent community systemically delimits access to membership and its
derivative benefits on the basis of a strict heredity system that effectively resembles an 'entail' structure of preserving privilege and advantage in the hands of
the few, those who are excluded have reason to complain.

'Entailed' property and birthright citizenship: analogous transmissions?

If we were to look for a pattern that closely resembles the structure of birthright
transmission of entitlement, we would find it – somewhat surprisingly – in the
inheritance regimes of property that date back to medieval England. There, we
find the (now long discredited) institution of the *fee tail* or *entail* – an effective
illustration of just how much of an outlier the reliance on birthright transmission
of entitlement is in the current era.[27] In the language of the early common law,
fee tail involved a landed estate that automatically descended from person A to
person B 'and the heirs of his body' and continued so passing through the
descending line only in order to keep the landed estates squarely in the hands of
a small echelon of powerful and wealthy families.[28] Practically, then, 'entail'
was a legal means of restricting future succession of property to the descendants
of a designated estate-owner. It offered a tool to preserve land in the possession
of dynastic families by entrenching birthright succession, while at the same time
tying the hands of future generations from altering the estate they inherited from
their predecessors.

The history of entail dates back to thirteenth-century Britain. The English
Parliament formally adopted the entail regime in the *De Donis Conditionalibus*
statute (1285 AD) in response to petitions from 'landowners who wanted to
bestow on a child and the heirs of his or her body an inheritable estate in land
that could not be alienated by fee simple'.[29] The *De Donis* statute thus secured a
special interest in land, which created a distinctive pattern of succession,
whereby each successive holder was limited to use of the land for life, without
the power to alter the chain of transmission or to dispose of the property.[30] It was
also deeply gendered, commonly limiting the entail to male descendants alone
(in the form of primogeniture).[31] The entail was to keep the estate strictly within
the possession of the heirs of landed aristocracy in a social order where the hold
on land was intimately tied up with political authority.[32] The birthright transmission it upheld was designed to be infinite in duration, transferring the land from
one generation to another in perpetuity.

The successive generations, the progeny of aristocracy, were not always
pleased with the restriction that entail attached to the inherited estate. English
lawyers eventually developed a method known as 'common recovery', which
permitted one to 'dock' (or 'break') the entail and 'seize' the estate, thus
effectively removing the original restraint that ran to A for life, then to B and the
heirs of his body, then to C and the heirs of his body, and so on.[33] Such legal

manoeuvring, which permitted cutting off the chain of transmission from one generation to another, was eventually approved by the English courts in the landmark decision of *Taltarum's Case* (1472 AD).[34]

Interestingly, the legal institution of entail later migrated to North America with English colonists who created estates in fee tail, primarily in the southern colonies such as Virginia, Georgia and North Carolina.[35] One of history's little ironies was that it became harder for descendants of landed estates in the American colonies to 'dock' or cut off the entail than it was for their wealthy aristocratic brethren in England, because certain colonies, such as Virginia, specifically enacted statutes that prohibited the option of 'common recovery'.[36] Thus, once an entail was created, the transfer of property to the heirs of one's body – and to them only – 'was of indefinite duration – the original perpetuity, in fact'.[37]

It should come as no surprise that this aristocratic method for preserving land in the sole dominion of certain families, which effectively perpetuated their disproportionate wealth and political power, sparked the ire of American revolutionary reformers. Thomas Jefferson, for example, led the effort to abolish entail in Virginia, his home state, by putting forward a motion in 1776 to the Virginia Assembly to extinguish entailed estates by law. As many legal historians have observed, Jefferson counted this legislation among his foremost achievements. What is less well known is that James Madison, the champion of property rights in the new republic, also supported the abolition of fee tail in Virginia and elsewhere in the United States. Madison, like Jefferson, held the position that '[a]bolishment of fee tail [would] shorten the longevity of inherited wealth and thereby lesson the "proportion of idle proprietors" in Virginia society'.[38]

For American republican lawyers, hereditary transfer of privilege such as the 'entailment of land appeared to be the most glaring vestiges of a corrupt past'.[39] It was associated with feudal-like encrustations on the common law that preserved and perpetuated social hierarchy in England. For Jefferson, explains John Hart, abolishing entail 'was a key part of a "system" of reforms 'by which every fibre would be eradicated of ancient ... or future aristocracy and a foundation laid for a government truly republican'.[40] It was a central component of this project because entailed transfer of estates, by creating a bloodline of land owners, diminished opportunity for those who did not enjoy such inheritance. It therefore defeated a broader social and economic agenda of 'republican laws of descent and distribution' designed to gradually contribute to 'equalizing the property of the citizens'.[41] What is more, the concern was not only with accumulation of great wealth, but with the *permanence* of such riches in the hands of certain families. Such permanence was the result of the *birthright* nature of entail, which guaranteed entitlement to successive descendants simply by virtue of their status as 'the heirs of [the original landholder] and his body'. No other criteria were imposed, nor could a later generation alter this automatic grant. This lead to a concern, already expressed by William Blackstone in his magisterial 1765 *Commentaries on the Laws of England*, that the Nth generation of heirs to an entail might become morally corrupt and 'disobedient when they knew they could not be set aside'.[42]

In the American version of this critique, three main reasons can be identified in support of the abolition of the automatic birthright entitlement in estates: concerns about 'moral corruption' (or what we would label today as the decline of civic virtue); reservations about the inefficient allocation of resources that is preserved when the land is held by 'idlers'; and repudiations of antiquated legal instruments that perpetuated social privilege and inequality. The eighteenth-century republican discussion of 'moral corruption', or decline of virtue, revolved around the concern that those who have a guaranteed birthright to inhere entailed estates will become 'idlers' with tainted habits and manners. Instead of being productive republican citizens, these idlers visited 'suffering' on American society in their individual extravagance and excessive consumerism, which Madison described as the wasteful 'capacity to purchase of costly and ornamental articles consumed by the wealthy only'. As Madison saw it, a core cause for such tainting of manners was the 'too unequal distribution of property, favoured by laws derived from the British code, which generated examples in the opulent class inauspicious to the habits of other classes'.[43]

Instead of cultivating a civic republican ethics of virtue, the perpetuation of property in certain families through mechanisms such as entailment of land created a nascent American aristocracy. What is more, heirs of such families knew that they could not be cut off from the chain of birthright transmission; as a result, the republican concern was that they would become 'disobedient' and socially unproductive members of the polity. The abolishment of entail and the creation of more equal partition of property were thus seen as a crucial ingredient in diminishing the prospect of individuals inhering great wealth in perpetuity irrespective of their talent, work ethic and virtue.

Another dimension of the critique of entail focused not so much on the moral character of the birthright recipient, but on the lack of efficiency of this allocation scheme, which created little incentive for those who are guaranteed such wealth as matter of birthright to 'maximize' the value of their estate. The preamble to the 1776 Virginia statute, which abolished entailed estates, did not shy away from explicitly expressing such concerns:

> the perpetuation of property in certain families, by means of gifts made to them in fee taille, is contrary to good policy, ... [it] discourages the holder thereof from taking care and improving the same [the estate], and sometime does injury to the morals of the youth.[44]

An even more pointed argument about inequality is articulated in the 1784 legislative act of North Carolina, which similarly abolished the fixed and perpetual transfer of wealth and opportunity by birthright, stating in its Preamble that, 'entails of estates tend only to raise the wealth and importance of particular families and individuals, giving them an unequal and undue influence in a republic'.[45]

This opposition to the perpetual birthright transmission of entitlement was extended, at least historically, into the realm of citizenship. As James Kettner argues, *naturalization* – the process of volitional admission to the polity *rather than* birthright citizenship – provided the model of republican citizenship at this period.[46] On this model, a non-member who voluntary and affirmatively decided to become a citizen of the republic was, after becoming part of its social and economic life and taking an oath of allegiance, adopted into the polity as a full member. This process of *post*-birth admission, which emphasized agency and volition, indeed seemed to better reflect the ideal of political membership as conceived by the republican and liberal traditions, which emphasized choice and consent of the governed as the root of legitimate authority.[47] This sentiment informs an oft-cited passage in John Locke's *Second Treatise of Government*: 'a child is born a subject of no country or government'. When that child comes to the age of discretion, continues Locke, 'then he is a free-man, at liberty what government he will put himself under; what body politick he will unite himself to'.[48] This rejection of imposed, or ascriptive membership, finds striking parallels in early American republican thought, which, as Jefferson's formulates in the context of access to volitional citizenship, holds that 'all men [have a right to] depart from the country in which chance, not choice has placed them'.[49] Such insistence on severing the accidents of station of birth in assigning political membership (an ideal, we must not forget, which was initially conceived to apply merely to a small fraction of the population, namely free, white men) still remains a far cry from the reality that is in place under the current world system. What is particularly surprising is that the alternative path that has been chosen – reliance on automatic and hereditary transfer of membership entitlement – resembles some of the most deeply criticized, and ultimately abolished, feudal mechanisms of inheritance: the entail.

Whereas the archaic institution of hereditary transfer of landed estates has been discredited in the realm of property, in the most unlikely of places, we still find a structure that resembles it: that is, in the conferral of political membership. Birthright entitlement to citizenship not only remains with us today, but it is by far the most important venue through which individuals are 'sorted' into different political communities. Birthright principles strictly regulate the *entail* of citizenship for the vast majority of the global population. They secure the transmission of membership entitlement to a limited group of beneficiaries: 'heirs-in-perpetuity' who automatically gain access to the body politic on the basis of bloodline or birthplace. These beneficiaries, in turn, gain the right (and are bound by the duty) to pass it on to the next generation of 'natural-born' citizens, and these children will then pass it on to their children, and so forth: this structure effectively recreates the fee tail in the transmission of membership titles.[50]

To recognize the surprising similarities in form and function between birthright citizenship and inherited property of this particular kind is to identify a striking exception to the modern trend *away* from ascribed statuses.[51] This birthright-transmission mechanism, which is still exercised today, cannot be dismissed as a mere historical accident, given that the question of legitimizing political authority and property is central to the liberal, democratic and civic-republican intellectual traditions. This only makes the link that persists between *political membership and station of birth* – a connection that has been both ignored and taken for granted – ever more surprising and in urgent need of a coherent explanation.

One possible explanation, which grows out of our analysis here, is that birthright citizenship remains in operation – despite its tension with the core tenets of the leading political theories of our times – at least in part because it permits the perpetuation of unequal 'estates' in the descending lines of different political communities. As we have seen, such reliance on birthright entitlement camouflages the dramatically unequal voice and opportunity implications of this extremely important – yet only seldom discussed – allocation system.

Whereas the delineation of enforceable membership boundaries (citizenship's gate-keeping function) has been challenged in recent years as an offense to the universality of our shared humanity, both proponents and opponents of bounded membership have surprisingly paid scant attention to the crucial 'wealth-preserving' aspect of hereditary citizenship – the dramatically different opportunity structures to which individuals are entitled, based on the allocation of political membership according to predetermined circumstances of birth. This is a blind spot – if not the 'black hole' – of citizenship theory. Unlike the critical accounts of entailed property regimes, from Blackstone to Jefferson to Madison, scholars of citizenship have to date failed to turn their gaze to the largely analogous form of strict intergenerational transfer that still persists in the realm of birthright transmission of membership entitlement. Our account, which has established a conceptual and descriptive analogy between inherited property and birthright citizenship, brings to the fore familiar criticisms that has been levelled against antiquated and unequal transfer regimes of property in order to highlight the global distributive implications of prevalent structures of citizenship transmission. Such an inquiry is ever more urgent given that a transmission mechanism of this kind has, in a world like our own, particularly pernicious influences that interfere with the distribution of voice and opportunity on a global scale.

The legal category of entailed bequests from generation to generation without restraint belongs to a social world that has long been succeeded by other relationships and values. Indeed, it stands in tension with the deepest liberal and democratic tenets of the revolutionary proclamation that we are all born free and equal.[52] This only makes the persistent link between political membership and station of birth in distributing rights, opportunities and wealth – the 'entailed' transmission of the life-long good of citizenship that is conducted in feudal-like terms of birthright entitlement – even more puzzling. Thinking about citizenship as a special form of inherited entitlement is an intriguing way to defract our current limited categories into a new set of possibilities.

Notes

1 This set of themes is developed in considerably greater detail in Shachar (2009; 2011) and in Shachar and Hirschl (2007).
2 See Global Commission on International Migration (2005).
3 See Shachar (2003).
4 See Vink and de Groot (2010).
5 Most of the data in this section are compiled from the *World Development Report 2006* (World Bank, 2006) and the *Human Development Report 2005* (UNDP, 2005).
6 For a detailed analysis, see Pogge (2002).
7 See e.g. Sachs (2005: 20–31).
8 Data drawn from the *OECD Health Data* (OECD, 2011).
9 Data drawn from the *Child Mortality Indicators 2012* (World Bank, 2012).
10 See the *World Development Report 2000/2001* (World Bank, 2000).
11 This argument is powerfully advanced in the classic essay by Haslett (1986).
12 For a discussion of the distinction between 'narrow' and 'broad' concepts of property, see Shachar (2009: 27–33).
13 Treating citizenship as a 'precious good' is central to Michael Walzer's (1983) analysis of membership.
14 We make this statement as a descriptive observation of the reality we find in practice, not as normative judgment about whether or not this is a desirable state of affairs.
15 See Stevens (1999).
16 Brubaker (1992: 31).
17 See Shachar (2007).
18 See Held (1991).
19 The security that attaches to full membership is thought to nourish our sense of identity and belonging, with important 'returns' in terms of our ability to fully exercise our autonomy and freedom.
20 An emphasis on the right not to be excluded is found in MacPherson (1977). Clearly, acquisition of citizenship status per se is no guarantee against the persistence of inequalities between members of the same polity. But it does anchor certain basic interests as non-revocable once a person is counted in the innermost circle of members.
21 A related argument is developed by Eisgruber (1997).
22 See Harris (1996).
23 The idea of fair value of equal liberties is drawn from Rawls (1971: 227).
24 The latter interpretation draws on Sen's capabilities approach, see e.g. Sen (1992); Roemer (1998); Nussbaum (2000). Nussbaum makes explicit the claim that these capabilities ought to be fulfilled by governments.
25 See e.g. Zucker (2001, chaps. 9–11).
26 See Murphey and Nagel (2002, chap. 3).
27 Importantly, we are not relying here on the historical precedent of treating ownership of real property as a precondition for full membership in the polity. As is well recorded, such reliance has worked to drastically restrict access to citizenship, excluding the vast majority of the population from full inclusion as equals. Our focus is different: we are exploring the conceptual and functional analogies between the regimes of protected property and bounded citizenship.
28 On the deeply gendered aspects of these intergenerational transfers, see e.g. Wright (2004) and Fellows (1991).
29 Hart (2001: 171–172).
30 See Orth (1992).
31 This strict pattern of transfer often put women in the precarious situation of reliance on marriage as the core means for ensuring financial security and social respectability (in a highly stratified society) for themselves and their children. In this respect, the entail was part of a larger system of laws that regulated monogamy, patriarchy and

inheritance. Of the vast body of feminist critique of this hierarchical social order, see e.g. Spring (1993).
32 See Alexander (1997).
33 See Orth (1992: 38).
34 Y.B. 12 Edw. 4, Mich 25 (1472).
35 See Morris (1927: 24–51).
36 We draw this argument from the elegant analysis offered by Orth (1992).
37 Orth (1992: 40).
38 For an illuminating and meticulous study of Madison's position on entail, see Hart (2001).
39 Alexander (1997: 39).
40 Hart (2001: 168).
41 Ibid.: 189.
42 Blackstone (1765–1769).
43 Madison (1792).
44 Act of Oct. 1776, ch. XXVI, reprinted in Waller Hening (ed.) (1823: 9 *Laws of Virginia* 226).
45 Orth (1992: 42–43).
46 See Kettner (1978).
47 Obviously, at this time the definition of eligibility for inclusion in the body-politic was itself deeply laden with race and gender-based exclusions. Full membership was reserved exclusively for 'free white persons'. See Smith (1997).
48 Locke (1988: 347, §118).
49 Jefferson (1994[1774]: 4).
50 This perpetual structure of hereditary transfer also appears to violate the common-law rule against 'perpetuities', which has been in effect for centuries, dating back to at least the 1682 decision in the *Duke of Norfolk's Case*.
51 This notion is perhaps best captured in Henry Maine's and later Emile Durkheim's 'from status to contract' typology.
52 See Yack (2011).

References

Alexander, G.S. (1997) *Commodity & Propriety. Competing Visions of Property in American Legal Thought, 1776–1970*, Chicago, IL: University of Chicago Press.
Blackstone, W. (1765–1769) *Commentaries on the Laws of England*, Oxford: Clarendon.
Brubaker, R. (1992) *Citizenship and Nationhood in France and Germany*, Cambridge, MA: Harvard University Press.
Eisgruber, C.L. (1997) 'Birthright citizenship and the constitution', *NYU Law Review*, 72: 54–96.
Fellows, M.L. (1991) 'Wills and trusts: "The Kingdom of the Fathers"', *Law and Equality*, 10: 137–162.
Global Commission on International Migration (2005) *Report of the Global Commission on International Migration*, Geneva: GCIM.
Harris, J.W. (1996) *Property and Justice*, Oxford: Clarendon Press.
Hart, J.F. (2001) 'A less proportion of idle proprietors: Madison, property rights, and the abolition of fee tail', *Washington & Lee Law Review*, 58: 167–194.
Haslett, D.W. (1986), 'Is inheritance justified?', *Philosophy and Public Affairs*, 15: 122–155.
Held, D. (1991) 'Between state and civil society: Citizenship,' in G. Andrews (ed.) *Citizenship*, Lawrence & Wishart, pp. 19–25.

Jefferson, T. (1994[1774]) 'Summary view of the rights of British America', in *Jefferson: Writings*, ed. by M.D. Peterson, Literary Classics of the United States.

Kettner, J.H. (1978) *The Development of American Citizenship, 1608–1870*, Chapel Hill: University of North Carolina Press.

Locke, J. (1988) *Two Treatises of Government*, ed. by P. Lasle, Cambridge: Cambridge University Press.

MacPherson, C.B. (1977) 'Human rights as property rights', *Dissent*, 24: 72–77.

Madison, J. (1792) 'Fashion', *National Gazette*, March 22.

Morris, R.B. (1927) 'Primogeniture and entailed estates in America', *Columbia Law Review*, 27: 24–51.

Murphey, L. and Nagel, T. (2002) *The Myth of Ownership: Taxes and Justice*, Oxford: Oxford University Press.

Nussbaum, M. (2000) *Women and Human Development: The Capabilities Approach*, Cambridge: Cambridge University Press.

OECD Health Data (2011) OECD Health Division, 30 June.

Orth, J.V. 'After the revolution: "Reform" of the law of inheritance,' *Law and History Review*, 10: 33–44.

Pogge, T.W. (2002) *World Poverty and Human Rights: Cosmopolitan Responsibilities and Reforms*, Polity.

Rawls, J. (1971) *A Theory of Justice*, Cambridge, MA: Harvard University Press.

Roemer, J. (1998) *Equality of Opportunity*, Cambridge, MA: Harvard University Press.

Sachs, J.D. (2005) *The End of Poverty: Economic Possibilities for Our Time*, Penguin Press.

Sen, A. (1992) *Inequality Reexamined*, Oxford: Clarendon.

Shachar, A. (2003) 'Children of a lesser state: Sustaining global inequality through citizenship laws', in S. Macedo and I.M. Young (eds) *NOMOS: Child, Family, and State*, New York: NYU Press, pp. 345–397.

Shachar, A. (2007) 'The shifting border of immigration regulation', *Stanford Journal of Civil Rights-Civil Liberties*, 3.

Shachar, A. (2009) *The Birthright Lottery: Citizenship and Global Inequality*, Cambridge, MA: Harvard University Press.

Shachar, A. (2011) 'The Birthright Lottery: Response to interlocutors,' *Issues in Legal Scholarship*, 9.

Shachar, A. and Hirschl, R. (2007) 'Citizenship as inherited property', *Political Theory*, 35: 253–287.

Smith, R.M. (1997) *Civic Ideals: Conflicting Visions of Citizenship in U.S. History*, Yale University Press.

Spring, E. (1993) *Law, Land and Family: Aristocratic Inheritance in England, 1300 to 1800*, Chapel Hill: University of North Carolina Press.

Stevens, J. (1999) *Reproducing the State*, Princeton University Press.

UNDP (2005) *Human Development Report*, New York: UNDP.

Vink, M.P. and de Groot, G.-R. (2010) *Birthright Citizenship: Trends and Regulations in Europe*, EUDO Citizenship Observatory Comparative Report, Florence: EUI, Robert Schuman Center for Advanced Study.

Waller Hening, W. (1823) *The Statutes at Large, Being a Collection of All the Laws of Virginia*, J & G Cochran, Vol. 9.

Walzer, M. (1983) *Spheres of Justice: A Defense of Pluralism and Equality*, Basic Books.

World Bank (2000) *World Development Report 2000/2001, Attacking Poverty: Opportunity, Empowerment, and Security*, Washington DC: World Bank.

World Bank (2006) *World Development Report 2006: Equity and Development* Washington DC: World Bank.

World Bank (2012) *Child Mortality Indicators 2012*, Available http://data.worldbank.org/indicator/SH.DYN.MORT.

Wright, N.E. (2004) *Women, Property, and the Letters of the Law in Early Modern England*, Toronto: University of Toronto Press.

Yack, B. (2011) 'Birthright, birthwrongs: Contingency, choice and cosmopolitanism in recent political thought', *Political Theory*, 39, 406–416.

Zucker, R. (2001) *Democratic Distributive Justice*, Cambridge: Cambridge University Press.

7 Equal inheritance

An anti-perfectionist view

Matthew Clayton

Bequests and inheritance raise difficult questions about how to combine two attractive political ideals: liberty and equality. Bequeathing property and goods to others seems to be morally acceptable to the extent that freedom matters. Restrictions on bequests place limits on individuals with respect to how they spend their justly earned income, which many regard as an unacceptable diminution of their freedom to pursue the goals they affirm. On the other hand, unequal inheritance, which produces unequal life chances, appears to be problematic from the point of view of egalitarian justice. True, many egalitarians allow certain socioeconomic inequalities – those which are the product of differences in merit, effort, or choice, for example. Nevertheless, the sheer good luck of being born to wealthy parents, for example, is not, according to most egalitarians, a cause of inequality that justifies the inequality it causes (Cohen, 2008: 89; Lazenby, 2009).

The question we confront is whether there is a principled way of combining considerations of freedom and equality to fashion a plausible approach to inheritance. In this chapter, I outline an approach to inheritance founded on a conception of what citizens owe to each other, a conception in which individuals have interests in obtaining the means to act as free and equal citizens and to reflect on and pursue their own particular view of what gives life value. This conception offers from the start a particular interpretation of what we ought to care about in caring about liberty and equality, and my primary aim is to explain how this attractive conception of political morality might justify significant legally enforced restrictions on bequest and inheritance.

The chapter has two parts. In the first part, I argue that if we embrace a particular conception of political morality that has received considerable support over the last 30 years – *anti-perfectionist egalitarian liberalism* – then we need to develop a new approach to questions of bequests and inheritance. After outlining it central features, I argue that adopting an anti-perfectionist political position transforms the debate about inheritance, because it requires us to avoid certain arguments that are often deployed by those on the left to defend significant restrictions on inheritance or bequests. In the second part of the chapter, I attempt to redeem the leftist view by elaborating a different approach to inheritance that draws on the anti-perfectionist ideal of resource egalitarianism, an approach that generates reasonably radical proposals for inheritance tax policy.

How anti-perfectionism transforms the inheritance debate

The justificatory restraint of anti-perfectionist liberalism

Anti-perfectionist liberalism can be characterized in several ways. Since I do not want to get involved in exegetical disputes that would take our focus away from issues concerning inheritance, I shall set out what I consider to be an attractive conception of the ideal with a view to using it as a basis for theorizing inheritance.

Anti-perfectionist liberalism is a conception of the kinds of reason to which it is legitimate to appeal when defending political principles or policies. It draws a distinction between the reasons tied to our status as 'free and equal citizens' and those given by more general ethical considerations. With respect to the first kind of reason, liberals typically argue that we have certain interests as citizens. In Rawls's version of political liberalism, we have interests (a) in developing and deploying a sense of justice, and (b) in reflecting on, revising, and pursuing our 'comprehensive' goals. Comprehensive goals are, in this view, goals an individual believes she has reason to pursue that are relevantly non-political. They might relate to her religion, her attitude to work and leisure, her sexuality, or the reasons given by her relationships with others. The liberal view is that our interests as citizens, to act justly with respect to others and to deliberate rationally about and pursue our particular comprehensive goals, justify the provision of certain rights. In the first place, they support the maintenance of the familiar liberal rights to freedom of conscience, expression, association, and democratic participation. Second, because the promotion of these interests requires other goods, liberal egalitarians argue for a fair distribution of social and economic benefits and burdens such that everyone has the wherewithal to pursue the particular comprehensive goals they reflectively endorse (Rawls, 1996).

While anti-perfectionist liberals work with reasons connected with our status and interests as citizens, they argue that general ethical or 'comprehensive' reasons are inadmissible within political morality.[1] Plainly, these more general reasons are of vital importance in individuals' lives as a whole: if a person realizes that she has spent her entire life worshipping a god that does not exist she might think, and be right to think, that her life would have gone much better had she pursued different goals. However, anti-perfectionists say that political morality should not draw on the truth or falsity of these kinds of belief. Our political institutions should not take a stand on which of the competing comprehensive conceptions are true or false. The upshot of this is that the fact that a particular god does not exist is not a reason for us to use the powers available to us through the state to attempt to prevent individuals from developing an allegiance to the associated religion. Instead, the reasons that should guide political activity are, to use Rawls's term, 'public reasons', reasons that are capable of acceptance by individuals who share interests as citizens but who disagree about religion, art, our place in the universe, and the value and implications of different kinds of personal relationship.

Since my aim is to consider the implications of anti-perfectionist liberalism for issues concerning inherited wealth, I shall not provide a detailed defence of this account of political morality or engage in the many interpretive disputes about it. Suffice it to say that anti-perfectionism is attractive because it serves the *ideal of political autonomy* under conditions of pluralism. Even people committed to acting according to norms of justice that maintain a fair distribution of benefits and burdens will, Rawls claims, inevitably disagree about comprehensive ethical questions. Given what he calls 'the fact of reasonable pluralism', the exclusion from political argument of comprehensive ideals that divide people is a condition of everyone being able to affirm the laws that constrain her. If laws were justified on the basis of a particular controversial religious ideal, for example, those who reject that ideal would be unable to identify with the constraints under which they live. Only when the principles governing society are justified on the basis of reasons they share can citizens realize political autonomy.[2]

Anti-perfectionist objections to certain leftist arguments

Anti-perfectionism treats certain arguments that are sometimes deployed to defend the taxation of bequests as inadmissible within political debate, because they rest on controversial comprehensive premises. To the extent that this is the case, those who favour restrictions on, or the taxation of, bequests or inheritance need to find alternative arguments for their proposals. In this section, I suggest that two arguments for reasonably restrictive policies with respect to bequests fall foul of the constraints of anti-perfectionism.

Posthumous interests

Consider, first, the simple leftist argument that a confiscatory tax on bequests is, in principle, just because there are no posthumous interests.[3] The argument is that such a tax cannot be unjust because the interests of the deceased are not violated by the confiscation of the property she justly held while alive. Interests, the argument goes, must be related to an individual's experience, but if an individual is dead then the conduct of others cannot affect her experience. Accordingly, she cannot be benefited or harmed by events that occur after her death and, therefore, the state's appropriation of her estate after her death for the purpose of egalitarian redistribution cannot set her interests back.[4]

Anti-perfectionists reply that the claim that we cannot harm the dead is too controversial to serve as a basis for a political conception of inheritance. For it is clear that many conceptions of well-being reject this view. Consider, for example, an alternative ethical conception that views leading a good life as the successful pursuit of valuable goals (Raz, 1986: 288–307). A common way of elaborating this view incorporates the idea of ethical luck, that one's well-being can be affected for better or worse by events that are entirely beyond one's control, events that prevent one's goals from being realized. A bolt of lightning that destroys the beautiful building Ann built might, according to this view, make Ann's life go worse. But it is irrelevant whether the lightning occurs before or after Ann's death. In either case, her ambition that her building continues to serve the community remains unfulfilled, which makes her life less successful.

Or consider Dworkin's account of ethics, which distinguishes between 'living well' and 'having a good life'. In his view, roughly speaking, a life well lived is one marked by a successful performance of the task of living. That 'adverbial' good is not affected by events that occur after one's death, because death marks the end of the performance. Nevertheless, as he says, 'whether someone has had a good life can be influenced after his death by anything that adds to or takes away from its achievements or hopes'. His examples include Hector who suffered after his death by being dragged by Achilles in front of the battlements of Troy. 'How good a life you have had waxes and wanes after you are no more', Dworkin insists (2011: 201).

The purpose of presenting these alternative accounts of well-being that affirm the possibility of posthumous interests is not to establish what is the right conception of our interests from which we might generate a conception of justice in inheritance. Rather, it is to illustrate that in a free society there will inevitably be significant disagreement about ethics and well-being. If our aim is to offer an account of just inheritance that is justifiable to reasonable citizens, that account must be one that refuses to take sides with respect to such disagreements.[5] If this is right, then if there is a case for a confiscatory tax on estates of the dead, that case should be prosecuted in a way that does not depend on controversial claims about posthumous interests.

Bequests and legitimate partiality

Consider another approach to questions concerning gifts and bequests that suffers from a similar problem. As I suggested at the outset, a popular way of addressing these issues is to view them as involving a conflict between two values, equality and liberty. More precisely, many on the left regard the conflict as being between securing equality of opportunity, on the one hand, and allowing the expression of legitimate partiality, on the other. Equality of opportunity is often understood as the ideal that there should be equal access to educational and economic success for those with similar natural ability and similar ambitions (Rawls, 1999a: 63). To the extent that this is valuable there are good reasons to restrict gifts and bequests that generate unequal opportunity. However, the ideal of equal opportunity conflicts with the view that it adds value to our lives to favour our nearest and dearest. The right view of justice in inheritance, it is claimed, requires us to scrutinize the basis of these values and to articulate an account that reaches the right balance between the competing ideals of equality and partiality.

The general problem with this approach to gifts and bequests is that, because reasonable people disagree about the ethical basis and importance of the good of acting partially, some reasonable citizens will inevitably reject any particular resolution. Let me illustrate the point by reference to perhaps the most developed version of this kind of account, offered by Brighouse and Swift (2009). In their conception, expressions of partiality towards one's children have value because they are constitutive of the realization of what they call 'familial relationship goods'. These are goods that are characterized in terms of an intimate bond between parent and child that is valuable for both parties. There is a distinctive value in parents and children loving each other and sharing a life together. The production of this good, they argue, requires the maintenance of opportunities for parents to be with their children, to share their enthusiasms and to devote certain resources to their children that are not offered to other children. Pursuing this thought further, they suggest that we should distinguish between different kinds of opportunity for parental partiality. Certain kinds of partiality cannot be denied to parents without jeopardizing the familial relationship good. One example they offer is the reading of bedtime stories. Even if it is the case that parents reading stories to their children is a significant cause of inequality of educational opportunity, because the value of the family clearly outweighs that of equality of opportunity, reading stories is permissible on grounds of justice. However, in other cases, such as leaving a large legacy to one's children, there is a more distant connection to familial relationship goods and the corresponding reason to favour one's children is less weighty. Brighouse and Swift accept that parents suffer some loss if they are denied the opportunity to benefit their children by leaving them their estate, because they are prevented from acting on their love for their children. However, the loss is less significant for two reasons. First, there are alternative ways of loving their children and, second, the general desire that one's child's life goes well is not as integral to the production of a valuable familial relationship as is sharing a story together. For these reasons, although a parent has valid reasons to improve her child's prospects, these reasons are less weighty from the perspective of family values than other kinds of partiality and, Brighouse and Swift argue, do not defeat our reasons to promote equal opportunity.

This conception of the conflict between equality and partiality is perfectionist. Brighouse and Swift try to resolve the tension between liberty and equality by assessing the relative importance for well-being of three concerns individuals often have. First, people value opportunities afforded to them by education and monetary resources. Call this the interest in being the recipient of resources. Second, many value having the opportunity to give or bequeath their holdings to those they care about. Call this the interest in giving. Finally, we value the maintenance of an intimate relationship with our children. Call this the interest in familial intimacy. Now Brighouse and Swift argue that, although it is defeated by our interest in familial intimacy, our interest in being recipients of resources outweighs our interest in giving. Their judgement seems to be the ethical one that a person loses less by being denied the opportunity to give to others than she does by receiving fewer educational opportunities or monetary resources. That is what motivates their claim that providing equal opportunity for all to receive education and monetary resources overrides granting everyone the opportunity to give to their nearest and dearest (except where that giving is an inseparable part of the maintenance of an intimate family unit).

As I argue below, anti-perfectionist egalitarian liberals should share many of Brighouse and Swift's conclusions. Nevertheless, their defence of these conclusions dismisses too quickly alternative ethical views that permit more parental partiality than theirs. Consider, for instance, parents who, understanding their own limitations, propose to express their love for their child by hiring a more able carer to attend to her daily needs. Even if these parents are making an ethical mistake, it is not obvious that their claim to have the opportunity to favour their child in this non-intimate manner should be treated as less important than people's interest in being the recipient of education or income. To be sure, I am not claiming that parents *are* entitled to the opportunity to advantage their children in these, perhaps inequality-generating, ways. The point is that that issue needs to be resolved in a way that does not depend on controversial claims about the ethical significance of different kinds of parental love.

The central tension: giving versus receiving

Robert Nozick made at least one profound observation about a particular kind of left-wing political morality. It is worth quoting him at length:

> Apparently, patterned principles [principles of the form 'to each according to her...'] allow people to choose to expend upon themselves, but not upon others, those resources they are entitled to (or rather, receive) under some favoured distributional pattern D1. For if each of several persons chooses to expend some of his D1 resources upon one other person, then that other person will receive more than his D1 share, disturbing the favoured distributional pattern. Maintaining a distributional pattern is individualism with a vengeance! Patterned distributional principles do not give people what entitlement principles do, only better distributed. For they do not give the right to choose what to do with what one has; they do not give the right to choose to pursue an end involving (intrinsically, or as a means) the enhancement of another's position.
>
> (Nozick, 1974: 167)

Whilst there is widespread agreement that Nozick's 'entitlement' conception of justice fails to give adequate consideration to the plight of the poor or relatively disadvantaged, it is worth pausing to attend to a thought that is implicit in Nozick's complaint, that left-wing politics err because they focus exclusively on our interests as *recipients* of certain goods and fail to attach any weight to our interests as *agents* whose aims might include benefiting particular individuals who are close to us. Plainly, one objection to Nozick's account is that it commits the opposite mistake, by treating our interest in choosing how the resources we possess are spent as the only, or overriding, interest we have. A plausible account, it seems, should give due consideration to both interests.

If this is right, then justice with respect to gifts, bequests and inheritance must attend to our interests as both recipients and agents. Unfortunately, like the issues reviewed above, it is not obvious that there is any consensus as to which combination of giving and receiving makes our lives go better. While some individuals value benefiting particular others far more than they value the enjoyment of goods themselves, others take the self-help view that it is better for each to enjoy what she can obtain through her own efforts. As in many other respects, people exhibit a range of different convictions about the value of giving and receiving, and, in exercising political power over people, we should be reluctant to make claims about whether giving or receiving, or which trade-off between them, makes one's life go better. Instead, we ought to offer an account of justice that is acceptable to individuals who hold diverse, and sometimes conflicting, views about those issues.

An anti-perfectionist egalitarian conception of inheritance

The place of political interests and ethical ambitions

There are at least two ways of trying to identify principles of justice that are acceptable to people who hold different ethical convictions and ambitions. One approach, championed by Rawls, is to elaborate a conception of our interests as 'free and equal citizens' and to *disregard* the comprehensive disputes that divide us. As I sketched his view above, we proceed from a conception of our interests as citizens in developing and deploying a sense of justice and deliberating, revising and pursuing our comprehensive ambitions.

The interest-based approach produces some plausible results, because it restricts bequests or gifts *inter vivos* that threaten important freedoms and rights. Rawls rightly suggests that we have a right to participate in democratic political arrangements that are free of the malign influence of wealth. Plainly, preventing the wealthy from having too great an influence on elections and legislative decisions might be achieved through restrictions on the financing of political campaigns or lobbying activity. It is an open question, however, whether these restrictions are sufficient. If it turned out that democracy flourishes best in a society without significant inequalities of wealth, then that would constitute a weighty reason to limit inequality-generating bequests and *inter vivos* gifts for the sake of preserving our interest in participating in the right kind of democratic politics. Similar considerations apply in the case of the second fundamental interest Rawls ascribes to free citizens – the interest in rationally reflecting on one's comprehensive conception. If that interest were served poorly by an inegalitarian society that allowed the media to be dominated by a small number of very wealthy individuals, then restrictions on inequality-sustaining bequests and other gifts might be required on grounds of justice.

However, the interest-based approach encounters difficulties in identifying what is owed to citizens with respect to their interest in pursuing their distinctive views of the good life. The chief difficulty arises because some people's comprehensive ambitions include a desire to benefit particular others, an ambition which, as noted above, can diminish the opportunities available to others. Rawlsians might say that the desire to help another is unreasonable if it sets back third-party interests with respect to the enjoyment of certain goods, such as educational opportunity. Nevertheless, this reply seems to rest on a particular view of how we ought to weigh our ambitions to receive and to give. It asserts that the enjoyment of an environment in which one receives a certain kind of good is more important than is having the opportunity to give to particular individuals. But without an argument, that assertion appears unmotivated. Suppose a citizen complained that Rawls's 'fair equality of opportunity' and the 'difference' principles neglect her ambition to give to her family and friends. It is not clear that Rawlsians have a convincing answer to this complaint. They cannot appeal to the view that, on the right conception of well-being, the diminution of her opportunity to give is an acceptable price to pay for the benefits she gains from the resources she receives, for that would be a controversial judgement about well-being; and they do not want to appeal to people's ambitions with respect to giving and receiving. But it is hard to see what other basis there is to motivate the priority Rawlsians attach to ensuring that people receive monetary resources to pursue their goals over the protection of their opportunities to give to others.

If Rawls's interest-based approach to justice is incomplete, perhaps it can be buttressed by incorporating an account that rests, in part, on judgements that reflect people's actual ambitions. The second, Dworkinian, strategy for developing an account of justice acceptable to everyone does precisely this, through elaborating a conception that *accommodates* or *includes* individuals' diverse ambitions in the formulation of public policy. On this view, when we assess what equality requires we allow individuals to bring their own ambitions to the table, to assess whether a distribution is equal by taking into account their distinctive goals in life. To be sure, certain ideals are treated as given. In Dworkin's view, the fundamental ideal is to treat individuals with 'equal concern and respect'. Equality, then, is not up for discussion as it is in other accounts of justice. However, because the aim is to elaborate a *liberal* egalitarian account, that is, an account that is acceptable to everyone, the right way to formulate what counts as an equal distribution is to assess whether the distribution is one in which individuals regard themselves as no worse off than others given the distinctive ambitions that drive them (Dworkin, 2000: chs 2, 3, 7, 8, 9).

I have suggested that the anti-perfectionist aim of seeking principles of justice in inheritance that do not rest on disputed comprehensive foundations places in doubt certain prominent arguments deployed by those on the left: those that deny the existence of posthumous interests, or those that rest on controversial claims about familial relationship goods, or the relative ethical importance of receiving compared to giving. Instead, we should, I have argued, develop a conception of justice in inheritance that appeals to a *hybrid* conception of egalitarian justice that (a) rests on our interests as free and equal citizens, that (b) is, at least to some extent, sensitive to the views people hold with respect comprehensive issues concerning posthumous interests and the value of giving and receiving, and (c) that incorporates these interests and ambitions in a way that treats everyone as an equal.

Gifts, bequests and inheritance from a resource egalitarian perspective

I have suggested that a hybrid conception of justice is the best approach to inheritance policy.[6] In the remainder of the chapter, I focus on merely one part of this hybrid view: the aim of ambition-sensitivity. Our question is this: to the extent that it ought to reflect what real people value what should be our approach to questions of justice with respect to bequests and inheritance? Our approach, I suggest, should be to follow Ronald Dworkin's conception of equality of resources and to try to determine its implications for the taxation of inherited wealth.

Equality of resources

Dworkin's conception of equality operates with two devices: first, the so-called 'envy test', which is a test for equality between individuals in their possession of external resources, such as their bundles of land, monetary resources and occupation; and, second, 'the hypothetical insurance' scheme, which deals with inequalities in people's enjoyment of personal resources, such as differences in health or natural talent. The ambition-sensitivity of equality of resources is evident in the envy test, which proposes that a distribution of external resources is equal only if no one prefers anyone else's set of resources to her own. The envy test matches our intuitions concerning the injustice of many cases in which wealth and income is unequally distributed. Nevertheless, it also coheres with the view that inequality of wealth is not always unjust. Suppose, for example, that an inequality in monetary resources is explained by a difference of ambition, rather than of circumstance or opportunity. Imagine Carla and Dan are equally placed so far as their abilities and other circumstances are concerned, but Carla invests for monetary gain while Dan prefers to teach philosophy which commands lower monetary remuneration in the market. In this case, there is a difference of wealth, but no unjust inequality according to equality of resources, because Dan does not believe that Carla's mix of occupation and income makes her life go better than his.

As Dworkin notes, equality of resources 'allows us to cite, as disadvantages and handicaps, only what we treat in the same way in our own ethical life' (2000: 294).[7] His conception is attractive to anti-perfectionists because it avoids appealing to a controversial account of the good life. The envy test avoids using a metric for interpersonal comparison that can be rejected by reasonable individuals and, instead, allows individuals to bring their own convictions to the egalitarian table. In this way, the different ambitions and convictions of individuals are accommodated, because each is permitted to express her claim for compensation by citing a lack of items that *she* regards as helpful given her distinctive ethical convictions.[8]

To deal with inequalities of personal resources, such as inequalities in health, disability or wealth-producing talent, Dworkin suggests that just arrangements are those that mimic the outcome of hypothetical egalitarian insurance scheme. He illustrates this at length by asking how we ought to set the size and decide the distribution of the health care budget (Dworkin, 2000: ch. 8; 2002a). Dworkin's ambition-sensitive solution is to ask what insurance policies would be bought by equally situated rational individuals if they had perfect information about the costs and benefits of different treatments and policies, enjoyed a fair share of wealth and income, and lacked information about their particular susceptibility to having or developing different medical conditions. Under Dworkin's 'veil of ignorance' although the insuring parties retain information about the *average* probability of having or developing certain conditions, no one knows whether she is more or less likely to be beset by those medical problems than the average.

In Dworkin's scheme the medical risks individuals face are equal, they are perfectly informed, and no one enjoys more or less than a fair share of income with which to insure. Dworkin asks us to try to identify what insurance policies with respect to health care individuals would purchase in such a context and claims that, because the background conditions are suitably equal, whatever size and distribution of the health care budget is the outcome of the scheme should be matched by social policy here and now.[9] This solution is ambition-sensitive because the insuring parties consult their own preferences and aims in life and, specifically, they ask themselves how much they value good health compared to other goods, such as wealth and income, education, good pensions, and so on. In addition, they might attach higher priority to certain kinds of health care over others. For example, many would value expensive life-saving treatment for conditions that affect them earlier in life more highly than similarly expensive life-saving treatment for conditions that affect them towards the end of their lives. Thus, insuring parties would purchase insurance packages that protect their health to a particular extent, and they would buy greater protection against certain health risks compared with others.

Dworkin's thought experiment provides us with a defence of a health service that is funded out of taxation and free at the point of delivery. It may also have revisionist implications for how health care budgets are spent. For example, he argues that it is highly unlikely that the medical insurance decisions of equally situated individuals would match the current distribution of medical services in the USA, in which 40 per cent of the health care budget is spent on people in the last six months of their lives. Individuals in the insurance scheme would, he suggests, decide to buy more extensive health care earlier in life at the expense of services that would generate only small benefits at the end of a life. In particular, insurers would not, he suggests, buy policies to provide life-support in the event of lapsing into a permanent vegetative state or expensive medical treatment when in the late stages of Alzheimer's. The resources that might be used to purchase such medical provision would generally be regarded as better spent pursuing other goods (Dworkin, 2002a: 212–213).

One of the distinctive features of Dworkin's hypothetical insurance scheme is that it is modelled on a particular conception of equality that reflects people's actual ambitions.[10] As he explains, the hypothetical situation renders individuals equal in terms of the *ex ante* risks they face, but the choice they make in this context might not be (and probably would not be) such that their *ex post* circumstances are equal. Some have criticized resource egalitarianism for precisely this feature, but Dworkin is clear that he regards this as one of the key attractions of his conception of resource egalitarianism.[11] Equality of Resources does not, then, *eliminate* inequality that stems from unequal propensity to disability or ill health, but *softens* it by identifying appropriate compensation for those disadvantages by reference to what equally placed individuals consulting their own ambitions and attitudes to risk would, on average, insure to provide.

Applying hypothetical insurance to bequests and inheritance

It is natural to extend the hypothetical insurance scheme to issues concerning gifts *inter vivos* and posthumous bequests, because the inequalities such transfers create are, *prima facie*, unjust. If Eric's parents bequeath him a large sum of money, according to resource egalitarianism that creates an inequality of resources between Fran and him, because both would prefer to have Eric's lucky inheritance.

If the hypothetical insurance market is adopted as the appropriate ambition-sensitive solution to the problem of how to respond to this inequality, the question is: what kind of protection against inequalities caused by unequal bequests would equally situated individuals insure to provide?

However, before I try to answer that question, the nature of the hypothetical insurance scheme for bequests needs some clarification in light of the distinctive problems presented by gifts and bequests. One complication arises because decisions to give or bequeath are made at a particular point in adult life. If we ask adults what they would insure to provide for if they possessed equal resources and lacked information about the particular advantages they enjoy in life, one period of their lives would not be included in their deliberations – their pasts. However, this would render any decisions they might take of questionable relevance for justice, because one of the central questions about intergenerational transfers is that they produce inequalities in the formative years of people's lives. A second issue concerns how an ambition-sensitive conception of equality can cater for the claims of children on the assumption that the ambitions of children are not the product of the right kind of rationality or critical reflection to command our respect.

Given these problems, if we want to run an ambition-sensitive hypothetical insurance market to deal with intergenerational transfers, that scheme must involve a reasonably complicated thought experiment, in which people's ambitions for different stages of their lives are accommodated. We might think about the issue in the following way. *What kinds of protection against disadvantage at different stages of their lives would individuals choose on the assumption that they will relive their lives from birth to death?*

Elsewhere, I have run a similar thought experiment to deal with inequalities between parents and children that relate to the costs of, and resources for, raising and educating children (Clayton, 2006: 61–75). The fundamental feature of that scheme is that to identify how we ought to respond to unequal circumstances, individuals choose principles and policies that determine certain entitlements of children and particular rights and duties of parents on the assumption that they will relive their lives, first as children and then as adults. In doing so, they consult their ambitions with respect to childhood and parenthood.[12] Working through various outcomes of the scheme, I speculate that individuals would insure against the possibility of having a child who is difficult or costly to bring up. They would also insure against the possibility of being born into a family that is poor or neglects their needs as children. They would take out insurance, that is, to pay for a range of measures – public education campaigns, social services provision, child benefit, well-financed compulsory public education, and so on – that ensure that their opportunities to enjoy parenthood and their opportunities as children are not unduly limited.

A similar thought experiment is, I think, a promising way to identify just rules regarding bequests. Suppose, then, that each adult knows she is to relive all the stages of her life. She knows she enjoys a fair share of monetary resources, which is the product of her pursuing her particular ambitions with respect to labour and leisure in the context of a competitive market. To simplify the choice problem, I shall stipulate that no one is more or less disadvantaged with respect to the genetic lottery. Nevertheless, each insurer knows that her society exhibits inequality of wealth that is not unjust but, rather, reflects people's pursuit of different ambitions, which translate into different labour-leisure-income trade-offs. Suppose, in addition, that the individual in question does not have information about whether, in her life to come, she will be a low or high earner, in either absolute or relative terms; neither does she does know whether her parents or friends will be rich or poor. Finally, the choice is stipulated as being an informed choice, in which the insurer has complete information about the costs and benefits of different policies.[13]

Given this equal choice situation, individuals must decide whether or not to adopt laws that permit various gifts or bequests and, if they do, which tax regime ought to operate for such transfers. In doing so, they consult their own ambitions for their lives as children and adults. As noted above, individuals will come to the choice they face with different views concerning the importance for them of giving to particular individuals who are close to them and of ensuring that they or their children receive monetary resources, and it is their view of the relative importance of these ambitions that will guide their insurance decisions. In this resource egalitarian conception, whatever insurance decisions would be taken within this equal choice situation should guide inheritance policy here and now. If, for example, individuals would heavily constrain the inequality of wealth that might arise as a product of *inter vivos* gifts or posthumous bequests, then that justifies a steeply progressive tax on gifts and estates here and now, or a different tax regime that would produce a similar result.

Implications for the taxation of bequests

I have argued for a particular approach to issues concerning gifts, posthumous bequests and inheritance that is both egalitarian and anti-perfectionist. The simple thought is that the rules governing bequests should be those that equally situated people would, on average, choose on the basis of what matters to them. This view is hostile to approaches that proceed from a controversial account of what makes one's life go well or claims about whether we can be harmed or wronged after death. But the account also refuses to pander to the current ambitions of people in our society, which are heavily influenced by unjust inequalities. Giving free reign to people's ambitions is consistent with justice only if their ambitions are not held because of their place in the distribution of good and bad luck. Accordingly, our policy with respect to bequests should mimic what would be chosen within the hypothetical insurance scheme in which individuals do not know whether they are advantaged or disadvantaged in the social lottery.

Let me conclude, then, by making a few tentative suggestions about what the outcome of the hypothetical insurance scheme would be with respect to posthumous bequests. First, following Dworkin's suggestion, there are good reasons to believe that the insurance conception of inheritance supports a steeply progressive tax on bequests so that everyone's inheritance is roughly equal. This argument trades on the observation that individuals would choose to protect themselves against having less wealthy or less generous benefactors. They might, that is, agree to limit the extent to which would-be benefactors can benefit particular people through bequests in favour of a more equal distribution of assets between individuals (2000: 346–349; 2006: 117–118).

One objection to this suggestion is that individuals would choose to protect the right to bequeath because they are more concerned about the welfare of their children than they are about their own. But, as Dworkin suggests, concern for one's child is 'double-edged' (2000: 348). Although freedom to bequeath to one's child is, indeed, one way of benefiting one's child, in the thought experiment under consideration, it is not the only way, because one's child's prospects might be advanced by buying protection against her not receiving inheritance from oneself that takes the form of a payment that is funded by a progressive tax on bequests or inherited wealth.

It is important to distinguish between two ambitions that might move parents who are partial towards their own child. First, they might think that the opportunity to give to their child is valuable because they want her to do well. Second, they might treat the opportunity give to their child as valuable independently of whether their gift promotes her well-being. To the extent that individuals are moved by the first ambition, a concern for their respective children's well-being, they should be aware of the fact that some parents would exercise the freedom to give to their children more than others would, and some children would, thereby, benefit more than others. In the hypothetical insurance scheme, individuals would take steps to prevent or compensate for the outcomes of both unequal family circumstances and different parental preferences. Even if we limit our attention to individuals who care very much for their children, under the equal conditions stipulated by the insurance scheme, the rational choice for the average parent who is reluctant to gamble with her child's future might be to constrain inequality-generating parental gifts. To the extent that we are concerned about the *recipients* of gifts or bequests – the legacies our children might receive – it seems that hypothetical choice supplies an argument for restricting gifts for the reasons Dworkin suggests.

The argument for a relatively unconstrained right to bequeath is better served by appealing to the second ambition described above, our ambition as *agents* to give or bequeath wealth to particular individuals. It might matter to people that *they do the best they can with the resources they have* to promote their child's well-being, rather than that their child's life goes well: I fail as a parent on this view if I could do more for my child but do not do so because of weakness of will or because the law prevents me from so doing. We can imagine a society in which people held this belief. People in that society might choose not to prohibit or tax inequality-generating gifts, because they would not want to reduce inequalities or protect their children from unequal gift giving *by denying themselves the opportunity to fulfil their ambition to do the best they can for their child.*

However, it is unlikely that more than a very few people are moved by this kind of ambition. Even if an individual were so moved, she would have to consider her prospective life as a whole, in which she is not merely (a) a parent with that desire, but also (b) a parent who wants her child to be protected against the harms that other parents' gift-giving might produce for her child, and (c) a child whose prospects are affected by her own and other children's parents being free to act on such desires. She would have to take into account the different circumstances that would influence how that freedom would affect her and her child if it applied generally.[14] For these reasons, then, it is likely that individuals facing equal risks and consulting their own ambitions for how their lives as children and adults should go would not choose principles that protect the opportunity to leave large legacies to particular individuals.

If the hypothetical insurance scheme is the right device to identify what justice demands with respect to gifts, then further questions arise. In particular, the derivation of a progressive estates tax from the scheme needs further defence because it is incomplete. It considers only a limited number of variables and does not consider the possibility that a tax on bequests would generate perverse incentives that might turn out to be worse for everyone or upset the demands of justice. For example, some argue that a significant tax on bequests would encourage more giving or exchange *inter vivos*, which may reduce saving from the optimal rate and, thereby, be detrimental to the economy.[15] A related argument is that encouraging transfers of wealth *inter vivos* would be worse from the point of view of equality. This might be the case because, other things equal, *inter vivos* gifts benefit recipients earlier in life and the value of such receipts might be multiplied through investment. For instance, the purchase of expensive education for one's child, some argue, buys a positional advantage with respect to access to higher education and the job market. It, thereby, generates more inequality than if the gift is received later in life when the chances of investing it in that way are diminished (Brighouse and Swift, 2006).

Both these arguments raise relevant considerations that individuals in the equal insurance scheme must take into account in deciding the schedule of tax rates for bequests. Since I do not have the expertise to consider the empirical claims on which these arguments rest, I simply offer two comments about these arguments. First, fears such as these would be diminished if the rate of saving were inelastic with respect to different rates of estates taxation. If individuals were, on average, precautionary savers who save to fund their lifestyles after work given the indeterminacy of the time of death, then taxing bequests highly would not produce perverse incentives. I leave the details of these empirical matters for others to consider. Second, the concern that taxing bequests would lead to a more worrying inequality shows that rational individuals in the hypothetical insurance scheme would choose policies that are age-sensitive. Recall Dworkin's observation that when choosing medical insurance individuals would not insure to pay for expensive treatment in the final stages of their lives. Similarly, the issue of the regulation of gifts might display *age-relativity*. For example, it might be that insurers would buy protection against having a diminished education or diminished employment prospects by restricting unequal gifts in their formative years, but would not protect against having less wealth than others to the same degree in their later adult lives. If so, the hypothetical insurance scheme might favour a regime in which the consumption of particular goods at certain stages in life (e.g. private schooling) is taxed more heavily than the use of bequests to consume other goods in other parts of the life cycle. In addition, judgements about which goods are worth pursuing at particular stages in one's life might inform how the receipts from the taxation of bequests or inheritance are used. I simply raise these issues to illustrate how the hypothetical insurance scheme might be applied.

I want to finish my brief discussion of the implications of equal inheritance by addressing the issue of the kind of harm that individuals would protect against and, relatedly, whether an estates tax should be hypothecated. Dworkin's own discussion of inheritance suggests that a tax on bequests should be hypothecated and directed to reduce the unequal influence of class on people's life prospects. It is worth quoting him at length:

> The harm such insurance protects against is, we might say, relative rather than absolute. We assume that people have decided how much health and unemployment insurance to buy: they have decided, let us assume, that it makes sense to provide for helpful but not speculative medical care, and for income, if unemployed, somewhat above the poverty line in their

community. They have decided that further insurance to guarantee more medical care or a higher income would not be worth its premium cost. Inheritance insurance would make sense, therefore, to guarantee not a higher standard of living in absolute terms, but against the different and distinct harm of occupying a low tier in a class system – against, that is, a life in a community where others have much more money, and consequently more status and power, than they do and their children will. But it does not make sense for them to pay premiums out of current income to guard against that relative disadvantage, because, as I just said, they have already decided that spending more to guarantee a higher absolute income would be unwise.

(Dworkin, 2000: 348)

Dworkin's position with respect to gifts and bequests has two notable features. First, he claims that the point of taking out insurance against the possibility of misfortune with respect to inheritance is to avoid occupying a lower position in the class structure. And second, he has a particular view of how the tax receipts that would be generated by a tax on bequests should be spent. Because he takes the harm to be avoided to be the harm of social stratification, the receipts from the tax are to be spent to fund measures that improve social mobility. We are to use these tax revenues to fund better public provision of education, and to improve access to higher education and professional training for those from less advantaged social backgrounds. These revenues are not to be used, he insists, to improve health care provision or to fund higher incomes for the unemployed: our entitlements with respect to these goods are already fulfilled through income tax (ibid.: 349).

Dworkin's view depends on accepting a particular alignment of two distinctions. The first is between different causes of inequality. Certain inequalities are the product of different individuals giving unequal amounts of resource to the next generation: the 'social lottery', which benefits individuals directly and also indirectly by affording them greater opportunity to develop marketable skills. Certain other inequalities are the product of unequal natural endowment, which enables some to offer more marketable skills than others do. This is the genetic or natural lottery.

The second distinction is that between absolute and relative advantage. One response to fact of inequality of advantage is to display a concern for individuals' *absolute* advantage. This can involve two kinds of concern: first, the concern of 'beneficence', that individuals should enjoy more rather than less advantage; and, second, the 'prioritarian' concern that resources are directed to the less advantaged.[16] A different response is to display a concern for individuals' *relative* advantage by limiting the extent to which some have more than others. To clarify this position we must attend to another distinction. Our worry about the relative standing of individuals with respect to income, for example, might be *derivative* or *non-derivative*. It is derivative if it refers to goods other than income, such as power or status. It is non-derivative if we attach fundamental value to the narrowing of income inequalities.

Dworkin's claim is that when the source of inequality is the natural lottery then our concern to compensate individuals for their inferior circumstances (genetic inheritance) involves a concern for their absolute advantage, but not their relative advantage. But it is unclear why that should be the case.

Consider, first, the derivative concern for limiting income inequality. Understood in these terms, Dworkin's claim about inequalities that arise from the natural lottery seems mistaken. Inequalities of income caused by the activity of individuals possessing unequal talents and different ambitions in a market could, it would seem, generate inequalities of power and status. If we are concerned about the latter, then surely this gives us a reason to limit the income inequalities that are generated by market exchange within a generation, and not merely the inequalities that arise across generations as a product of parents bestowing unequal gifts on their children.

Perhaps, though, we should interpret Dworkin's view as involving the claim that relative income inequalities are *non-derivatively* problematic when they are the product of gift giving (but not when they follow from the natural lottery). That is, they are problematic even when they do not produce further inequalities in terms of power or status. But if this is his view, the defence of it remains unclear, because the natural and social lotteries share one feature that is of considerable importance from the point of view of resource egalitarianism: both unfavourable natural endowment or disadvantageous social origins are types of bad 'brute' luck that call for compensation.

It is also puzzling why insuring individuals should be concerned about only their relative fortune when thinking about the inequalities produced by the *social* lottery. Considering the prospect of a vast fortune being given to the children of wealthy parents while those born to poor parents receive very little, it seems clear that one might bring one's desire for more rather than less wealth and income, or one's desire to avoid certain absolute disadvantages, to bear on the decision of whether to take out insurance in the face of this possible unequal distribution of luck.

The resource egalitarian accepts that the inequalities of income that are the product of both the social and natural lotteries are prima facie unjust and call for regulation by suitable principles of justice. Dworkin's preferred solution with respect to these lotteries is to model compensation on the basis of his hypothetical insurance scheme. However, it is a mystery why in that scheme we should have a concern for the absolute fortunes of individuals in response to the natural lottery, but a concern for their relative fortune in response to the social lottery. In the absence of a plausible defence of this position, the right approach seems to be that insurers should be free to protect against both absolute and relative disadvantage irrespective of whether the disadvantage has a social or natural cause.

The second element of Dworkin's proposal for dealing with the social lottery is his claim that the tax revenues produced by taxing gifts, bequests, and inheritance should be spent in a particular way, to enhance the public provision of education, to subsidize higher education and professional training, and to develop other initiatives that improve social mobility. However, if we reject Dworkin's claim that our concern with the social lottery is purely relational, then we might also reject his restrictions on the use of funds obtained through taxing gifts. We might instead simply view gifts as a cause of inequality that is not immune from taxation, because it tends to produce brute luck inequalities. How we use those tax receipts is a further question. We could use them in the way Dworkin envisages, but we might also use such funds to improve the absolute advantage of those who suffer different kinds of bad luck, including accident or genetic misfortune.

No doubt, many more questions arise if my interpretation of resource egalitarianism is adopted as the right approach to inherited wealth. My brief remarks suggest that this view has reasonably radical implications for the taxation of bequests. However, even if I am wrong about that, there remain good reasons to investigate the implications of resource egalitarianism for inherited wealth. In virtue of its commitment to impartiality and its sensitivity to the values people affirm, equality of resources offers an attractive approach to issues of distributive justice that integrates the ideals of equality and freedom.

Acknowledgements

Earlier versions of this chapter were presented at the Conference on Justice between Age Groups at the University of Essex and the Workshop on Inherited Wealth, Justice and Equality at UCSIA, University of Antwerp. I thank the audiences at both events for their helpful comments. For instructive conversation or written comments, I am grateful to Doug Bamford, John Cunliffe, Guido Erreygers, Tim Fowler, Axel Gosseries, Hugh Lazenby, Martin O'Neill, Fabienne Peter, Victor Tadros, Andrew Walton, and Andrew Williams.

Notes

1 This puts the view rather strongly and some anti-perfectionists, like Rawls, allow comprehensive reasons a place within political morality under certain conditions. For clarification, see Rawls (1999b: ch. 26).
2 There is an issue about the scope of public reason, which I lack the space to discuss fully. It might be claimed that Rawls's ideal of political debate on the basis of public reasons applies to 'constitutional essentials and matters of basic justice' and that issues concerning inherited wealth fit neither of these descriptions. That claim appears mistaken, however. Because inheritance policy has the potential for producing significant involuntary inequalities between individuals, it surely counts as a matter of 'basic justice'. For a nice examination of this issue, see Quong (2004).
3 The argument that confiscation is, in principle, just is, of course, compatible with more or less restrictive rules regulating bequests. For example, it may be irrational, if not unjust, for the government to disallow bequests if that would produce a lower yield than would allowing and taxing them at a rate below 100 per cent.
4 I draw on Fabre (2008). Fabre's argument denies posthumous rights, which, for the purposes of that paper, she understands as normative devices that protect people's interests.
5 In this context, 'reasonable' citizens are taken to be citizens who acknowledge the two basic interests in having and exercising a sense of justice and reflecting on and

pursuing their particular comprehensive goals. Of course, many actual citizens reject the ideals of freedom and equality as the starting point for a conception of political morality. But these citizens count as unreasonable in the liberal view.

6 For further elaboration of this kind of hybrid view as a general conception of justice, see Clayton (2006: 28–35) on which I draw in presenting the elements of resource egalitarianism.

7 Dworkin's claim, that an adequate account of advantage should be one which squares with people's particular ethical judgements, is a key part of his critique of equality of welfare and equality of access to welfare. Welfarist conceptions take into account the preferences of different people. But welfarists aim for equality of preference-satisfaction, which produces very different results compared to Dworkin's appeal to preferences in equality of resources. Dworkin's central objection to welfarism is that it is committed to asserting the counter-intuitive claim that if Dan's preference-satisfaction is lower than Carla's then we ought to compensate Dan for this, even when Dan believes that his philosophical life is far superior to a life devoted to monetary enrichment. For the debate between Dworkin and welfarists as represented by G.A. Cohen, see Dworkin (2000; 2004: 339–350), Cohen (1989; 2004), Williams (2002) and Clayton (2000).

8 Note that Dworkin himself defends equality of resources on the basis of an account of ethics and political morality as 'integrated'. That is, he believes that equality of resources and the right account of ethics are mutually supportive. He distances himself from the Rawlsian account of anti-perfectionism, the conception of anti-perfectionism advanced here, which asks us not to take a stand on the merits of different accounts of ethics (Dworkin, 2011). Notwithstanding the merits of his ethical defence of equality of resources, my claim is that it can be nested within a Rawlsian conception of anti-perfectionist political morality.

9 Dworkin adopts the averaging assumption because of the epistemic difficulties in tailoring health care provision to individuals when what a person is due is determined by what she would have insured for in a situation of equality in which she lacks information about the particular risks that she faces. The averaging assumption is a second-best solution given the unfeasibility of an individualized insurance market.

10 But not their convictions with respect to justice or their views about the legitimate extent of inequality: it is the role of the insurance scheme is to shed light on what justice demands of us.

11 For criticism of hypothetical insurance, see Otsuka (2002); Fleurbaey (2002). For defences, see Dworkin (2000: 340–346; 2002b: 120–125); Williams (2004).

12 Dworkin presents the insurance scheme for dealing with inequalities affecting children by introducing 'prudent guardians' (2000: 338–339, 347–348). I shall not consider the extent to which replacing such guardians with individuals who will live another life as child and adult would affect the results of the scheme. However, one reason for preferring the account as set out here is that it makes more vivid the ambition-sensitivity at the heart of equality of resources.

13 Like others, resource egalitarians stipulate that the choice should be rational and fully informed. But, as Dworkin notes, this does not assume any particular view of how individuals ought to choose, such as expected utility maximization or disaster avoidance. Those are further questions concerning optimal choice that are left to individuals to answer for themselves.

14 The issue here is the one Hart raises in discussing Rawls's defence of particular liberties by reference to the choice of representatives in the 'original position':

> Any scheme providing for the general distribution in society of liberty of action necessarily does two things: first, it confers on individuals the advantage of that liberty, but secondly, it exposes them to whatever disadvantages the practices of that liberty by others may entail for them. ... So whether or not it is in any man's

interest to choose that any specific liberty should be generally distributed depends on whether the advantages for him of the exercise of that liberty outweigh the various disadvantages for him of its general practice by others.

(Hart, 1989: 247–248)

15 For an exploration of these issues from the perspective of political liberalism, though not the kind of anti-perfectionist liberalism that informs this paper, see Edward J. McCaffery (1994).
16 For these distinctions and relevant discussion, see Parfit (2002).

References

Brighouse, H. and Swift, A. (2006) 'Equality, priority, and positional goods', *Ethics*, 116: 471–497.

Brighouse, H. and Swift, A. (2009) 'Legitimate parental partiality', *Philosophy and Public Affairs*, 37: 43–80.

Clayton, M. (2000) 'The resources of liberal equality', *Imprints*, 9: 63–84.

Clayton, M. (2006) *Justice and Legitimacy in Upbringing*, Oxford: Oxford University Press.

Cohen, G.A. (1989) 'On the currency of egalitarian justice', *Ethics*, 99: 906–944.

Cohen, G.A. (2004) 'Expensive taste rides again', in J. Burley (ed.) *Dworkin and His Critics*, Oxford: Blackwell.

Cohen, G.A. (2008) *Rescuing Justice and Equality*, Cambridge, MA: Harvard University.

Dworkin, R. (2000) *Sovereign Virtue: The Theory and Practice of Equality*, Cambridge, MA: Harvard University Press.

Dworkin, R. (2002a) 'Justice in the distribution of health care', in M. Clayton and A. Williams (eds) *The Ideal of Equality*, Basingstoke, Palgrave.

Dworkin, R. (2002b) 'Sovereign virtue revisited', *Ethics*, 113: 106–143.

Dworkin, R. (2004) 'Ronald Dworkin replies', in J. Burley (ed.) *Dworkin and His Critics*, Oxford: Blackwell.

Dworkin, R. (2006) *Is Democracy Possible Here? Principles for a New Political Debate*, Princeton, NJ: Princeton University Press.

Dworkin, R. (2011) *Justice for Hedgehogs*, Cambridge, MA: Harvard University Press.

Fabre, C. (2008) 'Posthumous rights', in M. Kramer *et al.* (eds) *The Legacy of H.L.A. Hart: Legal, Political and Moral Philosophy*, Oxford: Oxford University Press.

Fleurbaey, M. (2002) 'Equality of resources revisited', *Ethics*, 113: 82–105.

Hart, H.L.A. (1989) 'Rawls on liberty and its priority', in N. Daniels (ed.), *Reading Rawls: Critical Studies on Rawls' 'A Theory of Justice'*, Stanford, CA: Stanford University Press.

Lazenby, H. (2009) 'One kiss too many? Giving, luck egalitarianism and other-affecting choice', *Journal of Political Philosophy*, 18: 271–286.

McCaffery, E. (1994) 'The political liberal case against the estate tax', *Philosophy and Public Affairs*, 23: 281–312.

Nozick, R. (1974) *Anarchy, State and Utopia*, Oxford: Basil Blackwell.

Otsuka, M. (2002) 'Luck, insurance, and equality', *Ethics*, 113: 40–54.

Parfit, D. (2002) 'Equality or priority?' in M. Clayton and A. Williams (eds) *The Ideal of Equality*, Basingstoke, Palgrave.

Quong, J. (2004) 'The scope of public reason', *Political Studies*, 52: 233–250.

Rawls, J. (1996) *Political Liberalism*, New York: Columbia University Press.

Rawls, J. (1999a) *A Theory of Justice*, revised edition, Cambridge, MA: Harvard University Press.

Rawls, J. (1999b) *Collected Papers*, ed. S. Freeman, Cambridge, MA: Harvard University Press.

Raz, J. (1986) *The Morality of Freedom*, Oxford: Clarendon Press.

Williams, A. (2002) 'Equality for the ambitious', *The Philosophical Quarterly*, 52: 377–389.

Williams, A. (2004) 'Equality, ambition, and insurance', *Aristotelian Society Supplementary Volume*, 78: 131–150.

8 Favouring wealth intergenerational mobility by increasing the inheritance tax

Putting the case for France

Luc Arrondel and André Masson

There is a paradox about wealth transfer taxation. Although the economic arguments in favour of taxing at least *post-mortem* bequests appear quite convincing, the majority of the social and political systems, following their national opinions, have adopted the opposite view. It thus seems that, for a number of years, we have reached a dead end. Is there a way out? Which tricks are there to use in order to make an inheritance tax system politically acceptable?

To some extent, this chapter can be linked to the subsequent analysis of Cremer and Pestieau (Chapter 10 of this volume). Their theoretical discussion of the merits of wealth transfer taxation on both efficiency and equity grounds leads to the unsurprising conclusion that there is a strong case for an inheritance or estate tax. The authors acknowledge that the desirability of a wealth transfer tax depends on the dominant bequest motive (whether accidental, altruistic, 'joy of giving', exchange-motivated, etc.) within the population considered. But if one is looking for a tax system to finance government services that is 'as efficient, fair and painless as possible', then, '[o]n all accounts, it is difficult to imagine a better tax than the estate tax' (Cremer and Pestieau, Chapter 10: 168). Note that similar conclusions could be, and have been drawn over the past 20 or 30 years. If anything, the case for wealth transfer taxation is stronger today, owing to increasing wealth inequalities and a rising weight of inheritance in wealth accumulation in most occidental countries.

Yet, as noted by Cremer and Pestieau, most (American) economists favour a reduction of the wealth transfer tax. Moreover, the general policy trend over the last years has been a decrease if not an abolition of this type of taxation in most occidental countries. The authors point out three reasons for this paradoxical state of affairs: avoidance and evasion; the transmission of family businesses; and tax competition within and between countries leading to a 'race to the bottom' regarding any wealth taxation. And last but not least, political systems have to take into account the fact that wealth taxation has become so *unpopular* nowadays.

These arguments are not really compelling, though (for example, you could have a particular legal and fiscal regime for the transmission of family businesses). More specifically, they do not take into account the French situation, where there is an efficient and popular wealth tax. It was established by the left government in 1981 (under the name of IGF), with strong support from the majority of the population (except for the richest households). In 1986, the newly elected right government suppressed the wealth tax ... which is one important reason why it lost the following election. The wealth tax was later restored (under the name of ISF) and has since expanded, the population covered increasing from 0.5 per cent of households at the start to at least 2 per cent today. In the meantime, however, the tax rate of both gifts and inheritances has decreased – especially in recent years – and more and more beneficiaries are exempt from any taxation. Moreover, the wealth transfer tax is as unpopular as ever: in the 'Pater' recent surveys that we conducted with the TNS-Sofres Institute in 2002, 2007 and 2009, this negative attitude was found to be massive, with over 90 per cent of interviewees saying they were in favour of an across-the-board reduction in inheritance tax (see Arrondel and Masson, 2007b).

The former French president Nicolas Sarkozy is highly representative (much more in any case than academics) of the point of view of the man in the street in those matters. During his 2007 electoral campaign, he basically used two arguments when stating his economic programme.[1] First:

> I want 95% of the French people to be exempt from inheritance tax. When you have worked your entire life to build up capital, you should be able to leave it to your *children* tax free.
>
> (our emphasis)

And second:

> Life is badly designed: when you're older, you have fewer needs and more income [and goods]. When you're young, you have a lot of needs and little income. I believe in the *mobility* of capital, of wealth. The problem in France is that we *inherit too late* on in the day.
>
> (our emphasis)

Note that these two harsh statements are typical of a French mentality and may not have universal value.

The first one introduces a key consideration: you should not tax saving made for *family* purposes. It is not (only) that you should not interfere with family relations which are private matters, or that saving per se should not be taxed. The underlying rationale is that you should not discourage accumulation for such a noble objective as increasing the well-being of your progeny, an objective that satisfies the human desire for prosperity or immortality. It is perfectly in line with the French saying: *toucher à l'héritage c'est comme toucher à la famille* – 'interfering with inheritance is tantamount to interfering with the family'.

The case for inheritance taxation may thus vary from one country to another and should appear less pervasive in 'family-oriented' nations. Instead of considering only the different types of motivations for wealth accumulation and transmission that have been proposed in the economic literature, we shall therefore adopt a slightly broader perspective borrowing from sociological analyses of the different social cultures and welfare states in Europe and the United States. To be more specific, we refer here to the trilogy put forward by Esping-Andersen (1999) who defines three different welfare 'worlds' – the 'liberal', 'conservative' and 'social-democratic' – assimilated at the end to three geographic areas – respectively English-speaking, continental or Mediterranean, and Scandinavian. In this setting, France can be qualified as 'moderately conservative'.

Yet the Weberian 'ideal' typology developed by the Danish sociologist has a number of flaws, inducing followers to distinguish four, five or more ideal types of welfare states. Moreover, it is not perfectly suited for our purpose. We shall rather contrast, at a more abstract level which preserves parsimony and coherence, three 'visions' (*Weltanschauungen*) of the welfare state, that is to say three philosophical schools of thought or *paradigms* based on incompatible 'metaphysical' priors or postulates (Masson, 2009). The three paradigms basically diverge on the hierarchy stated between the three 'pillars', the market, the family and the state, looking especially at their respective roles in securing the specific needs and covering the risks of the two periods of economic dependency, youth and old age:

- the *free agent* paradigm (dominant in the 'liberal' world) believes in markets and advocates the freedom and responsibility of the individual; it wants to reduce or limit state intervention;
- the *equal citizenship* paradigm (dominant in the 'social-democratic' world) believes that the state should grant a high level of welfare to any citizen and conduct equalising redistributions; it wants to reduce or limit family links in favour of the individual direct link between the state and each citizen;
- the *multi-solidarity* paradigm (dominant in the 'conservative' world) believes in the virtues of intergenerational family solidarity and places limited trust in market mechanisms.

Interestingly enough, each paradigm implicitly favours one (or several) specific motives of wealth transmission introduced in the economic literature (first section).

On the other hand, our trilogy will not alone solve the problem. It will indeed *not* explain why Sweden, for instance, where the dominant equal citizenship paradigm is in favour of wealth transfer taxation, has recently abolished its estate tax as well as its wealth tax (admittedly both were old-fashioned). As suggested by the dead end reached in the chapter by Cremer and Pestieau (Chapter 10 of this volume), it turns out that a universal defence of inheritance taxation, and especially of *increased* inheritance taxation, may prove difficult or even vain at present. Perhaps a more promising way out would be to look for arguments that are more country specific and/or circumstantial. This is the objective of our chapter which focuses on the French situation.

Granted that the first argument of Nicolas Sarkozy against inheritance taxation, based upon family consideration, is especially strong in our country, let us now consider his second argument. The fact that we inherit later, due to increased longevity, is also true elsewhere. But the bulk of the argument, although stated like a universal truth, refers to a specific feature of the French context, namely a strong intergenerational imbalance: seniors and the elderly have enjoyed an increase in their assets and incomes whereas the living conditions of the youngest households have tended to deteriorate, at least in relative terms (second section).

How should we cope with such an undesirable gap between French seniors and their children which may foster intergenerational tension or conflict? This chapter goes against current trends in France (see appendix) by making the case for heavier and more progressive inheritance taxes in order to raise differential tax relief on gifts, thereby encouraging a more widespread use of these *inter vivos* transfers. The desired effect would be to speed up the circulation of assets (which are at old age more often of a rent type than investment capital) in favour of the young generations.

The rationale most frequently put forward to justify increasing taxes on capital transfers is that inheritance is a major factor behind the concentration of assets and a prime vehicle for the reproduction of inequalities. Indeed, at the top of the wealth ladder, the richest are often the children of rich individuals, and vice versa.[2] We use a different, complementary justification. If we really want the family to continue to free up transfers of assets to the new generations (second section), the suitable solution would be to considerably *raise* the inheritance tax. Admittedly highly unpopular in our country, the grounds for the measure would no longer be equity considerations as before. Basically, unless one is prepared to subsidize gifts and other *inter vivos* transfers, the only efficient way to give the latter a significant tax incentive is through a heavier and more progressive tax on post-mortem inheritances *alone*.

In favour of such a reform, there are some proven facts:

- A large number of French senior households have sufficient financial means to make these early transfers (third section).
- These households have reacted in the past to such tax incentives to earlier transmission by substantially increasing the sums of gifts to their children (fourth section).
- By easing the recipient children's cash constraints, early transfers significantly facilitate these children's plans to buy housing, start up a business, etc. – whereas the average age of inheritance is currently nearly 50 years old (fifth section).

Lastly, what can be done to guarantee the *social* utility of these freer flowing *family returns* through capital transfers to the young, which still present the shortcoming of benefiting already-advantaged children when they are made through family channels? The solution would be to allow the wealthiest parents to escape inheritance tax by a means other than the family, by fostering the development of charitable gifts or bequests to duly registered *charity* works and foundations. To encourage such donations would require increasing the freedom to bequeath *outside of the family* in our country (sixth section).

All in all, the proposed tax and legislative mechanism would be a socio-political hybrid, using a mix of free agent ('liberal'), multi-solidarity ('conservative') and equal citizenship ('social-democratic') measures (seventh section).

Three paradigms of the welfare state: three views of 'family returns'

The disagreement does not so much concern the diagnosis of the intergenerational imbalance, particularly pronounced in the French case, when it comes to its magnitude and length. The debates focuses rather on the underlying causes of this imbalance and, more importantly, on the desirability of increased wealth family 'compensatory returns' to the young. That explains why the proposed solutions differ so greatly.

The free agent paradigm: capitalist or joy of giving transfers

The 'liberal' or rather *free agent* school of thought believes in markets, whose functioning is said to be hindered by social security burdens and brakes on innovation. Its solution to the intergenerational imbalance is therefore to reduce the size of the welfare state by substantially reducing upward government transfers, especially pensions, replaced partly by private pension funds, and the public debt, which weighs on the new generations. Remaining spending is to be channelled into young people's education and training – at least the 'worthy' young – in the name of equal opportunities and prioritising investment.

Obviously, the model of *capitalist* intergenerational transfers (see Arrondel and Masson, 2006) fits in the best with the free-agent world view. This model concerns large fortunes which cannot be used up in a single lifetime. The capitalist intergenerational transfers are mainly wealth-motivated, driven by entrepreneurial motives, accumulation for its own sake, economic power, social prestige and sometimes even desire for posterity. The impact of taxation on the transfer will depend on the particular motivation of wealth ownership: tax relief on gifts could speed up the transfer of a business, but would have no effect on wealth accumulated for economic power. Legislation in support of foundations and other charitable works could appeal to certain fortunes while preventing expatriation.

The same holds true to a lesser extent for the *paternalistic* transfer model where the donation or inheritance comes simply from the 'joy of giving' for its own sake – whether to family or society – without thinking too much about the situation or needs of the beneficiaries. This motivation is likely to be concentrated among the more well-off strata of society. The sums transferred are thought to be generally sensitive to tax relief and greater freedom of bequest. Gifts reportedly increase, albeit in a limited way, with the differential tax breaks granted.

The equal citizenship paradigm: accidental bequests

The 'social democratic' or rather *equal citizenship* school believes that the state should grant a high level of welfare to all citizens and conduct equalising redistributions. It does not trust family solidarity and capital transfers to solve the imbalance between young people and seniors since it deems them to be insufficient, unequal and a source of perverse or arbitrary dependence. It advocates the idea of tapping into rich seniors by raising wealth taxes and social contributions paid by pensioners while reducing cash transfers such as family allowances and especially pensions: it would be preferable to put the money into collective personal services deemed more efficient and fair. This leaves the welfare state to prioritize the 'new risks' – unskilled young people, lone parent families, young parents, etc. – and 'active' investment spending (education and vocational training).

The *accidental* bequest model fits in best with equal citizenship reasoning, in particular because inheritance taxation in this case creates the least behavioural distortions. Deemed 'involuntary', the accidental bequest arises as a result of precautionary behaviour prompted by uncertainty over the length of life combined with life annuity market imperfections, i.e. the desire, in these circumstances, to protect oneself against the risk of becoming penniless in old age: we leave behind what we would otherwise have consumed had God given us a longer life. This motive only gives rise to *post-mortem* bequests whose amount is influenced neither by taxation (at least within given margins) nor by inheritance legislation. It concerns mainly the lower and middle classes, life cycle savers (for retirement and precautionary motives), who form a significant proportion of the population, but only hold a modest share of the national wealth.

The multi-solidarity paradigm: altruistic motives or indirect reciprocities

Conversely, the 'conservative' or rather *multi-solidarity* school believes in the virtues of intergenerational family solidarity and parental altruism,[3] and places only limited trust in (savings and life annuity) markets in order to satisfy the needs of the elderly. Consequently, it argues in favour of high state pensions and advocates often a complementary division of roles between the family and the state, with the former looking primarily after the young (education and various assistance) and the latter looking after the old (health and retirement). It would solve the generational imbalance by developing incentive policies to increase and/or speed up 'family returns' through capital transfers to the young-family returns which it paints in glowing colours.

Becker's (1991) *altruistic* model fits in best with the multi-solidarity paradigm: family transfers are eminently virtuous because they are driven by altruism on the part of the parents who know and do what is best for their children. The parents are assumed to be altruistic towards their children to the extent that they derive a utility gain from the potential increase in their offspring's well-being following the transfers granted. Transfers here aim to bring standards of living closer between parents and children – compensation between generations – and between brothers and sisters – compensation within generations. The greater a child's own resources compared with those of his or her parents or siblings, the less s/he will receive. Moreover, transfers are supposed to be made when the children need them the most, in the form of assistance or *inter vivos* gifts. Tax relief measures on gifts have maximum efficiency if this model prevails: the parents opt more for this alternative rather than bequeathing their fortune when they die.

A brief discussion: bequest models and (French) empirical facts

We have said nothing about models of intergenerational transfers based upon an (intertemporal) exchange between self-centered parents and children. Arrondel and Masson (2006) show that these exchange-motivated bequests do not fit (French) data.

Consider the most relevant *KCPG* intergenerational composition: *K* for young kid at home, *C* for adult child, *P* for parents of mature age (middle generation) and *G* for retired grandparent. We find that the only *upward* transfers of economic importance, whether in time or financial form, are given to the old, retired generation (*G*) by their children of the middle generation (*P*): adult children (*C*) do not make any significant transfers. Moreover, financial and time transfers made to old parents (*G*) cannot be explained by any observable (past, present or future) counterpart, given or promised to their children (*P*): helpers have not received more than others and do not expect higher inheritances – helped retired parents are actually poorer in (bequeathable) wealth and in income. In fact, the counterpart for the upward transfer from *P* to *G* comes from a third generation, meaning that the exchange, of an *indirect reciprocity* type, takes place between *three* generations. The upward transfer made by *P* to *G* reimburses the latter generation for having done the same to its own parents (*GG*: great-grandparents) – co-residence with old parents tends thus to be reproduced from one generation to the next – or is explained by 'demonstration effects' (Cox and Stark, 1998) being made in expectation of similar support (from *C*) at old age.

When bequests are not of the accidental type, there is likewise significant evidence that downward transfers (financial help, gifts and bequest) are driven in part by indirect reciprocities. Each form of parent-to-child financial transfers appears strongly influenced by, and often only by, the same form of transfer received. Moreover, the Bevan and Stiglitz (1979) model of golden rule or retrospective bequests could explain why the propensity to bequeath out of capital receipts is significantly *higher* than the one out of life earnings. Note that contrary to pure altruism, downward indirect reciprocities should entail at most *limited* compensatory effects (as the data show), since the prime motivation for the (downward) transfer is not to increase relatives' well-being, but to keep on the intergenerational chain in order to benefit in turn from it. It follows that parent-to-child transfers will be sensitive to tax relief and greater freedom of bequest, and that gifts, especially, will increase with the differential tax breaks granted, but usually in a more limited way than under pure altruism.[4]

The French context: intergenerational imbalance and transfers

This section first highlights the worrying intergenerational imbalance in our country. It then tries to assess the potentialities of rebalancing through government and family transfers by comparing the amounts concerned.

A growing gap in standards of living between young and older adults

In France, in particular, the last 30 years have seen a relative, if not absolute, decline in the situation of young adults entering the job market: qualifications are worth less, starting wages have stagnated, and it has become hard to find a job in an environment of high unemployment and unstable employment. The so-called 'postponement syndrome' is especially pronounced in our country. The new generations seem to watch their elders on the conveyor belt of growth – even reduced growth – while they live the key phases of their lives in slow motion, as everything happens for them *late:* independence, entering the world of work, professional career, home ownership, settling down with a partner, having children and inheriting ... not to mention the possibility of later retirement. With the end of the euphoria of the post-war boom years, this turnaround has fuelled debates on the end of generational equity and the breaking of the 'generational compact': the issue is whether the problems encountered by young people are due solely to a temporary bad patch and time lags or whether there is cause for concern that the problems and mounting hold-ups could become irreversible, blocking the futures of the disadvantaged for life.

Although the finger points primarily at market shortcomings, the situation in which young French people find themselves is all the more worrying in that the government seems to be doing too little about it, concentrating most of its constantly rising spending on the older individuals (health and pensions). This explains a large part of the unprecedented improvement in the pensioner's condition and a growing gap between young and old – a phenomenon totally at odds with the long-standing trend that prevailed previously. Yet the most worrying factor is probably the spiralling rise in these upward public transfers due mainly to population ageing. This raises the question of the sustainability of the redistribution policies: would the government be able to keep its promises to current and future pensioners without raising social security contributions too much and overloading the young generations' already heavy burden?

Government transfers (upward) and family transfers (downward): the amounts concerned

How can the growing gap between young and old households' standards of living be reduced? Our purpose in the following is not to envisage how we could, in the name of greater generational equity, curb the drift in upward government transfers – which would be the purpose of free-agent reasoning. It is initially to encourage family transfers to new generations, which is more of a multi-solidarity stance and in definite contrast to the equal citizenship thinking. In this exercise, it is important first of all to assess the potential quantitative importance of such rebalancing by comparing the sums concerned, both government and family transfers.

Table 8.1 presents an approximation, as a percentage of gross domestic product (GDP), of the annual sums of upward and downward cash transfers made by the government and families in France today. It hence provides a snapshot of public and private intergenerational solidarity by giving an idea of the quantitative importance of the flows concerned.[5]

The right-hand side of the table concerning public redistribution shows that individuals aged 60 and over, making up one-fifth of the population, currently receive nearly 20 per cent of GDP mostly in pension and health transfers. This is more than all the other age brackets in terms of expenditures on health, education, family allowances, supplementary benefits, unemployment benefit, etc.

The left-hand side of the table concerning the family isolates the financial transfers among adults: the flows display a highly pronounced asymmetry, inverse to the government transfers, with beneficiaries being mainly children and grandchildren. To take just one example, financial help is ten times higher overall downstream than upstream.

Despite its imperfections,[6] Table 8.1 paints a general picture that provides valuable information on the general balance of public and private transfers, both upward and downward. Government financial flows tend to move upwards through the generations while private financial flows move downwards. Bear in mind, however, that behind this basic observation, the sums concerned are not comparable. Total family transfers or returns – help, gifts and inheritances – represent a sizeable 6.5 per cent of GDP, that is however only half of public pensions and long-term care expenses; on the other hand, they are now more often made before death, as *inter vivos* flows (financial help and gifts) currently exceed inheritances.

Of course, the total amount of family returns is only part of the story. Let us then say a few words about their composition or timing. The financial transfers to adult children within the family can be divided into three types in France: financial help (loan or transfer of money, payment of a rent, and freely providing a separate home), which is neither taxed nor regulated; declared gifts, which are taxed (but still less than inheritances) and regulated (there are limits to unequal sharing between children); and lastly, there is inheritance, which is both regulated and taxed. These intergenerational transfers exhibit a specific timing.

Table 8.1 Public and private transfers between generations in France (% of GDP)

Type	Family		Government	
	Direction		*Direction*	
	Downward	*Upward*	*Downward and under-60s (80% of the population)*	*Over-60s (20% of the population)*
Cash transfers	Transfers between adults • Declared transfers **5%** Inheritances **3%** Gifts **2%** • Financial help **2%** • Education spending **?**	Transfers between adults • Gifts ε • Financial help **0.2%**	• Family allowances + maternity **2%** • Health, disability, etc. expenditure **5%** • Welfare (child, housing), minimum integration income **1%** • Unemployment **2%** • Education + in-service training expenditure **7%** Total **17%**	• Public pensions + long-term care **13%** • Health, disability, etc. expenditure **5%** • Growth in the public debt **2%** Total **20%**
Transfers in time and in kind	• Help in kind • Education time • Grandchild care • Coresidence	• Care or services for aged parents • Coresidence	• Services to families (crèches, canteens) **1.3%**	• Services to the aged **0.2%**

Source: authors' calculations based on various sources (INSEE, OECD and DGI).

Financial help is received by the children the earliest, in order to finance their college education and, especially, when they set up home with a partner and/or buy housing. Next come gifts received at an average of 38 years old in France, which is more than ten years before parental bequest received when the children are around 50 years old.

Well-off seniors (have enough means to speed up family transfers)

The question therefore needs to be put as to whether there really are enough possibilities for increasing these family transfers: could a significant proportion of senior households, among the most well-off, give more to their children during their lifetimes, i.e. would they have enough assets to shed some without undermining their own interests? We find this to be particularly the case in France for a number of reasons.

It is often said that there is too much saving in France (the saving rate is at the top of the list of European countries along with Germany and Italy). As a matter of fact, these savings exhibit above all an unequal age distribution since they are generally overly concentrated in the 50 to 70-year-old age brackets – and even older. There are, however, large disparities within these senior age brackets. Some appear to have too few savings.[7] Yet many other households reportedly save 'too much': late in life, they have ever more assets, on average well above levels observed in other developed countries (despite what is seen as a generous French social security system compared with the rest of the world), and much too high for their own consumption in their old age. Part (but only part) of this accumulation most probably comes from precautionary savings due to the uncertain future of pensions and health insurance, but it would be somewhat far-fetched to invoke a greater concern for the future among our compatriots than elsewhere in order to justify the differences observed with other countries.

Basically, based on the (admittedly demanding) assumption that the pension and health systems in France will remain generous towards the elderly, the ammunition is there to accelerate family transfers. And there are also legitimate reasons to do so: reasons specific to our country – young households' integration and savings problems – and reasons associated with the widespread lengthening of life expectancy. Inheritances are received later and later in life: from 1984 to 2000, French tax (DGI) statistics show that the average age at death rose five years and the average age of heirs rose the same. Today, we are inheriting from our parents at 48 years old or more on average.[8]

In an exercise to gauge the extent of the imbalance between generations, Figure 8.1 presents the rates of home ownership – purchased in own right or inherited – based on the head of household's age over the last 20 years (1986–2010): barely more than 10 per cent of the under-30s age bracket is concerned, whereas the rate of ownership is 70 per cent among households aged 50 to 70 years old. Moreover, the percentage of owners has risen among the 50 to 70 years old, while it has decreased among the under-40s since 1986: rising

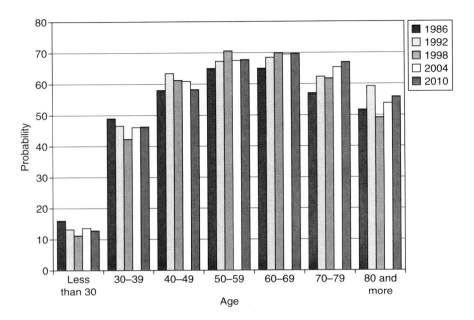

Figure 8.1 Probability of homeownership by age (source: Enquêtes Patrimoine Insee).

housing prices in the large cities have pushed up the average age of first-time home ownership among the young generations.

It is obviously hardly likely that people would pass on their usual residence while still alive.[9] Yet the generational imbalance concerns just as much the other elements of wealth, especially financial. Figure 8.2 presents the 2010 *median* (more representative) gross wealth for the different cohorts compared with the median wealth for the population as a whole. Households aged 50 to 70 years old have the greatest wealth, 55 per cent higher than the total median assets (at approximately €150,000). The over-70s stand nearly at this overall median level, whereas the 30 to 40 years old stand at just two-thirds and the under-30s are barely on the chart. These deviations partially reflect the uneven spread of home ownership, but the findings in terms of median *financial* assets reveal a comparable age imbalance: although the under-30s have some financial assets representing 40 per cent of the overall median, the 60 to 70 year olds tower 60 per cent above and the over 70s still have a median wealth that is 40 per cent higher than the overall median.

Finally, Arrondel, Masson and Verger (2009) find that, between 1992 and 2007, the gap in net wealth has widened between the households aged 50 and over and those below 30 years old, especially owing to the relative enrichment of home owners.

In short, there is even greater reason for an increase or acceleration in family transfers in the recent period insofar as it saw seniors becoming relatively

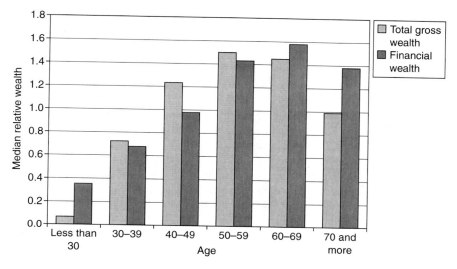

Figure 8.2 Median relative wealth by age (source: Enquête Patrimoine 2010 Insee).

wealthier. To become richer during this period, it was better to already be an owner and shareholder, and therefore over 50 years old. The concentration of stocks and shares is particularly striking: today, the over-65s own as many stocks and shares as all the other age brackets put together.

Can early transfers be encouraged and how?

How can senior households that can afford to pass on their assets to their children and grandchildren, be encouraged to do so sooner? The natural solution is to make *inter vivos* transfers, financial help and gifts, more advantageous compared with inheritances by means of taxation and legislation.

Theoretically, the effectiveness of such measures depends primarily on the reason for the transfer and capital market imperfections (non-liquid or indivisible assets): it is zero if the transfers are accidental, maximal in the case of operative (Beckerian) parental altruism, limited but positive in the case of 'joy of giving' motivations or indirect reciprocities mechanisms.

Empirically, both in France (Arrondel and Laferrère, 2001) and in the US (Bernheim *et al.*, 2001), estate data show that the frequency or amount of gifts with respect to inheritance is highly sensitive, over the short run, to the relative tax advantage granted to gifts relative to bequests or inheritance; yet, Poterba (2001) and McGarry (2001) claim that most US households fail by a substantial margin to exploit the advantages of gifts to the full extent permitted by law. This is evidence that wealth gifts and bequests are considered by parents as substitutes, but only as *partial* substitutes, for a number of reasons: uncertainty concerning future health or longevity, desire to monitor children and to have the last word, etc.

The lessons from past changes in differential taxation of gifts and bequests

In Arrondel and Masson (2007a), we obtain similar qualitative results from a different perspective: drawing on various sources covering a long period (INSEE assets surveys starting in 1986, DGI statistics starting in 1950, etc.) and more recent experiences ('donations Sarkozy'), we show that French households' transfer practices respond positively, in the short and long run, to tax relief on gifts. The efficiency of tax incentive measures has been considerable, albeit far from being as high as predicted by the Beckerian model of parental altruism.

For example, the 'donations Sarkozy' measure introduced in the summer of 2004 to make gifts of money (to children, grandchildren, nieces and nephews) exempt from taxation was a categorical success.[10] Initially intended to run until May 2005 for gifts of up to €20,000 (per beneficiary and per donor), the measure was extended through to December of the same year with the threshold raised to €30,000. The measure designed to 'encourage consumption by the young generations' was supposed to make up for the fact that children, assumed to have a higher propensity to consume, inherit later and later in life. This type of gift appealed to a large audience. By the end of 2005, nearly 1,600,000 deeds had been registered corresponding to a total sum of €26 billion, which is approximately the sum of the assets handed down every year on death in the recent period.

As shown by Figure 8.3, this sensitivity of transfers *inter vivos* to tax legislation is found just as much over the long run for 'wealth' gifts.[11] For example, the number of gifts rose 28 per cent in 1981 as households pre-empted the

Figure 8.3 Number of estates and inter vivos gifts (declared) (source: DGFip).

introduction of the wealth tax. A rumour was also going around at the time that the tax relief might be withdrawn. The reduction in the number of donors from 1981 to 1987 likewise corresponds to a period in which some breaks advantaging gifts were phased out. The number of gifts rose again from 140,000 in 1992, when gifts made at least ten years before death were withdrawn from the calculation of the inheritance tax[12] to a peak of 345,000 in 2000. This increase was also driven by the extension of tax relief on gifts to grandchildren in 1996. However, this sharp growth (11 per cent per year on average) stopped short in 2000 and plummeted (–8 per cent per year on average) in a trend reversal that could be explained by a phenomenon of 'saturation' among the parents liable to anticipate the transfer of their assets on the back of these tax breaks.

An iconoclastic proposition

A whole host of indices point to the end of this tax/legislative incentive logic for early transfers in France: the number of gifts fell in the 2000s and the spurt prompted by the 'donations Sarkozy' could well turn out to be transitory. What's more, the sharp increase (tripling) in identical tax allowances for transfers *inter vivos* and on death has substantially reduced the *relative* advantage of gifts over inheritance. The fact that many *inter vivos* transfers (financial support, small cash gifts and various services) are already neither taxed nor even regulated gives an additional justification for a low taxation of (early) gifts. On the other hand, this leaves only one way to really give *inter vivos* wealth transfers the edge – excluding subsidising them – and that is to *substantially raise taxation on (large) family inheritances*.

This measure is admittedly unfashionable and would also appear to be highly unpopular. So, before embarking on a reform of this nature, steps need to be taken to ensure that it is 'really worth it' by checking firstly that early transfers really improve the well-being of the beneficiary children as expected.

Are early transfers useful to their beneficiaries?

In an ideal world, capital transfer timeframes would have little effect on the behaviour of beneficiaries who could always borrow at the market rate based on what they expect to inherit. In the real world, the legislators and many donor parents try and help along young beneficiaries' integration plans – forming a family, entering the world of work, building capital (housing purchase) – by giving them 'a leg up'.

Economists identify two polar cases. The first one, the 'Carnegie effect', is when the transfers received drive up current consumption only and may even prompt a downturn in the labour supply – why bother working when you can live off private income? The opposite case is when an early transfer of assets furthers the young beneficiary's longer term integration plans – housing purchase, forming a family, stable occupation and even business start-up – by lifting credit constraints or providing the capital investment needed.

The biographical and recall data collected in INSEE's 2004 *Patrimoine* (Assets) Survey clearly show that the second option is the case, arguing in favour of early transfers. It is even close to the ideal situation for the purposes of our demonstration where the expected inheritance ('inheritance expectations') has a negative effect on the achievement of the investment project considered, the inheritance already received has a fairly positive effect, and the financial help or gifts received have a much greater positive effect (Arrondel and Masson, 2007a).

Home ownership and purchase (on one's own)

The probability of the representative household[13] being a home owner or first-time buyer is 59.8 per cent. This same probability is just 53.6 per cent for households that have received no transfer from their parents. It stands at over 75 per cent for households that have received a gift, but at just 56.9 per cent for households that have not. The effect is found to be positive, but less pronounced, between heir and non-heir: the respective probabilities are 67.3 per cent and 56.9 per cent. The role of receipts of financial help is smaller, but still significant (63.1 per cent as opposed to 59.4 per cent). On the other hand, inheritance expectations have somewhat of a negative effect (not significant).

The positive influence of capital transfers, in all their forms, on home ownership is thus clear, with gifts having a particularly strong effect. Yet the fact remains that other determinants play a prominent role (own resources, family composition, place of residence).

We come to similar conclusions regarding the probability of having purchased housing on one's own (without an inheritance or gift). Here again, the gift received is found to have a prominent effect: the probability of being an owner increases from 52 per cent for a household that has received nothing from its parents to 69 per cent for a household that has received a gift (see Figure 8.4).

Business start-ups and takeovers (non-family-run)

Do early intergenerational transfers foster business start-ups? Based again on the INSEE 2004 *Patrimoine* Survey, we tested this hypothesis on a sample of non-farmer individuals aged 20 to 50 years old – the most apt to become entrepreneurs. We found 4.3 per cent new entrepreneurs and 2.8 per cent buyers of non-family businesses within this population. Of the different transfers (financial help, gifts and inheritances), only the fact of being a gift recipient was found to foster the transition to entrepreneur status (see Figure 8.5): the probability of starting up a business is 4.1 per cent without the help of a gift, but 6.9 per cent for gift recipients. If we combine business start-ups and takeovers, the figure rises from 6.5 per cent for entrepreneurs not receiving a gift to 9.3 per cent for gift recipients (here again, inheritance expectations have a specific negative, but not significant effect).

Obviously, these gift effects need to be put into perspective since other factors, for given resources, play a greater role: the probability of starting up a

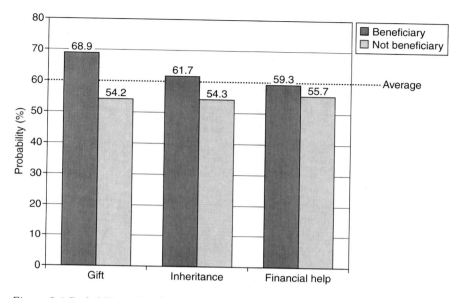

Figure 8.4 Probability of buying a home (estimated in %) (source: enquête Patrimoine 2004 Insee).

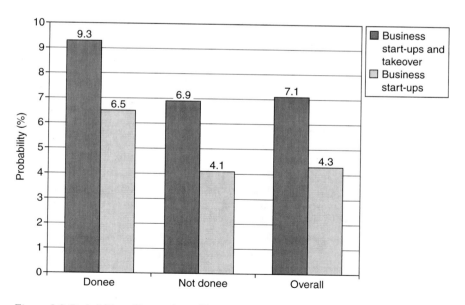

Figure 8.5 Probability of becoming self-employed (in %) (source: enquête 2004 Insee).

business stands at 19.1 per cent for the sons and daughters of entrepreneurs (four times higher than for the children of wage-earners); and postgraduates and top university graduates are twice as likely (nearly 9 per cent) to become self-employed.

How can the social utility of capital transfers be guaranteed?

Speeding up family transfers is therefore an efficient individual strategy. Yet is it a different story for society as a whole? Can we count on a *collective* benefit from incentive measures to make early transfers?

Two different arguments say so, especially in the French case. First, the earlier transfer of wealth and economic power to the young generations in itself carries a strong *symbolic* message regarding the importance that society places on young people and their future; it reveals its desire to hand over the baton to the young and set up a more harmonious succession of generations. The second argument is that it would have welcome and positive repercussions on French young people's job perspectives, especially if it is true, for example, that young managers tend to give precedence to hiring other young people.

However, the costs of the proposed incentive measures need to be compared with these probable gains: either in terms of efficiency and hence tax incidence, if the heavier inheritance tax discourages intergenerational savings for one's children or stimulates tax avoidance (including by means of expatriation); or, most importantly, in terms of equity since gifts appear to be so much a practice of the wealthy and a select vehicle for the reproduction of inequalities, giving young people from privileged backgrounds even more of an advantage.

How can the tax measures be shaped to avoid these two pitfalls, i.e. how can the positive effects of an earlier transfer of family assets be maintained without creating perverse reactions of the saver or adding to inequalities? The solution points to increasing not just the inheritance tax rate, but also its *progressivity*. This would entail, in return, increasing the possibilities for well-off parents to sidestep the tax, not just by having a low tax on family gifts (especially early), but also by introducing partial or total exemptions to foster donations or bequests to duly registered *charity* works and foundations – especially for the training and steady employment of young people from deprived backgrounds. This would entail increasing the freedom to bequeath *outside* of the family by further reducing the 'right to inheritance' and the children's reserved portion of the estate, especially over and above a certain sum (Masson, 2006).

Such is the guiding principle of this mechanism, which would not simply seek to 'take from the rich'. Whatever the choice made by wealthy seniors – to whom a wide range of options would be offered – the government would gain, either because its revenues would be boosted by the inheritance tax, or because the generational imbalance would be reduced somewhat by the increase in early family transfers, or again because private initiative would alone make investment deemed in the public interest and aimed at the most underprivileged.

Conclusions

We have proposed a seemingly highly unpopular measure in the form of a substantial increase in inheritance tax. Yet, the measure would be coupled with several more popular reforms: charity bequests and (especially) donations could be largely exempted; also (early) gifts, which are presumably prompted by a form of family altruism, would remain significantly less taxed than *post-mortem* transfers. Moreover, this tax and legislative arrangement could help rebalance the situation between generations efficiently, by increasing downward transfers of assets, and equitably, by averting the reproduction of inequalities.

Also, some remarkable conclusions are drawn when this somewhat disparate mechanism is judged in the light of our three welfare state paradigms, which present some similarities with the Esping-Andersen (1999) trilogy. All the measures proposed appear to cut across the three schools of social thought in some way, even though they are contradictory in their premises, borrowing from each school:

- The proposal to increase the inheritance tax and make it more progressive would be approved by Esping-Andersen and many 'equal citizenship' advocates (who would still not like tax relief on gifts), but would also be commended by a liberal-libertarian movement.
- Increasing the freedom to bequeath outside of the family, by encouraging gifts and bequests to charities, is a typically 'free-agent' measure.
- Yet the initial will to raise or speed up family transfers is clearly based on 'multi-solidarity' thinking.

Two obvious remarks to conclude. First, to be fully effective, the proposed transfer mechanism would need to be supplemented by other measures fostering the development of long-term nursing care insurance, the sustainability of the pension systems, etc. Otherwise, the stepping up of capital transfers, within or without the family, could be curbed by concerns over the future of the public pension and health systems or by the desire by seniors to protect themselves against the risks of old age.

Second, it is clear, once again, that this type of reform cannot be applied across the board: it is much more suitable for a continental European 'conservative' country such as France than for the Scandinavian nations, which would prefer to directly increase social transfers to the young.

Appendix: wealth transfer taxation in France and its recent trends

Without going into the details of a complex system, it is worth noting a few figures on inheritance taxation in France. As in most Western countries, the returns from the taxation of inheritances and gifts are minimal, representing around 1 per cent of total government revenues per year. Tax allowances and other subtleties mean that tax is paid on barely one in four inheritances and that the average tax rate for all assets inherited is around 6 per cent. The most heavily taxed are large fortunes (marginal rate back to 45 per cent) and especially non-lineal inheritances (the tax rate is already 55 per cent for a nephew or niece, 60 per cent for a non-relative).

In the French inheritance tax system, lineal descendants (children and represented children) are entitled to a portion of estate that legally devolves upon them as heirs. This 'reserved' share of the estate depends on the number of children: it is half for one heir, two-thirds for two heirs, and three-quarters for three or more heirs. The rest of the estate forms the 'disposable portion' that can be freely bequeathed. In the case of an intestate succession, the heirs share the estate equally amongst them. This notion of 'reserve' (to the children) comes from Roman law and is in sharp contrast to the inheritance rules in effect in the English-speaking countries where parents have the freedom to bequeath as they see fit with no distortionary taxation.

French inheritance taxation since the post-war period has displayed a decreasing trend, which has sharpened in recent years following the introduction of a series of measures with the explicit intention of reducing tax on capital transfers: the 'donations Sarkozy' measures in 2004, the 2006 reform of the French Civil Code, and especially the 2007 TEPA Act (standing for work, employment and purchasing power). The stated market-based objectives of these measures were to improve 'economic efficiency' in terms of stimulating and supporting household consumption, and encouraging the middle classes to work more and invest by raising the proportion of exempt family inheritances to 95 per cent. A more specific objective was also to offset the growing gap between the young and older generations' standards of living. There was a tendency to minimize the obvious drawback of these measures in terms of equity: a smaller inheritance tax would foster the reproduction of inequalities from one generation to the next, between well-born young people and the others.

The TEPA act of 21 August 2007 went a long way to fulfilling this promise. Inheritance taxes are calculated on the portion inherited inheritance tax, according to the amount received and the family link, and there are also tax allowances for certain heirs. In the case of children, the TEPA Act raised this tax allowance from €50,000 in 2006 to some €160,000. The surviving spouse's portion was made totally exempt from inheritance taxation (the previous allowance had been a mere €76,000).

As regards lineal gifts, each parent can now pay tax free up to €160,000 (as opposed to €50,000 in 2006) per beneficiary every six years: in other words, gifts below this threshold and bestowed at least six years prior to death are not brought back into the inheritance for the tax calculation. Other tax breaks on gifts have been tailored to cope with an increased longevity: 50 per cent tax break when the donor is less than 70 years old and 30 per cent between 70 and 80 years old.

Last but not least, the TEPA Act provides for tax breaks (75 per cent up to a ceiling of €50,000) for taxpayers liable to wealth taxation who make donations to public and private research establishments, to state-approved public utility foundations, and to professional integration companies, associations, workshops and projects.

It should be noted, however, that most of these exemptions on inheritance taxes have been reduced since 31 July 2011. For instance, tax exempt lineal gifts can be made only every ten years. Moreover, tax breaks for gifts according to the donor's age have been largely suppressed.

Notes

1 In the French newspaper *Le Monde*, 23 January 2007.
2 Yet the link is far from automatic, and factors other than inheritance play an important role in explaining wealth inequality within the bulk of the population: for example, wealth inequalities remain very high among households who have not yet received anything and only have modest inheritance expectations.
3 Parental altruism in the economic sense: parents are concerned about the well-being of their offspring. In the most family-oriented variants, parents are supposed to constantly know, want and do what is best for their children (in terms of education, assistance and capital transfers).
4 Note that Barro's dynastic altruism can be interpreted as a specific variant of downward (and forward) indirect reciprocity (see Arrondel and Masson, 2006).
5 Transfers in time or in kind are given for information only: the most important sums, of family origin, are hard to put a figure to as they are extremely sensitive to the calculation or accounting conventions used.
6 It is merely a snapshot that gives no information on past trends or the sustainability of the government transfer systems and does not include the corresponding structure of contributions.
7 In France, as in most of the developed countries, nearly one-quarter of households do not save enough for their old age given their pension entitlements, leading their consumption to plummet when they retire (Arrondel and Masson, 2007b).
8 French families have already reportedly made an effort to narrow this lag by speeding up transfers: the average age of donors rose less over the period and, helped by the intergenerational age difference, the average age of donees (beneficiaries) even *fell* from 39 years to 37.5 years old (Arrondel and Masson, 2007a).
9 The gift of housing subject to usufruct, promoted by tax incentives, is really only an incomplete transfer.
10 Tax relief was granted on these gifts only if the recipient had reached the age of majority. However, these breaks could be granted concurrently with relief on other gifts.
11 'Wealth' gifts exclude manual gifts which are subject to the same legislation but are not recorded by a deed and are made by physically transferring *moveable* property – cash, jewellery, car, bearer notes, etc. – from one hand to another.
12 Provided these gifts were not in excess of 300,000 FRF.
13 The given specific effects are calculated for given values of the household's other characteristics: income, inheritance expectations, social group, age, qualifications, place of residence, etc.

References

Arrondel, L. and Laferrère, A. (2001) 'Taxation and wealth transmission in France', *Journal of Public Economics*, 79, 3–33.

Arrondel, L. and Masson, A. (2006) 'Altruism, exchange or indirect reciprocity: What do the data on family transfers show?', in J. Mercier-Ythier and S.C. Kolm (eds) *Handbook on the Economics of Giving, Reciprocity and Altruism*, Amsterdam: North-Holland, Vol. 2, pp. 971–1053.

Arrondel, L. and Masson, A. (2007a) 'Solidarités publiques et familiales', in D. Cohen (ed.) *Une jeunesse difficile: portrait économique et social de la jeunesse française*, Cepremap, Paris: Éditions de la rue d'Ulm, 6, pp. 107–190.

Arrondel, L. and Masson, A. (2007b) *Inégalités patrimoniales et choix individuels. Des goûts et des richesses …*, Paris: Economica.

Arrondel L., Masson, A. and Verger, D. (2009) 'Le patrimoine des Français: État des lieux, historique et perspectives', *Économie et Statistique*, 417–418, 3–25.

Becker, G.S. (1991) *A Treatise on the Family*, Enlarged edition, Harvard: Harvard University Press.

Bernheim, B.D., Skinner, J. and Weinberg, S. (2001) 'What accounts for the variation in retirement wealth among U.S. households?', *American Economic Review*, 91(4): 832–857.

Bevan, D.L. and Stiglitz, J.E. (1979) 'Intergenerational transfers and inequality', *Greek Economic Journal*, 1(1), 8–26.

Cox, D. and Stark, O. (1998) *Financial Transfers to the Elderly and the 'Demonstration Effect'*, Boston College – Harvard University, mimeo.

Cremer, H. and Pestieau, P. (2012) 'The economics of wealth transfer taxation', this volume, Chapter 10.

Esping-Andersen, G. (1999) *Les trois mondes de l'État-providence*, Paris: PUF; English edition: *The Three Worlds of Welfare Capitalism*, 1990.

Masson, A. (2006) 'Famille et héritage: Quelle liberté de tester?', *Revue Française d'Économie*, 31(2), 75–109.

Masson, A. (2009) *Des liens et des transferts entre générations*, Paris: Éditions EHESS, Collection En temps & lieux.

McGarry, K. (2001) 'The cost of equality: Unequal bequest and tax avoidance', *Journal of Public Economics*, 79, 179–204.

Poterba, J. (2001) 'Estate and gift taxes and the incentives for inter vivos giving in the United States', *Journal of Public Economics*, 79, 237–264.

9 Does the financial crisis create opportunities for wealth taxation?

Rajiv Prabhakar

Introduction

One impact of the recent financial crisis in the UK has been to slow efforts to weaken inheritance taxation. In 2007, the then Conservative shadow chancellor George Osborne promised at their party conference that a future Conservative government would raise the threshold of paying inheritance tax to £1 million. This move was widely seen as reviving the fortunes of the Conservative party and deterring Prime Minister Gordon Brown from calling a snap general election in October (Prabhakar, Rowlingson and White, 2008).

Since Osborne's statement, the UK had a financial crisis that involved government bailouts for banks such as Northern Rock and Royal Bank of Scotland. The public sector deficit began to rise and public sector borrowing became a topic of political controversy. The Office for Budget Responsibility's economic and fiscal forecast published in November 2011 noted that public sector borrowing as a percentage of Gross Domestic Product (GDP) had a post-war peak of 11.2 per cent in 2009–10. In 2011–12 it was 8.4 per cent and is forecast to drop to 4.5 per cent in 2014–15. Public sector net debt as a percentage of GDP is projected to rise from 52.9 per cent in 2009–10 to 78 per cent in 2014–15 (Office for Budget Responsibility, 2011). Although questions can be asked about how much of a problem the deficit poses for the UK economy (Arestis and Sawyer, 2009), the tension nevertheless between the main parties is how cuts in public spending as well as possible tax rises are needed to close it.

One result of all this is that the Conservatives had to drop their pledge on inheritance tax. On 6 May 2010, the UK had a general election. Prior to that election, both Labour and Liberal Democrat politicians had been increasingly critical of the Conservative promise. The charge was that in the financial crisis it was perverse that the Conservative party should be offering a tax cut that would only benefit the very wealthiest in society. At Prime Minister's questions in the House of Commons, on 2 December 2009, Gordon Brown quipped that the Conservative inheritance tax policy: 'seems to have been dreamed up on the playing fields of Eton' (reported in Treneman, 2009). During the 2010 general election, both Gordon Brown and Nick Clegg criticized David Cameron on inheritance taxation during the television debates between the party leaders.

In the 2010 general election the Conservatives won the largest number of seats but failed to win an outright majority in the House of Commons. A governing coalition was eventually agreed between the Conservatives and the Liberal Democrats. As part of the coalition agreement the Conservative party had to drop its inheritance tax pledge (HM Government, 2010). Arguably, the coalition presented the Conservatives with an opportunity to axe a pledge they increasingly saw as a problem. Rawnsley comments:

> two years is a very, very, very long time in politics. The cut to inheritance tax doesn't look so smart at all in the utterly changed political atmosphere of recessionary Britain. George Osborne's pledge has gone from being a lifesaver into an albatross around the necks of him and David Cameron.
>
> (Rawnsley, 2009)

The financial crisis has thus shaped the debate about inheritance tax. However, the main effect so far has been to stop this tax from being cut. This chapter asks whether recent events could also be used to create an opportunity for making a case for increasing wealth taxes. This considers how the causes and consequences of the financial crisis might be used to stimulate debates about wealth taxes. In the UK, a house price bubble is often seen as one of the chief causes of the financial crisis. The role played by the housing market might create an opportunity to discuss house or land taxation.

This moment may be opportune because it builds on current political debates about tax and spending. As noted above, a key debate among political parties is on the steps needed to cut the public sector deficit. A study of wealth taxes could be part of this wider debate. The discussion of how to reduce the deficit can be shaped in a variety of ways. One approach is to try to identify the cuts in front-line services needed the close the deficit as quickly as possible. An alternative tack is to use the deficit to open up deeper debates about why government tax and spending should be part of the economy. This latter path creates extra opportunities to discuss the role of wealth taxes.

What are wealth taxes?

Wealth taxes can mean a wide variety of things. Wealth usually refers to a stock of resources and contrasts with a flow of resources such as income. It can consist of financial wealth such as savings as well as non-financial wealth such as housing. Wealth can be taxed in several main ways. First, a tax can be placed on underlying holdings of wealth. For example, a tax might be placed on the value of property. This tax might be extended to cover other forms of financial wealth such as shares. Second, a tax can be placed on the income that comes from wealth. For example, government might tax the interest payments made to savings. Third, transfers of wealth could be taxed. Different taxes can be developed depending on whether a tax is placed on the donor or recipient of such a transfer. For instance, an estate tax arises if this tax is placed on the estate of a donor. If this tax is imposed instead on the recipient then this is an inheritance tax. If a tax on recipients is widened to include gifts as well as inheritances then this is a capital receipts tax. Different versions of a capital receipts tax (or other wealth taxes) can be fashioned depending on the regularity of such taxes. For example, a capital receipts tax could be set over a person's lifetime or it might be imposed on an annual basis (Atkinson, 1972; Boadway *et al.*, 2010).

Why focus on wealth taxation at all?

Perhaps the first question to ask is why it is worth looking at wealth taxes at all. Much of the debate in the UK is dominated by discussion of inheritance tax, although strictly speaking this is a misnomer as this tax is placed on the estate of the deceased rather than on the amount a person inherits. Taxes such as inheritance tax play a minor role in the public finances in the UK. Table 9.1 uses data from HM Revenue and Customs (2012) to show the contribution that inheritance tax and a selection of other taxes make to the overall tax revenues in the UK between 2001–2 and 2010–11.

This table shows that inheritance taxation plays a small role when compared to other taxes such as income tax, value added tax, fuel duty and corporation tax. This has not always been the case. Table 9.2 shows the role that a predecessor to inheritance tax, estate duty, played in public finances during the twentieth century. Estate duty was introduced in 1894 and paid on property that was transferred at death. The table shows that estate tax played a significant role in the opening decades of the twentieth century, although much of this occurred before the rise of the welfare state.

Estate duty was replaced in 1974 by a capital transfer tax. This occurred because of a concern that people were able to avoid estate duty by making lifetime gifts. By 1974, estate duty raised 2.4 per cent of tax revenue and was seen as largely voluntary. The capital transfer tax covered gifts, although there were exemptions for spouses (Boadway, Chamberlain and Emmerson, 2008). Boadway, Chamberlain and Emmerson (2008) record that capital transfer tax

Table 9.1 Specific tax as a percentage of overall tax receipts (%)

Year	Income tax	Value Added Tax	Fuel duty	Corporation tax	Inheritance tax
2001–2	33.6	19.0	6.8	10.0	0.7
2002–3	33.8	19.6	6.8	9.0	0.7
2003–4	33.1	20.1	6.6	8.1	0.7
2004–5	34.3	19.7	6.3	9.1	0.8
2005–6	33.9	18.3	5.9	10.5	0.8
2006–7	34.9	18.3	5.6	10.5	0.8
2007–8	33.6	17.9	5.5	10.3	0.8
2008–9	34.9	17.9	5.6	9.8	0.6
2009–10	35.4	17.2	6.4	8.8	0.6
2010–11	34.3	18.7	6.1	9.4	0.6

Source: author's calculations from HM Revenue and Customs (2012).

Table 9.2 Contribution of estate duty to overall tax revenue (%)

Year	%
1908–9	18.8
1918–19	5.0
1928–9	20.0
1938–9	14.8
1948–9	9.0
1958–9	6.2
1968–9	5.8

Source: Table T1.2 Net receipts of former Inland Revenue taxes, Available www.hmrc.gov.uk/stats/tax_receipts/1_2_v2_dec05.pdf.

was highly progressive with a top rate of 75 per cent for transfers over £2 million. They go on to argue that legal changes introduced by the Conservative governments after 1979 weakened capital transfer tax, and that this was replaced by inheritance tax in 1986.

Although inheritance tax makes a small percentage contribution to the public purse, it nevertheless appears to provoke considerable public hostility (Hedges and Bromley, 2001; Lewis and White, 2006; Prabhakar, 2009). For example, Hedges and Bromley (2001) report a survey of public opinion towards taxation for the Fabian Society. This survey covered 1,717 adults in 2000. They found that about half of respondents thought that inheritance tax should be abolished, while roughly 20 per cent thought that the threshold at which it started should be raised from its then level of £250,000 to at least £500,000.

Does the combination of public opposition plus the minor role that inheritance tax plays in public finances mean that reformists would be better served by focusing their attention elsewhere? Although the above suggests that wealth taxes should be kept in proper perspective, there are at least two reasons why such a search is nevertheless worthwhile. First, taxes should be judged against a range of criteria and not just the revenue they raise. For example, a Fabian Society Commission on Citizenship and Taxation outlines ten principles that it argues should define a good tax system. These are: that taxes should be legitimate, being seen by taxpayers as part of a legitimate system; progressive, that is taking a higher proportion of income and wealth from those with higher incomes and wealth; promote economic efficiency; discourage social harms (such as pollution); foster horizontal equity, by treating people in similar situations similarly; respect individual independence by taxing people separately; have a broad base; be efficient to administer; foster international co-operation; and be sufficient to raise revenue for public spending (Commission on Taxation and Citizenship, 2000). An inheritance tax may advance other principles, notwithstanding the minor part it plays in overall tax revenue. For example, the Commission on Taxation and Citizenship argues that a capital receipts tax would satisfy horizontal equity as it would mean that a person whose receipts come from one source (an inheritance say) would be treated the same as someone else receiving the same value from gifts from a variety of sources (Commission on Taxation and Citizenship, 2000). Of course, there are lots of ways of combining these principles. Furthermore, one might dispute some of these principles, or point to others omitted by the report. However, the main point is that the tax systems can and should be judged according to a range of measures. A variety of arguments can be developed to outline why wealth taxes should be part of a set of a fair or just system of taxation (see other chapters in this volume).

Second, one may question whether there are alternatives to wealth taxes that can avoid controversy. One might accept that inheritance taxation should be part of a fair or just tax system but take a practical view that those interested in creating a more equal society would be better served by stressing policies unlikely to provoke as much public ire. This pragmatic challenge assumes that there are alternatives to wealth taxes that are unlikely to provoke as much opposition among the public and policy circles. However, Graetz and Shapiro (2005) maintain that arguments against wealth taxes are in fact part of a broader attack on policies aimed at advancing equality. Their book *Death by a Thousand Cuts* is a case study of the repeal of estate tax in the US. In 2001, a coalition involving Republicans and small businesses managed to wage a successful public campaign against this tax even though it only applied to 2 per cent of estates. Graetz and Shapiro chart how this conservative coalition managed to mobilize public support, which involved developing potent and compelling images and stories that triumphed over the statistics outlined by defenders of the estate tax. The title of their book alludes to this wider challenge to policies aimed at advancing equality. The repeal of the estate tax was seen as the first cut in a wider assault on policies for equality. An implication of this argument is that if reformists give up on wealth taxes, then criticisms of equality would not disappear but simply move to other targets. Indeed, critics may be emboldened if they feel they have had success in undermining wealth taxes (Graetz and Shapiro, 2005). A defence of wealth taxes thus carries a wider significance and importance for policies to advance equality.

Wealth taxes as a response to the current crisis

Wealth taxes might be considered as one of the policy tools to address current economic issues. The initial global financial crisis of 2007–8 has arguably prompted a series of other challenges such as a crisis in Eurozone economies and sluggish growth in national economies. One challenge facing economies such as the UK is a shortfall in aggregate demand as consumers rein back spending and consumer confidence drops. There is a tradition of economic thought that suggests that transferring resources to those with low wealth and income can stimulate demand. This is because those on lower income and wealth have a greater propensity to consume out of income and wealth than their richer peers (Keynes, 1936; Standing, 2011). Wealth taxes can play a role here by transferring wealth from low to high spenders. Keynes (1936) pointed to such arguments when he suggested that in an economy below full employment, total savings might not determine total investment in an economy as predicted by standard economic theory. This is because those with high savings might hoard their savings and cut back on investment. He says that wealth taxes could help address this by redistributing resources. Standing (2011) sketches similar arguments in his proposals for 'economic stabilization grants' as a response to the crisis. Standing argues that providing capital grants to all individuals could be used to pump-prime demand within the economy (Standing, 2011). Wealth taxes might be used to pay for such economic stabilization grants. This would chime with those strands of thought that supports using inheritance taxes to pay for capital grants (Ackerman and Alstott, 1999; White, 2003).

Wealth taxes as a way of stopping another crisis

Wealth taxes might also help stop another financial crisis as well as being an immediate policy response to current economic challenges. This is because wealth taxes might help address one of the key sources of the crisis in places such as the US and UK, that is problems in the housing market (OECD, 2009; O'Donnell and Keeney, 2010). In particular, mortgages were made easily available in the 'subprime' housing market. Although a boom could be sustained while house prices were rising, problems arose once this bubble burst. Individuals found it difficult to make mortgage repayments, and financial institutions with substantial holdings of such mortgages suffered heavy losses. These problems fed into and were mirrored in the UK. For example, the Northern Rock bank pursued an aggressive mortgage policy and suffered significant losses. Fears of a run on this bank as savers and depositors began to withdraw money prompted the UK government to intervene to nationalize the bank. The taxpayer thus had to bail out Northern Rock and other banks to protect the financial system.

Some commentators see the recent financial crisis as part of a wider failure of the UK government to tackle systematic problems in the housing market (Watson, 2008). However, one might use recent events as a way of opening up debates about the taxation of housing as well as wealth more generally. Crawshaw notes that:

> the economic downturn has exposed serious failures at the heart of Britain's housing system. ... As housing and economic policies are now being reassessed in the light of the economic downturn, it is vital that we take the opportunity to consider housing taxation as one of the key ways to tackle these systematic failures.
>
> (Crawshaw, 2009: 6)

As well as being relevant for the housing market, housing taxation is also important for wealth taxation more generally. Property is an important part of household wealth. In 2011, the Office for National Statistics published the results of the second wave of its Wealth and Assets survey, which reported household wealth between July 2008 to June 2010. This survey notes that total household net property wealth (that is, the value for each household for the main residence and any other property minus the value of mortgage liabilities and equity release) was £3.375 billion in 2008/10. This fell though from £3,506 billion in 2006/8 (Office for National Statistics, 2011). A housing tax is thus an important form of wealth tax. Property also impacts on other types of wealth tax. For example, in the UK part of the public's concern with inheritance tax is that rising property prices will tip increasing numbers of estates over the inheritance tax threshold (Prabhakar, 2009).

One way that recent events might be used to open up debates is by discussing the fairness of taxing property price rises. Of course, while distinctions can be drawn between housing taxation and land taxation, there is nevertheless likely to be a close relation between land and house values. Taxing housing might act as a reasonable proxy for taxing the value of land. House prices have risen substantially over the recent past. Figure 9.1 draws on data as the Department for Communities and Local Government to show how the simple average house price in the UK has changed since 1991.

Between 1991 and 2010, the simple average house price in the UK, adjusted for inflation, more than doubled, rising from £62,455 in 1991 to £150,266 in 2010. It is plausible to suggest that home-owners have enjoyed a windfall gain to the value of their homes over this period (although there are regional variations). House prices have risen in significantly from factors beyond their control.

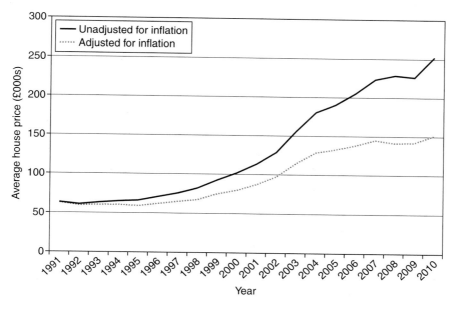

Figure 9.1 Simple average house prices in the UK (source: Department for Communities and Local Government, Available www.communities.gov.uk/housing/housingresearch/housingstatistics/housingstatisticsby/housingmarket/livetables/housepricestables/simpleaveragestables/).

Although personal investment and home improvements may have increased the value of their homes, it is unlikely to have more than doubled house prices over this period.

During the nineteenth century, Henry George outlined arguments that prefigure some of the debates today. In his book *Progress and Poverty*, George argues that land is the most important factor of production and that the bulk of material progress comes from rents for land rather than returns to labour or capital. He argues that it is unnecessary to remove private property in land in response to its unequal ownership. Instead, George supports a tax on the rents from, as well as the value of land (George, 1932). More recently, various commentators outline why a land tax is a fair tax (Maxwell and Vigor, 2005; McLean, 2006a; 2006b). For example, McLean argues that land values are based on three main sources: its scarcity value; the value created by the owner of the land; and the value added by the actions of public authorities. He argues that much of the value of land derives from the first and third of these sources. For example, a land value may rise because local authorities make an investment in local transport networks such as faster trains. He says the fact that much of the rise in land values come from communal rather than individual actions justifies taxing the value of land (McLean, 2006b).

Another way that property taxation can be linked to recent events is by considering how taxes might help manage demand for housing. Crawshaw (2009) provides an example of this in a policy report published for the housing charity, Shelter. He says that the focus of the report is how the: 'taxation system affects access to, and demand for, housing' (Crawshaw, 2009: 8). Crawshaw considers a range of tax reforms that might be used to manage demand and dampen the possibility of a future bubble. These ideas cover council tax, stamp duty, capital gains tax, taxation of rental income, inheritance tax and housing tax credits. He identifies two immediate reforms. First: abolishing council tax discounts to owners of second and long-term empty houses; and second, raising the threshold of rent-a-room relief to home-owners to boost the supply of low-cost rental accommodation. The aim of both of these proposals is to reduce the demand for owner occupied housing.

Prospects for reform

The above suggests that the financial crisis might create opportunities to boost a case for wealth taxation. These suggestions do not exhaust all possibilities, and they are not guaranteed to succeed. This section looks at what evidence exists to suggest they might work. This considers public opinion and public debates, particularly regarding housing or land taxation. It is a commonplace to say that the public shows hostility towards all forms of wealth taxation, especially inheritance taxes. Although such opposition should not be dismissed, focus group research suggests that there may be more prospects for shaping public opinion than often supposed (Prabhakar, 2009; 2012). Opposition to wealth taxation appears to be moderated when people are asked to view wealth taxes as part of the wider tax system. For example, in a focus group study conducted in England in 2006 respondents were asked to choose between a package that involved cuts in income tax but rises in the estate tax versus cuts in estate tax but rises in income tax (Prabhakar, 2009). Although respondents displayed strong hostility to estate tax when asked about this tax at the outset of the groups, these views were moderated when people were asked about this specific policy choice. The attitude to this policy choice was fairly evenly split, with around half preferring cuts in income tax but rises in estate tax while the remainder preferred the reverse. This suggests that attitudes to specific taxes could change if people are asked to compare taxes or make policy choices (Prabhakar, 2009). This finding has been confirmed in more recent focus group research in 2010 that asked participants to compare estate taxes to a wider range of taxes such as fuel duty, Value Added Tax and alcohol duty. Fuel duty attracted most hostility among the younger respondents, although older participants reacted negatively to inheritance tax. However, attitudes shifted when people were asked to make choices, with most respondents caring about their overall tax bill rather than the particular taxes that were used to make up this tax bill (Prabhakar, 2012). The focus group research also shows that moral arguments can shape attitudes to taxation. The studies found that support for a work ethic meant that people were more willing to tax unearned income or wealth more heavily than earned income or wealth. Similarly, support for housing taxes tended to increase when this was tied to arguments about the fairness of taxing home-owners for the windfall gains to property prices from things other than their personal investments.

The coalition government

2010 saw the creation of a Conservative–Liberal Democrat coalition government. Thus, any realistic prospect for wealth tax reform in the near future must involve engaging with the new government. The Liberal Democrats announced plans for housing taxation in the approach to the 2010 general election. On 30 November 2009, party leader Nick Clegg said that there would now be a 1 per cent levy on properties worth over £2 million (BBC News, 2009; Liberal Democrats, 2009). The Liberal Democrats had to drop this proposal as part of their coalition agreement with the Conservatives (although there is still interest among Liberal Democrats in this idea – see Winnett, 2012). This section now looks at recent conservative writing as winning support among Conservatives is probably the main hurdle for winning political support for wealth taxes within the coalition government. While there is interest in tackling wealth inequality in this writing, there is less support for using wealth taxes to achieve this.

Phillip Blond (2010) coined the term 'red Tory' to refer to the idea that conservative means are best placed to advance progressive goals. He heads a think-tank, ResPublica, that is examining the policy implied by this approach. Elsewhere, the think-tank Demos hosts a progressive conservatism project which explores this approach (Wind-Cowie, 2009). The Conservative Universities and Skills Secretary David Willetts (2010) has written a book called *The Pinch* which is relevant for debates about wealth taxes. This book focuses on how a generation of 'baby boomers' born between 1945 and 1965 have done well out of the post-war welfare state, and the obligations they should have for future generations.

An important theme within this literature is a focus on wealth inequality. Blond argues that under the 'market state', which adopts a free market approach to the polity and economy, wealth inequality has increased. He records that in 1976, the bottom half of the population owned 12 per cent of the country's liquid wealth, but this had dropped to 1 per cent in 2003. If wealth is extended to include property, then the share held by the bottom half of the population is only 7 per cent. Blond says that combating this is needed to extend real opportunity. Willetts (2010) focuses on what he says is a neglected topic – the inequality that exists between generations. He says that baby boomers have considerable advantages in the main parts of personal wealth – namely housing, pensions and savings – when compared with younger generations. For example, baby boomers have benefited from significant rises in house prices and have access to historically generous pensions. In contrast, younger people find it harder to buy a house and face more insecure retirements. Wealth is thus unevenly spread between generations.

The above strands of thought suggest that steps should be taken to counter wealth inequality. However, a notable omission in them is any detailed discussion of wealth taxation. Blond (2010) does not discuss that issue at all. He grounds his red Toryism within a wider debate about the role of the state. His aim is to replace the welfare state with the 'civil state'. For Blond, the welfare state involves the state funding and provision of welfare. He uses familiar neo-conservative complaints against the welfare state. He contends that state intervention creates as many problems as it solves by leading to a dependency culture that traps people into poverty. Personal responsibility is eroded as people come to rely on the state to tackle their welfare problems, and this erosion means that individuals lack the necessary independence to help themselves. Wealth taxes might form part of the welfare state that he opposes.

Similarly, Willetts (2010) mentions inheritance tax briefly, but only to suggest a general reason for reducing it: 'One argument for cutting Inheritance Tax is that it increases the incentives for older people to save rather than consume their wealth' (Willetts, 2010: 249). This means that older generations have less to pass on to their descendants. In the particular case of the baby boomers, Willetts suggests that some of this consumption takes place because people are running down their savings to pay their bills for social care, that is for going into a nursing home. Taxing wealth transfers would reduce the amount baby boomers could leave to their families even more. The outcome would be that inequalities between the baby boomer generation and its successors would be increased.

One might question whether this conservative thought is sufficient to reduce wealth inequality without wealth taxation. For Blond, tackling wealth inequality rests on the case for a civil state. One way that this might be done is by encouraging those without wealth to acquire and accumulate it. However, it is arguable how easy it is for people to build wealth within existing entrenched inequalities. Furthermore, any process of wealth accumulation is likely to be a slow process.

It is likely that any meaningful effort to reduce wealth inequality would have to involve wealth taxes. Similarly, Willetts does not address inequality within a generation. Existing wealth inequalities would be entrenched as assets pass down within particular families.

Political factors are another possible reason why wealth taxes are little discussed in these policy proposals. Conservative politicians had consistently used 'death taxes' to attack the previous Labour government. Although the financial crisis has made Conservative politicians more wary of using such arguments, these criticisms have not disappeared. Progressive conservative policy proposals might be shaped then to fit the current political climate. If this is the case, then the future does not augur well for building a coalition of support for wealth taxes among the right.

Conclusion

The financial crisis has altered the terms of the political debate. In the UK, debate between the main political parties centres on a new 'age of austerity' as they discuss the appropriate package of taxes and spending commitments to cope with the crisis. A key feature of these debates is the discussion between party leaders of the depth and extent of cuts needed to control the public finances. Government is entering a period of retrenchment in which services will be cut.

Although public spending cuts are perhaps the most obvious impact of the financial crisis on the public finances, it is possible that the crisis creates opportunities as well as threats. Government-led bailouts of the banks and the financial system arguably expose some of the flaws associated with a free market approach to the economy. This creates a space in which one can debate different ways of governing the economy and society. Part of this might focus on the case for greater wealth equality and a need for wealth taxation. This chapter has highlighted two ways in this might be done, namely by linking wealth taxation to housing taxation as well as wider debates about the economy.

Any such programme needs an organization or network to make a case for reform. This is needed to help build public support and backing for wealth taxation. There are signs that centre left networks and parties are beginning to play such a role (Wilkinson and Pickett, 2009). There is less certainty the coalition government will pursue this, although part of its language today involves support for spreading wealth more equally. However, more activity is needed if the opportunities offered by recent events are not to be lost.

Acknowledgement

The research in this chapter comes from a grant received from the Economic and Social Research Council on 'The Assets Agenda: transferring knowledge on assets, financial education and wealth inequality' (RES – 189 – 25 – 0002). I am very grateful for financial assistance received from the Economic and Social Research Council.

References

Ackerman, B. and Alstott, A. (1999) *The Stakeholder Society*, New Haven: Yale University Press.

Arestis, P. and Sawyer, M. (2009) 'The future of public expenditure', *Renewal*, 17(3): 32–42.

Atkinson, A.B. (1972) *Unequal Shares – Wealth in Britain*, London: Penguin.

BBC News (2009) *Liberal Democrats double planned mansion tax threshold*, Available http://news.bbc.co.uk/1/hi/8385575.stm (accessed 18 December 2009).

Blond, P. (2010) *Red Tory. How Left and Right Have Broken Britain*, London: Faber and Faber.

Boadway, R., Chamberlain, E. and Emmerson, C. (2010) 'Taxation of wealth and wealth transfers', in J. Mirrlees, S. Adam, T. Besley, R. Blundell, S. Bond, R. Chote, M. Gammie, P. Johnson, G. Myles and J. Poterba (eds) *Dimensions of Tax Design*, Oxford: Oxford University Press, pp. 737–836.

Commission on Taxation and Citizenship (2000) *Paying for Progress. A New Politics of Tax for Public Spending*, London: The Fabian Society.

Crawshaw, T. (2009) *Rethinking Housing Taxation: Options for Reform*, London: Shelter.

George, H. (1932[1879]) *Progress and Poverty: An Inquiry into the Cause of Material Depressions and of Increase of Want with Increase of Wealth*, London: Vacher and Sons Limited.

Graetz, M. and Shapiro, I. (2005) *Death by a Thousand Cuts. The Fight over Taxing Inherited Wealth*, New Jersey: Princeton University Press.

Hedges, A. and Bromley, C. (2001) *Public Attitudes Towards Taxation: The Report of Research Conducted for the Fabian Commission on Taxation and Citizenship*, London: The Fabian Society.

HM Government (2010) *The Coalition: Our Programme for Government*, Available www.cabinetoffice.gov.uk/media/409088/pfg_coalition.pdf (accessed 9 June 2010).

HM Revenue and Customs (2012) *HMRC Tax & NIC Receipts*, Available www.hmrc.gov.uk/stats/tax_receipts/tax-nic-receipts-info-analysis.pdf (accessed 9 February 2012).

Keynes, J.M. (1936) *The General Theory of Employment, Interest and Money*, London, Macmillan.

Lewis, M. and White, S. (2006) 'Inheritance tax: What do people think? Evidence from deliberative workshops', in W. Paxton, S. White and D. Maxwell (eds), *The Citizen's Stake: Exploring the Future of Universal Asset Policies*, Bristol: Policy Press, pp. 15–35.

Liberal Democrats (2009) *Liberal Democrat Tax Plans*, Available www.libdems.org.uk/siteFiles/resources/PDF/Tax%20Plans%20-%20Briefing%20Document.pdf (accessed 15 December 2009).

Maxwell, D. and Vigor, A. (eds) (2005) *Time for Land Value Tax?* London: Institute for Public Policy Research.

McLean, I. (2006a) 'Land tax: Options for reform', in W. Paxton, S. White and D. Maxwell (eds), *The Citizen's Stake: Exploring the Future of Universal Asset Policies*, Bristol: Policy Press, pp. 69–85.

McLean, I. (2006b) *The Case for a Land Value Taxation*, Compass thinkpiece number 2, Available www.compassonline.org.uk/publications/thinkpieces/ (accessed 22 December 2009).

O'Donnell, N. and Keeney, M. (2010) 'Financial capability in Ireland and a comparison with the UK', *Public Money and Management*, 30(6): 355–362.

OECD (2009) *Financial Education and the Crisis. Policy Paper and Guidance*, Available www.financial-education.org/dataoecd/48/31/48646555.pdf (accessed 18 January 2012).

Office for Budget Responsibility (2011) *Economic and Fiscal Outlook, November 2011*, Available http://cdn.budgetresponsibility.independent.gov.uk/Autumn2011EFO_web_version138469072346.pdf (accessed 9 February 2012).

Office for National Statistics (2011), *Wealth in Great Britain. Main Results from the Wealth and Assets Survey 2008/2010.* Part 1, Available www.ons.gov.uk/ons/rel/was/wealth-in-great-britain-wave-2/2008–2010–part-1-/index.html (accessed 14 February 2012).

Prabhakar, R. (2009) 'How can opposition to inheritance tax be weakened?', *Public Policy and Administration*, 24(3): 227–244.

Prabhakar, R. (2012) 'What do the public think of taxation? Evidence from a focus group study in England', *Journal of European Social Policy*, 72(1): 77–89.

Prabhakar, R., Rowlingson, K. and White, S. (2008) *In Defence of Inheritance Tax* London: Fabian Society.

Rawnsley, A. (2009) 'Gordon Brown's favourite Conservative policy pledge', *The Observer*, 29 November.

Standing, G. (2011) 'Responding to the crisis: Economic stabilisation grants', *Policy and Politics*, 39(1): 9–25.

Treneman, A. (2009) 'Brown finds his voice and gets Cameron in a right old Eton Mess', Available www.timesonline.co.uk/tol/news/politics/article6941540.ece (3 December, accessed 17 December 2009).

Watson, M. (2008) 'Constituting monetary conservatives via the "savings habit": New Labour and the British housing market bubble', *Contemporary European Politics*, 6(3): 285–304.

White, S. (2003) *The Civic Minimum*, Oxford: Oxford University Press.

Wilkinson, R. and Pickett, K. (2009) *The Spirit Level. Why More Equal Societies Almost Always Do Better*, London, Allen Lane.

Willetts, D. (2010) *The Pinch: How the Baby Boomers Have Stolen Their Children's Future – And Why They Should Give It Back*, London: Atlantic.

Wind-Cowie, M. (2009) *Recapitalising the Poor. Why Property is Not Theft*, London, Demos.

Winnett, R. (2012) 'Nick Clegg: "We'll stick to our guns on mansion tax"', *Daily Telegraph*, 26 January.

10 The economics of wealth transfer taxation

Helmuth Cremer and Pierre Pestieau

Introduction

Taxes are rarely popular but those on wealth transfers are particularly controversial. A number of countries are without an inheritance or an estate tax and some contemplate phasing it out in the near future. Opponents of the 'death tax' as they have dubbed it claim that it is unfair and immoral. It adds to the pain suffered by mourning families and it prevents small businesses from passing from generation to generation. Because of many loopholes, people of equivalent wealth pay different amounts of tax depending on their acumen at tax avoidance. It hits families that were surprised by death (and it is therefore sometimes called a tax on sudden death). It penalizes the frugal and the loving parents who pass wealth on to their children, reducing incentives to save and to invest.

Supporters of the tax, in contrast, retort that it is of all taxes the most efficient and the most equitable. They assert that it is highly progressive and counterweights existing wealth concentration. They also argue that it has few disincentive effects since it is payable only at death and that it is fair since it concerns unearned resources. For a number of social philosophers and classical economists, estate or inheritance taxation is the ideal tax.

Clearly, death taxation more than any other generates controversy at all levels: political philosophy, economic theory, political debate and public opinion. The truth probably lies between these two opposite camps. For economists this tax like all taxes should be judged against the two criteria of equity and efficiency to which one could add that of simplicity and compliance.

The chapter is organized as follows. It first deals with the popular debate that is dominated by American economists and which only concerns the US estate tax, one, among many, type of wealth transfer tax. It also discusses the lack of popular support for such a tax. Then the chapter adopts a more theoretical approach to explore the social desirability of a wealth transfer tax.[1] The main point is that the desirability of a wealth transfer tax depends on the motives of wealth accumulation and transmission.

The US estate tax debate

2010

'Give a dog a bad name, and hang him.'

Few topics in US tax policy rival estate taxation as a subject exhibiting simultaneously a considerable level of passion and a substantial degree of confusion. There, like elsewhere, tax analysts have a limited sense of humour. Yet, recently they have indulged themselves with the joke that 2010 may be the best year for wealthy Americans to die – at least from their heirs' point of view. Strangely enough federal estate taxes were due to go to zero in 2010 unless Congress acted. In 2010, the taxes were expected to disappear entirely before reverting in 2011 to an exemption for only the first $1 million of the estate with a top rate of 55 per cent above that level. This scenario was avoided at the last minute. On 17 December 2010, President Obama signed a law providing sweeping changes to the rules governing estate taxes and gift taxes for the years 2010–2012. For 2011 the exemption is $5 million for an individual and $10 million for a couple. The tax rate for estates valued above these exemptions is 35 per cent.

The pro and the con camps are furbishing their arms with the hope of pushing the President and Congress to go their way. In that confrontation, the camp of the con is clearly the more vocal and the more aggressive. Just looking at the Google entries shows many more items from opponents of the estate tax than from advocates. In November 2009 a forum on the subject was organized in Washington by the conservative think tank American Enterprise Institute and the moderator started by the statement: 'It comes roaring back for people who die in 2011. Some people joke about wealthy people being killed off by their heirs in 2010.'

In this chapter we will show what kind of tax on wealth transfer a social welfare maximizing government ought to choose. But before turning to this analysis, let us examine the kind of arguments the two camps exchange, particularly the critics. Opponents of the estate tax remind us of those people who criticize a dish such as *coq au vin* arguing that the last one they tasted was made with corked wine, that they did not eat it because they are vegetarian and that it was too expensive. Those three arguments are not without relevance but they miss the point. The same can be said of the estate tax. Most of the critiques are addressed to the way it is administered, rather than to the idea of taxing wealth transfers.

Standard critiques

Critics contend the tax distorts investment and other choices of the rich, and also affects owners of small family businesses. It raises very little revenue at a heavy cost to the economy. It generates complex tax avoidance schemes. The hardest hit by the tax are farmers and small business people, who work hard to pass on an enterprise of value to their children. From a number of recent publications, we have listed of the main charges addressed to estate taxation.[2]

The arguments against the estate tax

- It reduces the stock of capital in the economy.
- It is a leading cause of dissolution for family businesses.
- It obstructs environmental conservation.
- It is a 'virtue tax' that penalizes work and thrift in favour of consumption.
- It is ineffective at reducing inequality.
- It has little effect on charitable giving.
- It raises very little, if any, net revenue.
- It is complicated, unfair and inefficient.

None of these charges is entirely irrelevant or completely wrong. However, none of these arguments is entirely correct either. It is true that estate tax does not raise considerable sums for the federal government. It makes up about 2 per cent of total federal tax proceeds. But at the same time 2 per cent is not that negligible. It is clear that inheritances only explain part of wealth inequality and that moreover wealth and income are not perfectly correlated. Thus even a well-functioning tax on wealth transfer would only have a limited impact on income inequality. Even so, it remains that it would have some impact. It is well established that estate taxation violates principles of horizontal equity. People with the same estate can pay different taxes depending on the asset structure, the fiscal engineering employed, the suddenness of death, and the degree of conviviality within the family. Yes, but that calls for reforming the tax and not necessarily killing it. We all know that heirs can be 'asset-rich' but 'cash-poor'. This is the case of small business owners who can be stuck with impossible tax burdens. In this respect it should be remembered that family-owned businesses and farms may be valued in a special way that reflects the current use to which the property is put, rather than its market value. It is possible that the effect of estate tax deductibility on charitable contributions has been overstated. It still has a positive effect and in any case fostering charitable contributions should not be one of the main missions of estate taxation. One of the tenets of a fair tax system is that income is taxed only once. Income should be taxed when it is first earned or realized, it should not be repeatedly re-taxed by government. The estate tax violates this principle. In the theoretical section we show that this argument is not correct. Further, capital gains income is not taxed until the income is 'realized', that is, until the assets are sold. If an asset is held until the owner dies, the gain in the value of the asset is never subject to capital gains tax or any other tax. Finally there is the alleged harmful effect of estate taxation on the environment. It is hard to believe that some sort of arrangement between the heirs and the State could not avoid it.

It is interesting to observe a gap between popular publications and rigorous public finance economics. In the first, one can read statements such as:

A full repeal of the death tax would create 1.5 million jobs. This is half the number of jobs President Obama claimed the $800 billion stimulus package would create – at one-fifth the price. Additional benefits from full repeal of the estate tax include:

- Increasing small business capital by over $1.6 trillion;
- Increasing the probability of hiring by 8.6 per cent;
- Increasing payrolls by 2.6 per cent;
- Expanding investment by 3 per cent; and
- Slashing the current jobless rate by 0.9 per cent.[3]

It is needless to say that these forecasts are too rosy to be credible.

On the contrary most public economists, while acknowledging the negative supply side effects of estate taxation, would compare them with those of other taxes and would not recommend abolishing it. In any case, the final decision is in the hands of voters and in the US these do not seem favourable to estate taxation.

Unpopular taxes[4]

A large number of surveys have been conducted in the US on whether or not the estate tax should be repealed. As these surveys show, estate taxes are not a popular form of taxation, even though they typically hit only a minority of the population. It affects fewer than 2 per cent of decedents and is therefore of no direct concern to most taxpayers.

Recently the AEI (2009) provided what can be considered as the most comprehensive collection of polls ever compiled on the subject of taxes. In this document there is a section on estate taxation with a list of surveys that are consistently in favour of the repeal of the tax. Let us mention two examples. In questions asked by CBS News/New York Times pollsters after the estate tax threshold was raised to $3.5 million, around four in ten said the tax should be eliminated altogether. In a 2006 question by Harris Interactive for the Tax Foundation, people said the estate tax was the worst federal tax, ahead of the federal income tax. In 2009, the federal estate tax was declared as being not at all fair by more people than any of five other federal taxes.

Estate taxation is so unpopular that Auerbach (2006) writes, 'it might make little sense at the moment to argue in favour of the estate tax in the United States'. Most recent Public Finance or Public Economics textbooks do not even mention this form of taxation. Data are scarce with the exception of those coming from OECD. (See for example OECD, 2008.)

On the issue of unpopularity, Frank (2005) argues that the way questions are phrased in opinion polls is of crucial importance. He shows that voters would not favour repealing the estate tax if they took into account the policy changes that such a reform would necessarily have to entail (raising other taxes, cutting government services or increasing federal borrowing). When asked just about repealing the tax without mentioning its repercussions, respondents do favour the repeal by almost three to one. When respondents are reminded that the revenue shortfall would have unpleasant repercussions, these respondents opposed repeal by almost four to one. There is also the way questions are framed. In a recent paper, Fatemi *et al.* (2008) demonstrate that prior counter attitude reverses the expected framing effects. In sum, when respondents do not initially approve of an estate tax, favourable frames lead to more negative responses than do unfavourable frames.

Along the same line, Birney *et al.* (2006) analyse the polling data and show how the contours of public opinion were strategically used in the policy debate. When the issue was framed as a matter of fairness, misperceptions of self-interest and principled beliefs about fairness combined to yield apparently over-whelming support for repeal. However, when it was instead framed as a matter of priority, majorities supported estate tax reform options over repeal. Interest groups used the findings about public opinion in coalition-building and campaigns that changed the public image of repeal from extreme to mainstream. In sum, public opinion polls supporting repeal provided 'running room' for politicians to vote for repeal. Krupnikov *et al.* (2006) examine whether the broad support for repeal of the estate tax is a result of citizen ignorance. They find that increasing information about the estate tax, or about politics in general, has very different effects on Republicans and Democrats. They also show that standard surveys overestimate the extent of misinformation about the estate tax and conclude that 'ignorance' is not a compelling explanation of why so many people support estate tax repeal.

To conclude this section, it is clear that an estate tax like that implemented in the US is subject to a very effective and active campaign of disparagement, and is unpopular even among those who will never be subject to it themselves, or even their descendants. Let us mention some standard explanations for this puzzle. First, there is clearly the way survey questions are framed and the intense lobbying activities of the opponents to the estate tax. There is also the way the tax is organized with its numerous loopholes, which give a feeling of huge horizontal inequalities. But clearly there is something more in it which is outside of the scope of economics. The estate tax seems to touch upon family values that are so important in the culture of American society and to remind people of something they want to forget about, death. The reason can be the same as that behind the annuity puzzle. Accordingly, very few people do buy annuities even though this would be a rational move. This is because they want to avoid a double penalty: early death and wasted investment. This prospect is not compensated for in the least by the alternative outcome: late death and high return from annuities. In the case of estate taxation, people want to avoid the double loss: death and death tax. This prospect is so repugnant that many individuals neglect the simple fact that at death they will not have any estate deserving to be so taxed.

Types and importance of wealth transfer taxes

Types of wealth taxation

Most of the writings on wealth transfer taxation are based on the US setting. It is important to realize that the US estate tax is just one type of wealth transfer tax. There exist two major types of taxes levied on wealth: those applied sporadically or periodically on a person's wealth (net wealth taxes), and those applied on a transfer of wealth (transfer taxes). These taxes are presented in Table 10.1.

Net wealth taxes are typically assessed on the net value of the taxpayer's taxable assets (i.e. value of assets minus any related liability), either sporadically (often known as 'capital levies') or on an annual or other periodic basis. Net wealth taxation has almost disappeared everywhere, except in a very few countries including France. In this survey we study transfer taxes. These taxes are typically assessed on the net value of the taxable assets transferred, and fall into two basic categories: those levied on the donor, more precisely on his estate (typical in common law countries), and those levied on the recipient, namely the heir.

Donor-based taxes can be levied separately on *inter vivos* transfers (gift tax) and on transfers at death (estate tax), or together in a single integrated tax. Recipient-based taxes can also be levied on *inter vivos* transfers (gift tax), on transfers at death (inheritance tax), and on an integrated basis (accessions tax). The most common approach to taxing wealth transfers among OECD countries is an inheritance tax. The US is somewhat unusual in applying an estate and gift tax.

Importance and evolution

OECD (2008) provides data on wealth transfer taxation for the period 1965–2006. We will restrict our presentation to EU15, the US and Japan with Figure 10.1 and Table 10.2, which give the size and the evolution of the wealth transfer tax over the period 1965–2006. As it appears from these figures wealth transfer taxes play only a minor role in the total tax revenues of countries. Within our sample of OECD countries in 2006, Belgium, Japan and France reach with respectively 1.39, 1.06 and 1.04 per cent, the highest shares in total tax revenues. In Portugal, by contrast, the share is less than 0.2 per cent and is the

Table 10.1 Wealth taxes

Form	Examples
Net Wealth Tax	Periodic
	Sporadic (capital levy)
Transfer Tax	
Transferor-based	Estate tax, gift tax, unified tax
Recipient-based	Inheritance tax, gift tax, accessions tax

Table 10.2 Estate, inheritance and gift taxes as a percentage of total taxation

	1965	1970	1975	1980	1985	1990	1995	2000	2005	2006
Belgium	1.17	1.06	0.76	0.82	0.59	0.71	0.76	0.97	1.30	1.39
Denmark	0.65	0.36	0.38	0.44	0.47	0.56	0.47	0.45	0.40	0.43
Germany	0.22	0.23	0.14	0.18	0.22	0.34	0.26	0.39	0.53	0.46
Ireland	1.89	1.25	1.12	0.35	0.30	0.39	0.44	0.67	0.50	0.62
Greece	0.86	1.35	1.00	1.22	0.95	1.23	0.97	0.80	0.42	0.34
Spain	1.05	0.86	0.79	0.41	0.41	0.42	0.51	0.63	0.74	0.74
France	0.56	0.72	0.72	0.57	0.61	0.95	0.82	1.07	1.19	1.04
Italy	0.85	0.64	0.21	0.21	0.23	0.14	0.15	0.20	0.01	0.01
Luxembourg	0.38	0.48	0.32	0.32	0.27	0.29	0.27	0.27	0.39	0.39
Netherlands	1.08	0.59	0.37	0.48	0.44	0.50	0.61	0.90	0.86	0.86
Austria	0.26	0.23	0.19	0.17	0.17	0.14	0.11	0.01	0.14	0.12
Portugal	2.02	1.47	0.86	0.22	0.83	0.50	0.21	0.25	0.08	0.01
Finland	0.22	0.24	0.21	0.22	0.27	0.37	0.38	0.59	0.70	0.70
Sweden	0.39	0.36	0.25	0.21	0.26	0.19	0.16	0.22	0.07	0.01
United Kingdom	2.62	2.01	0.82	0.59	0.69	0.65	0.58	0.62	0.70	0.74
United States	2.06	1.68	1.45	1.15	0.82	1.00	0.98	1.22	0.90	0.89
Japan	0.71	0.94	0.97	0.71	1.18	1.47	2.02	1.31	1.14	1.06

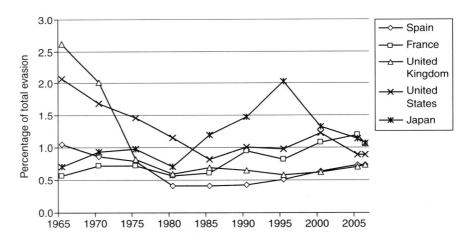

Figure 10.1 Estate, inheritance and gift taxes as a percentage of total taxation.

lowest. Sweden and Italy have abandoned it. As one sees from Figure 1, both the US and the UK experienced a huge decline, from 2.62 to 0.74 and from 2.06 to 0.89 respectively over the last four decades. France has experienced an increase with a peak in 1995. In Japan and Spain the evolution was less marked, increasing in the first and decreasing in the second.

Estate versus inheritance tax

In general, estate taxation gives one total freedom to bequeath one's wealth to anyone or anything. Disinheritance is possible, as long as the decedent prepares an explicit will. Inheritance taxation, on the other hand, often comes with the legal obligation to bequeath one's wealth to one's children, if any, and with an equal sharing rule for most of the estate. Donors have some freedom to allocate a small fraction of the estate, but this fraction declines with the number of children. As the relation between recipient and donor gets more distant, the inheritance tax rate increases.

The relative merits of the estate-type and the inheritance-type taxation are clear. The first is simple and relatively easy to administer, leaving all discretion to donors to dispose of their wealth as they wish. This means that it is possible to compensate some children over others for differences in income or need, and that it is possible to disinherit one's children. By contrast, the inheritance tax is more equitable than the estate tax in that it lightens the tax load of large families. Yet, it does not allow for compensatory treatment of children with uneven endowments.

Basically, estate taxation reflects a concept of the family and of the state that is quite different from the one that governs inheritance taxation. If one trusts parents to be fair in disposing of their estate, and if one believes that intrafamily inequality is as important as interfamily inequality, then what is desirable is a combination of freedom of bequest and a very low estate tax.

What do we learn from public economic theory?

We now turn to what public economic theory teaches us as to the desirability of wealth transfer taxation. And we start by looking at the reasons why people save and bequeath.

Wealth accumulation and transfer motives

It is now widely agreed that to understand the allocative and distributional effects of wealth and wealth transfer taxation one needs to have a better grasp of the saver's motives. Among these motives, one has to distinguish those which are purely selfish and those which concern intergenerational transfers (gifts and inheritance).

We examine briefly a number of motives that have been offered in the literature and sketch their implications. The first two motives are purely selfish. The last three concern bequests.

Consumption smoothing

This is the most traditional motive for saving over one's life-cycle, with or without uncertainty. It includes the need of replacement income after retirement, financing of children's education, precautionary saving and self-insurance. It is well known that this kind of saving decreases with social insurance and tends to be smaller when individuals are short-sighted. In case of imperfect annuity markets and 'premature' death, part of life-cycle saving is not consumed and leads to what is called accidental or unplanned bequests. This form of bequest is by its nature unaffected by estate or inheritance taxation.[5]

Preference for wealth

It is today widely agreed that neither life-cycle saving nor bequest motives can explain the top tail of the wealth distribution. This brings us back to Max Weber's theory of 'the spirit of capitalism' generalized by Kurz (1968): capitalists accumulate wealth for its own sake. To cite Weber (1958: 53):

> Man is dominated by making of money, by acquisition as the ultimate purpose of his life. Economic acquisition is no longer subordinated to man as the means for the satisfaction of his material needs. This reversal relationship, so irrational from a naive point of view, is evidently a leading principle of capitalism.

As argued by Carroll (2000: 463): 'the saving behavior of the (American) richest households cannot be explained by models in which the only purpose of wealth accumulation is to finance future consumption, either their own or that of heirs.' Then, to explain such a behaviour one has to assume that some consumers regard accumulation as an end in itself or as a channel leading to power, which is equivalent to assuming that wealth is intrinsically desirable; what we call here 'preference for wealth'.

Pure dynastic altruism: altruistic bequest[6]

Parents care about the likely lifetime utility of their children and hence about the welfare of future generations. Consequently, wealthier parents tend to make larger bequests. Conversely, holding parents' wealth constant, children with higher labour earnings will receive smaller bequests. When there are no rules restricting freedom to testate, there is also a tendency for parents to leave different amounts to different children, in order to equalize their incomes. Finally, pure altruism typically leads to the Ricardian equivalence: parents compensate any intergenerational redistribution by the government through matching bequests. In consequence, debt and pay-as-you go social security have no effect on capital accumulation.

Joy of giving: paternalistic bequest (bequest-as-last-consumption)[7]

Parents here are motivated not by 'pure' altruism but by the direct utility they receive from the act of giving. This phenomenon is also referred to as 'warm glow' giving. It can be explained by some internal feeling of virtue arising from sacrifice in helping one's children or by the desire to control their life. Formally, these bequests appear in the utility function as consumption expenditure incurred in the last period of life. *Ceteris paribus*, they are subject to income and price effects but do not have any compensatory effect, namely they are not intended to smooth consumption across generations. A crucial element is whether what matters to the donor is the net or the gross tax amount. In the first case, we can talk of some type of altruism; in the second, we rather have a selfish attitude.

Exchange-related motives: strategic bequests[8]

In their canonical form, exchange-related models consider children choosing a level of 'attention' to provide to their parents. In exchange, parents 'remunerate them' through a prospective bequest. The exchanges can involve all sorts of non-pecuniary services and they can be part of a strategic game between parents and children. Strategic bequests, as they were originally presented, imply that parents extract the entire surplus from their children by playing them off against each other. Strategic or exchange bequests depend on the wealth and the needs of the donor; they are not compensatory between parents and children and they do not need to be equal across children.

Existing evidence on wealth accumulation motives

There is a long history of research on bequest motives.[9] Initially researchers obtained widely divergent estimates. For example, Kotlikoff and Summers (1981) estimated that only 20 per cent of bequests are accidental. Hurd (1987) countered that households with children do not save more and, on this basis, concluded that bequests largely stem from life-cycle savings. Nevertheless, over time the literature appears to have reached a fragile consensus. Altruistic transfers appear to represent a minority of wealth transfers. The remainder would be egoistic, purely accidental or based on either exchange considerations or selfish joy of giving.

Desirability of taxation

We now turn to the desirability of taxation, particularly that of wealth transfers, for each type of wealth accumulation motive. Our theoretical discussion of wealth taxation will be organized in two stages. First of all, we assume that there are neither bequest motives nor preference for wealth. In that case, within the standard overlapping generations model there is no distinction between wealth and capital income. Then bequest motives and preference for wealth are introduced. In other words, it is recognized that saving is not motivated solely by retirement or precautionary concerns. We show that these other motives may have a significant impact on the rate and on the structure of taxation.

Pure life-cycle considerations

In this subsection we examine two propositions that lead to zero taxation of capital income. The first one, called the Atkinson–Stiglitz proposition, is discussed within the overlapping generations model. The second one, known as the Chamley–Judd theorem, is presented in a model with infinitely lived individuals.

1 THE OVERLAPPING GENERATIONS MODEL

The overlapping generations (OLG) model is the conventional setting to discuss capital income taxation when saving is exclusively motivated by consumption smoothing. It considers finitely lived generations that overlap, along with an infinitely lived government.[10] We use the two-period model, with labour supply in the first period and consumption in both the first and second periods. Saving from first-period earnings is used to finance second-period consumption, generating capital income that is taxable (in the second period). Since there is only a single period of work, the model can be viewed as shedding light on the taxation of saving for retirement. This model allows for the introduction of the Atkinson–Stiglitz (1976) (hereafter AS) proposition. It states that when the available tax tools include nonlinear labour income taxes, taxation of saving or of capital income is not optimal if two key conditions are satisfied: (1) preferences are (weakly) separable between consumption and labour and (2) all consumers have the same utility function.

To counter the AS result and its zero capital income taxation there are several angles of attack. The first one is clearly to question the assumption of separability or that of homogeneous preferences. Dropping the assumption of separability would not necessarily result in taxing capital income. Subsidizing is just as likely. Introducing heterogeneity in preferences appears to be more promising. It has been done in different ways. There are at least three potential sources of heterogeneity that can lead to a tax on capital income: time discount rates, longevity and initial endowments. Saez (2002) questions the Atkinson–Stiglitz theorem on the basis of differences in time preferences across individuals with different skills. He shows that capital income taxation becomes desirable under the plausible assumption that those with higher earning abilities discount the future less (and thus save more out of any given income). Cremer *et al.* (2009) use another stylized fact, namely the positive correlation between income and longevity to reach the same conclusion. Cremer *et al.* (2003) introduce an endowment (inherited wealth) as a second unobservable characteristic. They show that if ability and endowment are positively correlated then it is efficient to tax capital income.

If we discuss the AS proposition in the standard OLG setting, we have to keep in mind that there is no guarantee that the optimal accumulation of capital is achieved. If the government does not have direct control of capital, it can use tax policy to affect the capital labour ratio. In that case, even with separability and identical utilities, a tax on capital income is needed. This in itself is quite intuitive. However, the design of the appropriate tax rule is more complex. For instance, a need for additional capital accumulation, because the capital stock is below the modified golden rule level, will not necessarily lead to less taxation of capital income and more taxation of labour income. What matters is aggregate saving and this may depend much more on net of tax earnings than on the rate of interest.

Another variation of the standard model is to allow for uncertain earnings in the second period of life. Cremer and Gahvari (1995) have shown that if consumption decisions are to be taken before earnings uncertainties are resolved then the Atkinson–Stiglitz result fails to hold. Banks and Diamond (2010) discuss the implications of this result for capital income taxation. They argue that the case of uncertainty is similar to the situation (discussed above) where high wage individuals discount the future less. In the latter case, a high wage individual imitating someone with less skill saves more than a low wage individual. Taxing capital income is then an effective way to release an otherwise binding incentive constraint. Under uncertainty, this argument goes through. An individual who plans to earn less than the government planned amount in the event of high skill has a higher valuation of saving than the individual with the government planned income level. Consequently, a tax on savings continues to relax an incentive constraint. To illustrate this argument, Banks and Diamond (2010) point out that retirement age tends to be lower for those with higher savings. Consequently, taxing savings discourages earlier retirement.

Uncertain earnings are a central element of what is known as the New Dynamic Public Finance. This literature is quite complex and leads to a number of interesting insights. However, the basic case for taxation of capital income is based the same argument as in Cremer and Gahvari (1995).

2 THE INFINITE HORIZON MODEL

In the above models there is a contrast between finitely lived individuals, who are intergenerationally disconnected, and the government which has an infinite horizon and a different time preference. Let us now look at another class of models wherein individuals are infinitely lived and have the same discount rate as the central planner. For the purpose at hand the central finding of this literature, due to Chamley (1986) and Judd (1985), is the optimality of zero capital income taxation in the long term.

The intuition behind this result can be understood by looking at the wedge that a capital income tax introduces between the intertemporal marginal rate of substitution (MRS) and the intertemporal marginal rate of transformation (MRT). Let us illustrate this through a simple example.

Take a tax rate of 30 per cent and a rate of return of 10 per cent. In a year, the wedge between MRS ($=1+0.1*(1-0.3)=1.07$) and MRT ($=(1+0.1)=1.1$) is small and the distortion on the saving choice is negligible. After 40 years, the capital income tax generates a 67 per cent wedge between consumption today and consumption in 40 years. As a matter of fact, as the time horizon T goes to infinity, the ratio between MRS and MRT tends to zero. Consequently, when the investor has a very long time horizon the capital income tax becomes extremely inefficient.

The Chamley–Judd no capital income taxation conclusion has become the standard rule for a number of public economists and particularly macroeconomists. It has also been challenged on various grounds. It relies on a set of strong assumptions. As with the Atkinson–Stiglitz result, a key question is how robust their theorem is to realistic changes in the model. There is first the steady-state assumption; we know that during the transition capital income is subject to taxation. There is also the assumed equality between the private and the social discount rate and the absence of liquidity constraints. If one departs from these assumptions the tax is not any more equal to zero even in the steady state. Their model assumes also that there are no constraints on the tax tools. As shown by Coleman (2000) and Correia (1996), as soon as some taxes are constrained the zero tax result ceases to hold.

Uncertainty about earnings, along with borrowing constraints, is shown to lead to a positive tax. (On this, see Chamley, 2001, and Golosov *et al.*, 2003.) Finally let us mention a paper by Saez (2002) who introduces a progressive tax on capital income into the Chamley–Judd model. Under some plausible assumptions, he shows that such a tax is desirable; it drives all the large estates down to a finite level thus generating a truncated long-run wealth distribution.

To conclude this subsection, it seems that the case for a zero-tax on capital income when the only motive for saving is life-cycle consumption smoothing is rather weak. While Atkinson–Stiglitz, on the one hand, and Chamley–Judd, on the other, are often invoked to advocate a tax exemption on capital income, there appears to be a striking discrepancy between common beliefs and actual results. Under closer scrutiny, it is clear that neither of these zero tax results applies under 'plausible' circumstances.[11]

Bequests with or without motives

1 ALTRUISTIC BEQUESTS

We first consider the case where individuals save for their own retirement consumption needs and for making sure that their children's welfare is sufficiently high. The standard way of dealing with this problem is to adopt the infinitely lived individuals model. Instead of considering an infinite series of years of one individual life we consider an infinite series of generations (a dynasty), which are linked by bequests. We assume non-negative bequests, which correspond to the liquidity constraint in the infinitely lived individuals model, and the equality between the social and the individual discount factor. Then, one has the Ricardian equivalence implying the neutrality of the debt.[12] One also has the Chamley–Judd result. That is a zero tax on inheritance, but as we have just seen this result is subject to so many qualifications that it is not useful.

2 PATERNALISTIC BEQUESTS

These bequests are also called 'bequests as last consumption' or 'joy of giving' bequests. To obtain the social optimum, there is the issue of whether or not individual utilities should be 'laundered'. Harsanyi (1995) and Hammond (1988) have advocated 'excluding all external preferences, even benevolent ones, from our social utility function'. Advocates of a utilitarian approach, on the other hand, argue that the social planner cannot paternalistically modify individuals' preferences. Besides laundering there is the question of what is the argument of the parental utility function: before or after tax bequests. Quite clearly laundering and taking as argument the before tax bequests make a good case for a positive tax.

Bequests are potentially subject to a double tax: first, the tax on savings, and then the specific tax on transfers. This latter tax depends on the extent of laundering. When there is laundering, bequests lose their direct social utility and are thus subject to a relatively higher tax. In the absence of laundering it is not impossible to have a negative marginal tax. For example, Farhi and Werning (2009), who do not launder their utilities, study efficient allocations in a model with altruistic parents and focus on the implications for estate taxation. They show that the optimal estate tax rate is likely to be negative.

3 EXCHANGE-BASED BEQUESTS

In a two period model we have three tax instruments: a proportional tax on earnings, interest income and inherited wealth with rates. The overall tax on bequests may or may not be higher than that on future consumption. In other words, there is no particular reason to believe that the wealth transfer tax is positive. This will depend on the relative magnitude of the compensated derivatives which determine the overall tax on bequests and the tax on future consumption. For example if the demand for attention is much more elastic than that for future consumption, the tax on inheritance may turn negative.

4 ACCIDENTAL BEQUESTS

The accidental bequest case is not much different from the case without bequest. Saving is affected by survival probabilities. Accidental transfers are taxed at 100 per cent, without affecting the supply of saving. The part of public spending (if any) which exceeds the proceeds of the transfer tax is financed through labour and capital income taxes.[13]

5 PREFERENCE FOR WEALTH

The case with preferences for wealth is close to that of paternalistic bequests with one exception: here individuals obtain the same utility from saving for retirement and for bequests. As in the case of paternalistic bequests, wealth can be viewed as a consumption good and be taxed accordingly. The issue of laundering does also play an important role here.[14]

Table 10.3 Desirability of a wealth transfer tax under alternative bequest motives

Bequest motive	Laundering	Not laundering
Dynastic altruism	0/+	NA
Joy of giving – net of tax	+	–/+
Joy of giving – before tax	++	+
Exchange based	NA	+/–
Accidental	NA	100%

Note
NA: not applicable.

Efficiency and equity

The arguments developed so far are mostly concerned by efficiency considerations. The question dealt with is: given that some revenue has to be collected to finance public spending should we include a tax on wealth transfer in our tax toolbox? The answer to this question appears to be positive particularly in the case of accidental bequests and to a lesser extent when the bequest motive is the joy of giving. If we add the objective of redistribution, the case of wealth transfer taxation becomes even stronger.

In a recent paper Kopczuk (2009) adds another argument in favour of this tax. He posits that wealth concentration has negative social externalities and for that reason a tax that hits the top wealth is desirable.

Heterogeneity of preferences[15]

The theoretical literature on wealth transfer taxation tends to assume that individuals have only one type of bequest motive. In fact real life society consists of individuals with different motives; either they exhibit different motives of accumulation or different individuals have different motives. Two cases have been studied. First, there is the case of a society with individuals being either selfish or altruistic. Second, there is the case where the same individuals would leave bequests because of altruism and also in case of premature death. In those two cases, a wealth transfer tax happens to be desirable.

Conclusions

Our survey was limited to the normative aspects of wealth taxation and it would seem from this overview that the case for not taxing wealth and particularly wealth transfers is rather weak. Our basic goal is to finance government services with a tax system that is as efficient, fair and painless as possible. On all counts, it is difficult to imagine a better tax than the estate tax. Every euro we collect from it is one less euro we need to collect from some other tax that is worse in at least one of these dimensions.

There are a number of questions that we have not dealt with and which explain why wealth transfer taxation is today so unpopular that in some countries the political system is considering abolishing it.

There is first the issue of avoidance and evasion, which not only leads to poor tax yields but also to strong departures from both vertical and horizontal equality. Related to that, there is the issue of tax competition within countries and among countries. In federal states one observes a real race to the bottom regarding wealth taxation. In an economic union such as the European one there is an increasing tax competition for financial wealth and this includes wealth taxation. Another issue pertains to the alleged adverse effect of wealth taxation on family businesses.

Those three issues have a real political impact and yet there is little evidence on how important is their effect. What is certain is that they can be dealt with by reforming the tax on wealth transfer and not by repealing it.

Notes

1 There exist a number of surveys on the normative analysis of wealth transfer taxation: Cremer and Pestieau (2006; 2011), Boadway *et al.* (2010), Kaplow (2000), Kopckuk (2009), Masson and Pestieau (1997).
2 Saxton (1998), Holtz-Eakin and Smith (2009), Neese and Lowe (2009).
3 Dubay (2009).
4 See Rowlingson (2010) for a discussion of the public opposition to estate taxation in the UK.
5 Abel (1985), Davies (1981).
6 Becker and Tomes (1979), Barro (1974).
7 Bevan and Stiglitz (1979), Michel and Pestieau (2007).
8 Bernheim *et al.* (1986), Cremer and Pestieau (1996; 1998), Kotlikoff and Spivak (1981).
9 See Batchelder and Khitatrakun (2008). See also Arrondel and Masson (2004), Bernheim (1991), Altonji *et al.* (1992), Kopczuk and Lupton (2007).
10 Diamond (1975).
11 See Conesa *et al.* (2010).
12 Barro (1974).
13 Cremer *et al.* (2009), Blumkin and Sadka (2004).
14 Michel and Pestieau (2007).
15 Mankiw (2000), Michel and Pestieau (1998; 2000), Pestieau and Sato (2009), Pestieau and Thibault (2012).

References

Abel, A.B. (1985) 'Precautionary saving and accidental bequests', *American Economic Review*, 75(4): 777–791.
Altonji, J.G., Hayashi, F. and Kotlikoff, L.J. (1992) 'Is the extended family altruistically linked? Direct tests using micro data', *American Economic Review*, 105(6): 1121–1166.
American Enterprise Institute (2009) *Public Opinion on Taxes*, Available www.aei.org/publicopinion6.
Arrondel, L. and Masson, A. (2004) 'Altruism, exchange or indirect reciprocity: What do the data on family tranfers show?', in S.-C. Kolm and J. Mercier-Ythier (eds),

Handbook of the Economics of Giving, Altruism and Reciprocity, Amsterdam: North Holland.

Atkinson, A.B. and Stiglitz, J.E. (1976) 'The design of tax structure: Direct versus indirect taxation', *Journal of Public Economics*, 6(1–2): 55–75.

Auerbach, A. (2006) *The Future of Capital Income Taxation*, Berkeley: University of California, unpublished.

Banks, J. and Diamond, P. (2010) 'The base for direct taxation', in *Dimensions of Tax Design: The Mirrlees Review*, Oxford: Oxford University Press, pp. 548–648.

Barro, R. (1974) 'Are government bonds net wealth?', *Journal of Political Economy*, 82: 1095–1117.

Batchelder, L. and Khitatrakun, S. (2008) *Dead or Alive: An Investigation of the Incidence of Estate Taxes and Inheritance Taxes*, New York: NYU School of Law, unpublished.

Becker, G.S. and Tomes, N. (1979) 'An equilibrium theory of the distribution of income and intergenerational mobility', *Journal of Political Economy*, 87: 1153–1189.

Bernheim, B.D. (1991) 'How strong are bequest motives?', *Journal of Political Economy*, 99: 899–927.

Bernheim, B.D., Shleifer, A. and Summers, L.H. (1985) 'The strategic bequest motive', *Journal of Political Economy*, 93(6): 1045–1076.

Bevan, D.L. and Stiglitz, J.E. (1979) 'Intergenerational transfers and inequality', *Greek Economic Review*, 1(1): 8–26.

Birney, M., Graetz, M. and Shapiro, I. (2006) 'Public opinion and the push to repeal the estate tax', *National Tax Journal*, 109: 430–442.

Blumkin, T. and Sadka, E. (2004) 'Estate taxation', *Journal of Public Economics*, 88: 1–21.

Boadway, R., Chamberlain, E. and Emmerson, C. (2010) 'Taxation of wealth and wealth transfers', in *Dimensions of Tax Design: The Mirrlees Review*, Oxford: Oxford University Press, pp. 737–814.

Carroll, C.D. (2000) 'Why do the rich save so much?', in J. Slemrod (ed.) *Does Atlas Shrug? The Economic Consequences of Taxing the Rich*, Cambridge, MA: Harvard University Press, 463–485.

Chamley, C. (1986) 'Optimal taxation of capital income in general equilibrium with infinite lives', *Economica*, 54: 607–622.

Chamley, C. (2001) 'Capital income taxation, wealth distribution and borrowing constraints', *Journal of Public Economics*, 79: 55–69.

Coleman, W.J. (2000) 'Welfare and optimum dynamic taxation of consumption and income', *Journal of Public Economics*, 76: 1–39.

Conesa, J., Kitao, S. and Krueger, D. (2010) 'Taxing capital? Not a bad idea after all!', *American Economic Review*, 99: 25–48.

Correia, I. (1996) 'Should capital income be taxed in a steady state?' *Journal of Public Economics*, 60: 147–51.

Cremer, H., and Gahvari, F. (1995) 'Uncertainty, optimal taxation and the direct versus indirect tax controversy', *Economic Journal*, 105: 1165–1179.

Cremer, H., Gahvari, F. and Pestieau, P. (2009) 'Accidental bequests: A curse for the rich and a boon for the poor', *Scandinavian Journal of Economics*, forthcoming.

Cremer, H., Lozachmeur, J.-M. and Pestieau P. (2010) 'Collective annuities and redistribution', *Journal of Public Economic Theory*, 12: 23–41.

Cremer, H. and Pestieau, P. (1996) 'Bequests as a heir "discipline device"', *Journal of Population Economics*, 9: 405–414.

Cremer, H. and Pestieau, P. (1998) 'Delaying inter vivos transmission under asymmetric information', *Southern Economic Journal*, 65: 322–331.

Cremer, H. and Pestieau, P. (2006) 'Wealth transfer taxation: A survey of the theoretical literature', in S.C. Kolm and J. Mercier Ythier (eds) *Handbook on Altruism, Giving and Reciprocity*, Amsterdam: North Holland, Vol. 2, pp. 1108–1134.

Cremer, H., and Pestieau, P. (2011) 'Wealth and wealth transfer taxation: A survey', in E. Albi and J. Martinez-Vazquez (eds) *The Elgar Guide to Tax Systems*, Cheltenham: Edward Elgar, pp. 183-217.

Cremer, H., Pestieau, P. and Rochet, J.-C. (2003) 'Capital income taxation when inherited wealth is not observable', *Journal of Public Economics*, 87: 2475–2490.

Davies, J.B. (1981) 'Uncertain lifetime, consumption and dissaving in retirement', *Journal of Political Economy*, 89: 561–577.

Diamond, P. (1965) 'National debt in a neoclassical growth model', *American Economic Review*, 58: 1126–1150.

Dubay, C. (2009) *Estate Tax a Killer for Family-Owned Businesses and Their Workers*, WebMemo #2703, The Heritage Foundation.

Erreygers, G. and Vandevelde, T. (1997) *Is Inheritance Legitimate? Ethical and Economic Aspects of Wealth Transfers*, Berlin: Springer-Verlag.

Farhi, E. and Werning, I. (2010) 'Progressive estate taxation', *Quarterly Journal of Economics*, 125: 635–673.

Fatemi, D.J., Hasseldine, D.J. and Hite, P.A. (2008) 'Resisting framing effects: The importance of prior attitude on estate tax preferences', *Journal of the American Taxation Association*, 30(1): 101–121.

Frank, R. (2005) 'The estate tax: Efficient, fair and misunderstood', *New York Times*, May 12, 2005.

Golosov, M., Tsyvinski, A. and Werning, I. (2007) 'New dynamic public finance: A user's guide', *NBER Macroeconomics Annual*, 2006: 317–363.

Hammond, P. (1988) 'Altruism', in J. Eatwell, M. Milgate and P. Newman (eds) *The New Palgrave: A Dictionary of Economics*, London: Macmillan.

Harsanyi, J. (1995) 'A theory of social values and a rule utilitarian theory of morality', *Social Choice and Welfare*, 12: 319–344.

Holtz-Eakin, D. and Smith, C. (2009) *Changing Views of The Estate Tax: Implications For Legislative Options*, American Family Business Foundation, unpublished.

Hurd, M. (1987) 'Savings of the elderly and desired bequests', *American Economic Review*, 77(3): 298–312.

Judd, K.L. (1985) 'Redistributive taxation in a simple perfect foresight model', *Journal of Public Economics*, 28: 59–83.

Kaplow, L. (2000) 'A framework for assessing estate and gift taxation', in W.G. Gale, J.R. Hines Jr. and J. Slemrod (eds) *Rethinking Estate and Gift Taxation*, Washington, DC: Brookings Institution, pp. 164–215.

Kopczuk, W. (2009) *Economics of Estate Taxation: Review of Theory and Evidence*, Columbia University, unpublished.

Kopczuk, W. and Lupton, J. (2007) 'To leave or not to leave: The distribution of bequest motives', *Review of Economic Studies*, 74: 207–235.

Kotlikoff, L.J. and Summers, L. (1981) 'The role of intergenerational transfers in aggregate capital accumulation, *Journal of Political Economy*, 89(4): 706–732.

Kotlikoff, L.J. and Spivak, A. (1981) 'The family as an incomplete annuities market', *Journal of Political Economy*, 89(2): 372–391.

Krupnikov, Y., Levine, A. and Lupia, A. (2006) 'Public ignorance and estate tax repeal:

The effect of partisan differences and survey incentives', *National Tax Journal*, 109: 425–438.

Kurz, M. (1968) 'Optimal economic growth and wealth effects', *International Economic Review*, 9: 348–357.

Mankiw, G. (2000) 'The savers-spenders theory of fiscal policy', *AEA Papers and Proceedings*, 90: 120–125.

Masson, A. and Pestieau, P. (1997) 'Bequests motives and models of inheritance: A survey of the literature', in G. Erreygers and T. Vandevelde (eds) *Is Inheritance Justified?*, Berlin: Springer-Verlag, pp. 54–88.

Michel, Ph. and Pestieau, P. (1998) 'Fiscal policy in a growth model with both altruistic and non-altruistic agents', *Southern Economic Journal*, 64: 682–697.

Michel, Ph. and Pestieau, P. (2000) 'Tax-transfer policy with altruists and non-altruists', in L.A. Gérard-Varet, S.C. Kolm and J. Mercier Ythier (eds) *The Economics of Reciprocity, Giving and Altruism*, London: Macmillan and International Economic Association, pp. 275–284.

Michel, Ph. and Pestieau, P. (2007) 'Fiscal policy in an overlapping generations model with bequest-as-consumption', *Journal of Public Economic Theory*, 6: 397–407.

Neese, T. and Lowe, B. (2009) *Estate Tax Myths*, National Center for Policy Analysis, Brief Analysis N° 678.

Pestieau, P. and Sato, M. (2008) 'Estate taxation with both accidental and planned bequests', *Asia Pacific Journal of Accounting and Economics*, 15: 223–240.

Pestieau, P. and Thibault, E. (2012) 'Love thy children or money – Reflections on debt neutrality and estate taxation', *Economic Theory*, 50: 31–57.

Rowlingson, K. (2010) *Why is the British Public so Opposed to Inheritance Tax?*, unpublished.

Saez, E. (2002) *Optimal Progressive Capital Income Taxes in the Infinite Horizon Model*, NBER Working Paper No 9046.

Saxton, J. (1998) *The Economics of Estate Tax*, Joint Economic Study, Available www. house.gov/jec/fidcal/estattax/estattax.htm.

Stiglitz, J.E. (1987) 'Pareto efficient and optimal taxation in the new welfare economics', in M. Feldstein and A.J. Auerbach (eds) *Handbook of Public Economics*, Amsterdam: North-Holland, Vol. 2, pp. 991–1042.

Weber, M. (1958) *The Protestant Ethic and the Spirit of Capitalism*, New York: Charles Scribner's Sons.

11 Inheritance taxation, notions of legitimacy and Bourdieu

Ann Mumford

Introduction

This chapter aims to integrate some of the work of Pierre Bourdieu into reviews of the treatment of inheritance taxation, in some aspects of theoretical sociology. The objective is to forge a link between Bourdieu's writings on tax, power, legitimacy and inheritance, and the modern disquiet with taxation of inheritance.[1] This disquiet is approached from the perspective of a wide, cultural movement (on terms defined in Bourdieu's writings).

The motivation for this project is in some ways simple. Bourdieu, the second most cited writer in the humanities,[2] is one of the world's most acclaimed sociologists. His theories on power relations in society drew from an eclectic range of sources, and were celebrated and discussed widely, and not simply in scholarly circles.[3] Taxation did not escape his attention; and, indeed, he wrote in particular of the link between tax and war. This chapter will pursue this link, and a connection will be structured within the context of wider, sociological theories of inheritance, both cultural and economic (Mumford, 2007). The bases of these theories are described, briefly, below. It is not the intention of this essay to construct an essay which would attempt to forge an answer to the question, 'what would Bourdieu have thought of the inheritance tax debate, had he lived long enough to engage with it?' His work was vast, and often pursued the point that whilst mechanisms of power must be an analysed, this analysis should not be approached in a reductionist way. It is perhaps most accurate to suggest that he would have thought that the question of inheritance taxation is complex. The nature of this complexity will be introduced, here, and the object is to do so in a Bourdieusian context.

This chapter is in two parts. The first part introduces the questions surrounding popular resistance to inheritance taxation, and some of the arguments within Bourdieusian literature addressing the relationship between power and resistance. This is followed by a section constructing the link between death and taxation, on Bourdieu's terms. This section considers both the 'globalized' unpopularity of inheritance taxation, and the question of hereditary rights to power. Throughout this chapter, the question of social legitimacy, and Bourdieu's approach to it, is analysed. 'The man of great wealth', said Theodore Roosevelt, 'owes a peculiar obligation to the state' (Bartlett and Klein, 2008: III). It is the nature of the state's obligation to wealth, and its role in its creation and preservation – and the connection to power – that will be explored in this chapter. The thesis which this chapter will advance is that inheritance taxation resistance is the perfect Bourdieusian subject, both in that it is uniquely suited to an analysis in terms of a sociology of symbolic power, but also because, as with the anti-globalization activists who captured his attention in the 1990s, this movement reveals the often surprising irritants (especially where tax is concerned) that can arise in the relationship between state and citizen.

Narratives of inheritance, and natures of resistance

The resistance to inheritance taxation is difficult to classify, in that it does not necessarily appear to derive from wholly economic motives.[4] The response to the oft-asked question – why do taxpayers with relatively small estates resist a tax which they may never need to pay? – may of course, in some instances, be no more complicated than the response, 'because they have misunderstood it'.[5] Especially in taxation law, misunderstandings come easily, and in the case of inheritance taxation they may even be encouraged by the politicization of this tax, in a public debate which has not always valued accuracy (Schlachter, 1999).

The opponents of inheritance taxation, in classic political struggle, have simply wanted to win, and if it is possible to win by suggesting, 'this tax will not allow parents to provide for their children', then it cannot be surprising if such a slogan is adopted. To suggest that this slogan should be dissected, supported by research, or expressed more clearly, is perhaps expecting a bit too much of the political process. A more interesting question thus returns to the issue of classification. Why are such slogans so successful, when not necessarily accurate? Why, for example, has the slogan 'capital gains taxation prevents people from providing for their children' not been more successful? Given the inherent links between capital gains taxation and inheritance taxation, this, as was borne out in the 'emergency budget' from the UK's Chancellor of the Exchequer George Osborne, is a particularly relevant question. In his widely trailed Budget Speech on 23 June 2010, some increases in capital gains taxation were heralded as part of a project to introduce a new age of austerity for everyone – even those, ran the clear implication, wealthy enough to have capital (Burns and Landon, 2010). The presentation of cuts to the public sector, and increases in VAT, which are likely to have an impact on middle and lower earners, was frequently balanced by reference to increases in capital gains. (Elliott, 20 June 2010) The response to this increase in the UK was mixed, but it did not produce a discussion the intensity of which could be described as in any way approaching the level of inheritance tax public discourse. (Elliott, 22 June 2010)

The wealth of inheritance tax literature in recent years is testament to the fact that inheritance taxation is not always about money. In particular, Bourdieu's work has inspired a wide literature (Sallaz and Zavisca, 2007), some of which engages with questions of inherited wealth, and much of which is focused upon the extent to which inheritance is a source of gender inequality (Warren, 2006).[6]

In this, his work echoes Durkheim, although Durkheim focused instead on the extent to which inherited property was a source of inequality (Ramp, 2001: 100; Noble, 1980: 581; and Lamanna and Durkheim, 2001: 57, 60). A review of this literature suggests that the link between economic inheritance and gender inequality is a somewhat more common target of sociologists who do not always engage with this topic more widely.[7] There have been a range of fascinating responses to the question which naturally follows; i.e. what, then, does it concern?

Graetz and Shapiro, for example, focus attention on the political process, and how debates in the US have been influenced by constant legislative 'cuts', and the politicization of the motives behind these cuts (Birney, Graetz and Shapiro, 2008). Similarly, Batchelder (2007, 2008a, 2008b, 2009) has drawn attention to the target of inheritance (or, in the US, estate) taxation with her elegantly crafted 'comprehensive inheritance tax' proposal. Additionally, Beckert (2007, 2008, 2009) famously has forged the connection between legal approaches to property and ownership, and the impact upon taxation of these differing legal foundations. In many ways these descriptions, however, are overly simplistic. Graetz and Shapiro do not only address the political process. Batchelder's proposal stretches beyond moving the burden of taxation away from 'the dead', to the living. And, Beckert's study is enormously wide, and covers far more than comparative property law. A clue to the enormity of this topic is in the range of sources, and ideas, with which the leading pieces of work in this field engage.[8] Resistance to inheritance taxation, put simply, seems to be about a lot of different things.

The range of issues raised by inheritance taxation resistance would not have surprised Bourdieu, who would have suggested that the 'spheres' of politics, taxpayer and laws are not clearly delineated (Bourdieu, 1987). He would have predicted that it would be difficult to read any serious study of a topic such as inheritance taxation, and to single out or to select individual theses, because to do this would be to misunderstand how society operates – or, put simply, to misunderstand how society and inheritance taxation interact. Thus, important contributions to the topic, such as those listed, necessarily will engage with a spectrum of issues, from taxpayers, to governments, religion, communities, educational structures and the thorny question of 'a good death' (Mendenhall, 2008). As Swartz explained, 'Bourdieu rejects the idea that social existence can be segmented and hierarchically organized into distinct spheres, such as the social, the cultural, and the economic' (Swartz, 1996: 73) Thus, forging a connection between resistance to inheritance taxation and one, single cause would always be rejected in such a multi-faceted approach.

Bourdieu embraced what he described as the 'complexity' of 'social reality', and perhaps defensively insisted that he was not trying to complicate matters which are actually quite simple, or to simply indulge a 'decadent desire to say complicated things'.[9] Inheritance taxation is a part of this complicated 'social reality', or a fact of the continually reproducing process of symbolic power. He described symbolic power as resting upon two, crucial pillars. First, symbolic power is based upon 'symbolic capital', or, power that has been acquired by ruling groups in 'previous struggles' (Bourdieu, 2004: 23). Second, symbolic power depends upon the notion of 'symbolic efficacy', an admittedly complicated concept which consists of (1) the extent to which the 'vision' of power is actually based in 'reality,' which is discernible by (2) the 'objective affinities between the agents who have to be brought together' for power structures to perpetuate, and continually to reproduce (ibid.). Bourdieu argues that changing power structures ultimately involves seeking out the source of power, and resisting the temptation to be distracted by activities that occur as a result of this source. Thus, with inheritance taxation, the important issues would not be, why is it unpopular, and why do some taxpayers resist paying it? Rather, the question is, what is the symbolic capital upon which inheritance taxation depends?

Bourdieu's engagement with tax fraud is helpful at this point, as it points to a difficult history, challenging the legitimacy of taxation more generally. Indeed, one of his more famous quotes on the subject of taxation law, generally, is that '... [e]ven today *tax fraud* bears testimony to the fact that the legitimacy of taxation is not taken wholly for granted' (Bourdieu, 1999a: 59). His observation embraced both criminal tax fraud, which can be relatively simple, and extend no further than concealing or misleading (Green, 2004: 169); and, 'legal' tax avoidance. His observations are evocative of McBarnet, who moved the discourse of response beyond 'breaking it (crime) and obeying it (compliance)', and stressed the importance of 'non-compliance' (1988: 114). Noncompliance is achieved by separating the law's 'intent' from its 'content', and adhering as strictly as possible to the latter (Bourdieu, 1999a: 59). Tax avoidance is a difficult subject of study for sociologists (Mason and Calvin, 1978; Hasseldine and Li, 1999; Bergman, 2002), for, as McBarnet explains, the consequence of non-compliance is not a 'broken' law, but a law that has been 'rendered ineffective' (McBarnet, 1988: 113).[10] It is the seeming public acceptance of tax fraud, however, that attracted Bourdieu's attention.

A different approach to death and taxes

Bourdieu suggested that the violent history of tax (writing, it should be noted, of the twelfth century) threatened its modern stability. As a direct consequence of this history, Bourdieu argued, '[i]t is only progressively that we come to conceive taxes as a necessary tribute to the needs of a recipient that transcends the king; i.e., this "fictive body" that is the state' (Bourdieu, 1999a: 59) Additionally, of course, the sources of the revenue of a state have an important impact upon the form of the state itself.[11] The king first enforced taxation, in its ancient forms, through violence; whether through its enforcement through threats of violence to people who lived in the king's country, or, with confiscation of wealth as another form of taxation, in the outcome of war. Significantly, the driving purpose behind taxation often was the need to fund another war.

Although, as mentioned, Bourdieu studied the twelfth century, the relationship between taxation and war could be described almost as a classic friendship. Famous examples include England's ill-fated Charles I, whose need to fund wars with the French fundamentally changed the English constitutional landscape by resulting in his execution, and the insistence in the Bill of Rights that only Parliament may tax – which, for centuries, was the only limitation on parliamentary sovereignty (Patterson, 2004: 26–27; and Adams, 1999). A tax revolt led to the formation of the United States (Lowery and Sigelman, 1981). And, more recently, a property tax 'revolt' in Japan was traced to the American occupation after the Second World War (Jinno and DeWit, 1998). In such a context, the historical progress from viewing tax as inextricably linked to the violence of government, to accepting tax as a fundamental part of the state,[12] would be challenging in at least two respects. First, this requires viewing the state as in some ways independent from the king, or head of government. Taxes paid in the UK by 2010 at the request of the Labour Party Prime Minister Gordon Brown's Chancellor of the Exchequer, Alastair Darling, may now be spent by the Conservative Prime Minister David Cameron's Chancellor, George Osborne.[13] The state may change, and a change in political party leadership is a good example of this, but the state is also institutionalized, and unchanging.

The second respect in which it might be difficult to accept taxation as 'a necessary tribute to the needs of a recipient that transcends the king' concerns voluntariness. In the twelfth century, taxation was resisted at great personal cost. Today it is possible to resist taxation without risking death. Indeed, inheritance taxation 'revolts' are, today, not punished by death. But they are connected with increasingly diverse forms of nationalism, and it is this point which would have engaged Bourdieu, who argued that '...the progressive development of the recognition of the legitimacy of official taxation is bound up with the rise of a form of nationalism' (Bourdieu, 1998: 44). Similarly, in the US, critics of estate taxation have frequently invoked the imagery of the American Dream, part of which is predicated upon socio-economic mobility for one's children (Blatt, 1995). It is thus tied in to a conservative ideal, but also, intimately, connected to nationalism. Yet, the American Dream argument may be used against a claim to inherited wealth,[14] as inheritance makes hard work less necessary.[15] With the introduction of taxes on estates generally, a massive shift in law and culture followed in the US. The culture of dying assumed the importance of organising an estate so as to minimize tax. Ascher explains that '[i]n short, we [Americans] have a grand tradition of intricate and intrusive regulation of decedents' estates, and we have created and paid for a large, dedicated, and professional bureaucracy to do it' (1990: 115). It is for this very reason, he explains, that '[i]t is inconceivable that a federal attempt to curtail inheritance in the United States would go essentially unnoticed' (ibid.).

In the UK, the anti-inheritance tax movement has been no less nationalistic, but in a different way. The UK experienced the significant social upheaval of the inheritance tax of the mid-twentieth century, yet the public perception of this was that it was targeted at wealthy people. It may be suggested that there was insufficient preparation of the public for the extension of such a tax to taxpayers that did not consider themselves as falling within this category. It is less clear if the progressivity of inheritance taxation has influenced many taxpayers, in either the US or the UK, to support it. The reason for this is that whilst arguments in social science literature tends to focus on whether a tax is 'truly' progressive as described,[16] progressivity has not necessarily been accepted as a positive element of tax by those who must pay them. Thus, when supporters of inheritance taxation point to progressivity in its defence, the expected comparative debate (i.e. taxation of inheritance is more progressive than other taxes on capital, etc.),[17] they encounter instead objections about progressive taxation. Inheritance taxation targets some taxpayers who are not able to afford estate planning advice, yet may be avoided by some taxpayers who are able to afford such advice. It is in this context that the tax falls before the argument that it is unfair, and violates one of the ideals of British tax law; i.e. that it should be fair,[18] and above all accurate.[19]

If taxation came to be accepted as a result of burgeoning nationalistic tendencies, it is possible to advance three, alternative arguments. The first argument would be that that the lack of popularity for inheritance taxation is ascribable to unresolved, self-perpetuating problems at the heart of inheritance taxation's 'symbolic capital'. These problems have always existed, this argument would suggest, it is only now that politicians are attempting to deploy them. The second argument is that inheritance taxation is somehow set apart from other forms of taxation. This divergent path may only recently have been taken, or perhaps something unsettling has always existed at the heart of its symbolic capital. Politicians do not fight elections on a platform of repealing income taxation. They do, however, campaign to repeal inheritance taxation, as the 2000 US presidential election (Bartels, 2005: 19), the long campaign to retain power in the UK of former Prime Minister Gordon Brown,[20] and other European elections in the early years of the twenty-first century will attest (Mumford, 2007). The third argument would suggest that there has been a decline in nationalism, perhaps as a consequence of globalization. This argument would suggest that we are all global citizens now, and perhaps feel a diminishing kinship with national identities.

The problem with the second argument is presented in Bourdieu's work with tax fraud. He argues that tax fraud would not occur today if taxation were, truly, accepted. He is writing of all tax, generally, and not just inheritance taxation. The identified lack of 'legitimacy' is directly ascribable to an ancient, and very distant, historical moment. Interestingly, by reaching into history to explain modern 'tax fraud', Bourdieu writes like a true fiscal sociologist. Schumpeter would have approved of the desire to explain the modern state (and of course its budget) by looking back to the moment when a country moved from plunder and pillage, to an organized system of tax collection (Campbell, 1993: 163–164). The modern, fiscal sociology looks to budgets, and to tax law, to explain modern societies, but in a post-structuralist, neo-institutionalist way. Although of course it is led by the ground-breaking work of Schumpeter and Goldscheid amongst others (ibid.), in so many ways it reflects the work of Bourdieu. The 'fiscal sociology paradigm' (Moore, 2004: 297–298) endeavours to reveal the economic and social forces that propel social change (ibid.: 298). Tax does not exist simply within the realm of the public, as the 'tax apparatus' intercedes into the 'private economy' (ibid.).

Bourdieu might have expressed some support for the third argument, if only because it presents an opportunity to criticize globalization, of which Bourdieu was most certainly not a fan.[21] Swartz and Zolberg explain that, by the mid-1990s, Bourdieu used his position as a leading public intellectual to rally support for anti-globalization protests in France, including support for public worker strikes against the withdrawal of funding for the French welfare state (Swartz and Zolberg, 2004: 344). This was the privatization era, in both France and elsewhere, and Bourdieu's stance against the diminution of the economic state was strongly influential. His work is strongly reminiscent, for example, of Picciotto, who warns that 'privatization' is both 'misleading', and a 'misnomer' (Picciotto, 2000: 158). Privatization, rather, was driven by a desire to introduce 'market principles' into considerations about how to share public goods.[22] Within a growing and (then) expanding intellectual framework such as this, 'globalization' might not have been the only reason Bourdieu would have supported the suggestion that a decline in nationalism explains the modern unpopularity of inheritance tax. He might also have been sympathetic to the idea that, embedded within inheritance taxation, is an important symbolic power. Bourdieu expressed considerable sympathy for the 'honest taxpayer' who felt 'persecuted' by a government 'with its strict rules followed to the last dot' (Bourdieu, 1999b: 395). He noted the capacity of such taxpayers to get 'carried away' by 'conflicts' with the 'tax authorities, all of which only reinforces his resentment and his hatred of the government, politicians and bureaucracies' (ibid.). Anti-inheritance tax protest, thus, could be connected to a rupture between the citizen and the state, and the proliferation of 'social suffering in contemporary society'.

A 'globalized' unpopularity

An interesting question which arises at this point is whether this rupture is new or old. The fact that the repeal movement for inheritance taxation, in one sense, has gone global, would have captured Bourdieu's attention. He might have emphasized that the impact of such a movement will be noticed locally – for example, if '... [t]he rise in the inheritance-tax threshold ... is likely to reduce the supply of homes coming on to the market to settle estate taxes' (Muellbauer and Murphy, 2008), then the impact of complete repeal can be presumed to have an even greater effect. The problems of globalization and modernity which Bourdieu criticized are resolutely 'new', and reflective of his belief that some aspects of society have changed for the worse, and that these changes have clear and identifiable victims. Bourdieu's analysis of tax fraud, however, suggesting that something is amiss with a general 'acceptance' of taxation, is sourced in its violent history. Thus, the problem may be very old, in that tax, death and violence have always been connected; and, as a result, tax has always been mistrusted; and, unsurprisingly, a tax which is so intimately connected to death is simply too evocative of that past history to be palatable. Put directly, it is as if pillage and plunder have never been abandoned, and the rulers are still killing subjects for their wealth.

Or, it may be that these problems are new, the product of globalization and modernity, and simply indicative of taxpayers who are 'carried away' by inheritance taxation and what it represents; i.e. the state, and its failures. Although Bourdieu resisted reductionism, and insisted upon the multi-faceted nature of social life, the objection to inheritance taxation does appear to be targeted. The sources of the objection may be numerous, but inheritance taxation itself does appear to belong to the discussion. There may be something about this tax in particular that attracts resentment.

Bourdieu challenged traditional assumptions concerning the common good, particularly in the context of cultural inheritance. Taxation, he explained, was a key linking concept between cultural wealth and power. Thus,

> [t]he concentration of economic capital linked to the establishment of unified taxation is paralleled by a concentration of information capital (of which cultural capital is one dimension) which is itself correlated with the unification of the cultural market.
>
> (Bourdieu, Wacquant and Farage, 1994: 7)

Taxation led to the concentration of wealth within the state, which established a correlation between cultural, common wealth and its commodification. Although Bourdieu did not use the term in this way, commodification is used here to convey the process by which a monetary value is assigned to an object, activity or value that would not necessarily be viewed as part of the marketplace. This was a key process for Bourdieu, and one for which he frequently expressed mistrust, especially when elements of globalization are involved (Swartz, 2003). Bourdieu's concerns, however, for inequalities in power were not restricted to the 'big picture' of a globalized economy. On the question of access to education, for example, he emphasized that '…the inheritance of cultural wealth which has been accumulated and bequeathed by previous generations only really belongs (although it is *theoretically* offered to everyone) to those endowed with the means of appropriating it for themselves' (Bourdieu, 1973: 73). The link between cultural and economic inheritance is at this point most evident, as economic inheritance enables access to education, or cultural inheritance, or, more importantly, for Bourdieu, access to power.

Hereditary rights to power

Bourdieu forged the link between power, inheritance and – interestingly – education, clearly, arguing that a student's '…desire for a broad education to deal with problems in their human context … betrays a search for symbolic confirmation of their hereditary right to occupy positions of power and prestige' (Bourdieu, 1996: 101). He did not leave the question of power at the point of economic wealth; in other words, he did not conflate wealth with power, but approached power as a layered, or symbolic, concept. As Swartz explained, 'Bourdieu proposes a sociology of symbolic power in which he addresses the important topic of relations between culture, stratification and power' (Swartz, 1996: 72). Put simply, Bourdieu viewed power as working in different ways, for different people, at different times, and as deriving from a variety of sources.

On questions of class, wealth and power, Bourdieu often proceeds from familiar starting points, including Marxian analysis,[23] but then moves beyond this. Thus, as Swartz observed, '[l]ike Marx, Bourdieu emphasises the primacy of conflict and class-based social inequality in modern societies' (ibid.: 73). Bourdieu, however, is sharply critical of class reductionist accounts of religion and cultural life (ibid.), although he did provide the starting point of when it was appropriate to describe a given group of people as a class. As he explained,

> we will say that a 'class,' be it social, sexual, ethnic, or otherwise, exists when there are agents capable of imposing themselves, as authorized to speak and to act officially in its place and in its name, upon those who, by recognizing themselves in plenipotentiaries, by recognizing them as endowed with full power to speak and act in their name, recognize themselves as members of the class, and in doing so, confer upon it the only form of existence a group can possess.
>
> (Bourdieu, 1987: 15)

This is a useful point of integration for existing sociological, theoretical analyses of inheritance taxation, which have considered the extent to which inheritance tax avoidance benefits the wealthy, and the value of arguments that inheritance taxation is fair and 'targeted'. Thus, *inter alia*, Duff used elements of class-based analyses in outlining the 'political challenges' that may make the retention of inheritance taxation difficult in the UK, despite what he argues are its clear benefits (2005: 46). Similarly, Massone and Massone directly engage with class when proposing that earmarking funds collected for the benefit of 'the poor' might be a way of salvaging them (2001).

For Bourdieu, the pragmatic study of class and politics was more compelling. Thus, he devoted a great deal of intellectual energy to the educational system. He argued that the educational system is so much a part of, or responsible for, culture that he felt it was impossible to separate intellectually any attempts at a sociology of culture from a sociology of education (1990: 34). For example, he complained that '...[w]hen people write a social history of intellectuals, they almost always forget to take into account the structural evolution of the education system' (ibid.). This failure, Bourdieu argued, is pivotal, as '[t]he specific role of the sociology of education is assumed once it has established itself as the science of the relations between cultural reproduction and social reproduction' (1973: 71). Bourdieu's focus in his analysis of education and inheritance is the fluid nature of power.

The point is that this fluid, fast changing power may be taken from the citizen. The provision of education is a means by which the state may empower the citizen. The taxation of inherited wealth may be disempowering, both for the decedent who perhaps loses a sense of legacy, and an heir who loses wealth, and a feeling of connection with family prestige and advantage. Bourdieu's approach to power as a layered, symbolic question recognizes a multiplicity of potential responses, with perhaps a single element in common. The targets of inheritance taxation, lacking a connection with society or a sense of a commonality of purpose, may feel disempowered.

Conclusion

By restricting his observation to 'great wealth', Roosevelt, in the quotation in this chapter's introduction, did not say that every citizen is obliged to the state. He was focused upon a specific type of person, with a connection to a specific type of wealth – essentially, posthumous wealth. He considered whether society should allow this wealth to be perpetuated within a predefined set of people. Roosevelt may not have been as concerned with the fact that the nature of the property left after death may change, however, thanks to tax. Property shifts into a form most likely to escape tax, and perhaps it is what is left behind that should attract attention. Given that the shift may not be without consequences, is there a way of ensuring that the wealth that is left is both useful to the heirs, and useful to wider society?

On this, and other, questions about inheritance taxation, there should be little hope of immediate consensus. The battles of Gordon Brown in November 2007, and Al Gore in 2000, revealed that current battle lines on the subject of inheritance taxation are too deeply entrenched (Prabhakar, 2008; Mumford, 2007). Indeed, there is political profit in the current divisions.[24] The 'selling' of inheritance taxation could begin with analogies, and challenging desires. For example, parents may wish that many things that they enjoyed during their lifetimes should be enjoyed by their children, but should the simple fact of that wish be necessarily enough to demand that society will ensure its enforcement post-mortem?

From Bourdieu, however, one begins to learn more about the nature of this tax, and factors that go beyond its sheer marketing.[25] It is significant that inheritance taxation will never completely be able to banish the spectre of death from its assessment. It is more than a levy upon resources which a person might have consumed, had that person lived. It touches upon fundamental questions at the heart of inheritance taxation's 'symbolic capital'. It would be incorrect, however, to assume that the state is always the aggressor, and the citizen always the victim, in this relationship between death and taxation and the state (forged through violence). There are any number of cultural touchstones – the dying wish, even the dying declaration – which allocate a certain level of power, and control, to those facing death. The resistance against inheritance taxation could be portrayed as another way in which the taxpayer is mounting a challenge against the power of the state.

This chapter has argued that Bourdieu did not leave the question of power solely at the door of economic wealth, but instead structured a sociology of symbolism in which economic wealth was but one part of interlocking spheres of influence impacting upon the state. He worried about certain, specific problems, such as globalization, in terms of what practically might be accomplished to redress them, and also in terms of how they fit within culture, power and stratification. With inheritance taxation and its resistance, the perfect Bourdieusian subject emerges: power, means of appropriating it, challenges to the state, and a tax associated with death.

Notes

1 From a very wide literature, this project has consulted, *inter alia*, the following texts: P. Bourdieu, *Academic Discourse: Linguistic Misunderstanding and Professorial Power* (1996); P. Bourdieu and L.J.D. Wacquant, *An Invitation to Reflexive Sociology* (1992); P. Bourdieu, 'Cultural reproduction and social reproduction' (1973); Y. Dezalay, B.G. Garth and P. Bourdieu, *Dealing in Virtue: International Commercial Arbitration and the Construction of a Transnational Legal Order* (1998); P. Bourdieu, *Firing Back: Against the Tyranny of the Market*, (2003); P. Bourdieu, 'The force of law: Toward a sociology of the juridical field' (1986); P. Bourdieu and J.B. Thompson, *Language And Symbolic Power* (1991); P. Bourdieu, 'Marginalia: Some additional notes on the gift', (1997); P. Bourdieu, *Practical Reason: On the Theory of Action* (1998); P. Bourdieu, 'Rethinking the state: Genesis and structure of the bureaucratic field' (1999); P. Bourdieu, *Science of Science and Reflexivity* (2004); P. Bourdieu, 'Social space and symbolic power' (1989); and P. Bourdieu and R. Nice, *Sociology in Question* (1994).
2 See discussion of methodology in Cronin, Snyder and Atkins (1997).
3 This is discussed throughout Sallaz and Zavisca (2007).
4 Ventry summarized the position well when he argued that '[w]hile the rhetorical and political case against inheritance taxation is easy enough to dispel, the economic case against them requires more attention' (Ventry, 2000: 1164).
5 'Statistics can provide an important source of information, but in areas such as taxation, this can be supplemented usefully with metaphors and narratives.' (Prabhakar, 2008: 177).
6 An additional issue is that the continuation of this duty of care through inheritance may be based on gendered assumptions. Thus, '[w]omen, like men, pay income tax as individuals; but when it comes to tax and transfer arrangements for women with partners and women as mothers with dependent children, gendered circumstances enter the system of eligibility and entitlement' (Cass and Brennan, 2003: 38). Studies have suggested that societies which use primogeniture to distribute wealth suffer more inequality than those which divide wealth equally between the sexes (Menchik, 1980: 299). But cf. Binder (1973: 609), arguing that '[w]hile the popular wisdom probably overstates the quantitative importance of inheritance of nonhuman wealth, it is true that the distribution of inheritances is terribly unequal and, as such, is a contributor to the total inequality in incomes.' Families which do not discriminate on the basis of sex still may foster inequality with their intergenerational bequests – say, for example, where parents attempt to provide for one child, who may be perceived as disadvantaged, the expense of another; or where parents fear to 'spoil' children with wealth they have not earned, and thus impact upon the 'social mobility' of their descendants for generations to come (Tomes, 1981: 929).
7 Inheritance taxation, specifically, is not a frequent target of sociologists (Avery and Rendall, 2002: 1301; and Mullins, 2000: 685).
8 Thus, McCaffery has engaged with the Rawlsian view of liberalism in his defense of inheritance taxation. Writing that he considers Rawls to be his 'paradigmatic liberal', he notes that Rawls advanced his theory in favour of an estate tax in *A Theory of*

Justice (1971), (McCaffery, 1994: 281) although McCaffery points out that the (in 1994) 'recent *Political Liberalism*,' and Rawls' other works addressing 'socio-economic justice' do not engage with forms of inheritance taxation (ibid.) McCaffery explains that Rawls' preference for inheritance taxation stemmed from the argument that such a tax was solely about the redistribution of wealth. (ibid.) McCaffery concedes that Rawls makes a strong case, and observes that '[p]olitical theorists from Bentham to Mill, each of whom considered an estate tax to be the best possible form of taxation, to Bruce Ackerman, and just about everybody in between, have tended strongly to agree.' (ibid., citing Bentham, 1795). See also Levy (1983: 546): '[a] closer look the body of liberal egalitarian theory, however, reveals a similar, deeply rooted ambivalence'; and, Duff (2005).

9 Bourdieu (1989: 24). See also Bourdieu (2004: 85), where Bourdieu resists the effort to describe the sciences as uniquely complex, as compared, say, the physical sciences: '...exaltation of the "difference" of the social sciences is often no more than a way of decreeing the impossibility of a scientific understanding of their object.'

10 The appeal of tax avoidance is that is relieves a taxpayer from the 'necessity of compliance' (McBarnet, 1988: 113).

11 This is discussed throughout Moore (2004).

12 Based on a more or less collective agreement about a moral content to the tax law, as a now fundamental part of that state. As Copp (1999: 20) puts it, '...we are under a duty to pay the taxes required by a legitimate state assuming the moral innocence of the tax law.' As an interesting side note, this has been identified as a starting point for the law and economics movement. Indeed, one of the presumptions surrounding law and economics is that this field commits legislators to an agreed moral content in tax legislation (Hurd, 2002: 387–388).

13 For an introduction to the differences between Darling and Osborne, see 'Profile: George Osborne' (20 June 2010).

14 As Ascher (1990: 70) argued, '[o]ne of the most dominant themes in American ideology is equality of opportunity. In our society, ability and willingness to work hard are supposed to make all things possible.'

15 Support is provided by the argument that, '[i]n the popular imagination, the wealthy are the success stories, like Bill Gates or Oprah Winfrey, the sort of people you want to root for, not resent' (Birney, Graetz and Shapiro, 2008: 312).

16 Thus, '...[t]he abstract intent (or one of the abstract intentions) of the framers of a particular tax law might be to enact a moderately progressive or fair income tax scheme' (Brink, 1988: 122).

17 By contrast, however, '...given their collateral beliefs about, among other things, economic theory, the framers of a particular tax law have specific intentions to tax certain levels of income at certain rates and to allow particular deductions and credits to certain groups'. (ibid.)

18 But in a certain context. As Raz explains, 'Parliament is to distribute the burden of taxation in an equitable way, but it does not follow that the citizens had any reason to pay tax before the passing of the (just) tax law' (Raz, 1985: 11).

19 For more on the anti-inheritance tax movement in the UK, see, e.g. Bracewell-Milnes, who has argued that inheritance taxation causes a great deal of harm to the economy in the UK, and has long argued for its abolition. See Bracewell-Milnes (2002), and the review by Tiley (2003); also Bracewell-Milnes (1989, 1995, 1997).

20 'Profile: Gordon Brown' (10 May 2010).

21 See generally Fiss and Hirsch (2005: 33). See also Swartz and Zolberg (2004: 344).

22 Ibid.

23 Marx considered inheritance within his 'relations of production' (Swedberg, 2003: 6). Swedberg engages with (an earlier edition of) K. Marx and V.I. Lenin (1932). For more on the Marxian concept of the 'relations of production', see Lefebvre (1978), Edwards (1981) and Edwards (1975).

24 In this context, proponents of (supportive) estate tax reform will recognize Haslett's observation that '[o]ld ways die hard. A social practice may be taken for granted for centuries before humanity finally comes to realize it cannot be justified' (1986: 122).
25 As called for in Mumford (2010). Consideration of Bourdieu produces insights beyond simple marketing, or making arguments more effectively. It helps to advance a different sort of understanding of the tax itself.

References

Ackerman, Bruce (1980) *Social Justice in the Liberal State*, New Haven: Yale University Press.

Adams, C. (1999) *For Good and Evil: The Impact of Taxes on the Course of Civilization.* Lanham, MD: Madison Books.

Ascher, M.L. (1990) 'Curtailing inherited wealth', *Michigan Law Review*, 89(1): 69–151.

Avery, R.B. and Rendall, M.S. (2002) 'Lifetime inheritances of three generations of whites and blacks', *American Journal of Sociology*, 107(5): 1300–1346.

Bartels, L.M. (2005) 'Homer gets a tax cut: Inequality and public policy in the American mind', *Perspectives on Politics*, 3:15–31.

Bartlett, H.A. and Klein, D.B. (2008) 'Taking Stock of Paul Krugman's 654 New York Times Columns, 1997 through 2006', *Econ Journal Watch*, 5(1): I–XLV, Available www.econjournalwatch.org/pdf/KleinBarlettAppendix2January2008.pdf.

Batchelder, L. (2007) *Taxing Privilege More Effectively: Replacing the Estate Tax With an Inheritance Tax*, Available http://papers.ssrn.com/sol3/papers.cfm?abstract_id=993314.

Batchelder, L. (2008a) *Dead or Alive: An Investigation of the Incidence of Estate and Inheritance*, Available http://papers.ssrn.com/sol3/papers.cfm?abstract_id=1134113.

Batchelder, L. (2008)(b) *Reform Options for the Estate Tax System: Targeting Unearned Income, Testimony Before the US Senate Committee on Finance*, Available http://papers.ssrn.com/sol3/papers.cfm?abstract_id=1601652.

Batchelder, L. (2009) *Estate Tax Reform: Issues and Options*, Available http://papers.ssrn.com/sol3/papers.cfm?abstract_id=1320304.

Beckert, J. (2007) 'The longue durée of inheritance law: Discourses and institutional development in France, Germany, and the United States since 1800', *Archives of European Sociology*, 79–120.

Beckert, J. (2008) *Inherited Wealth*, Princeton: Princeton University Press.

Bergman, M. (2002) 'Who pays for social policy? A study on taxes and trust', *Journal of Social Policy*, 31: 289–305.

Binder, A.S. (1973) 'A model of inherited wealth', *Quarterly Journal of Economics*, 87(4): 608–626.

Birney, M., Graetz, M.J. and Shapiro, I. (2008) 'The political uses of public opinion: Lessons from the estate tax repeal', in I. Shapiro, P.A. Swenson and D. Donno (eds) *Divide and Deal: The Politics of Distribution in Democracies*, New York: NYU Press, pp. 298–340.

Blatt, W. (1995) 'The American dream in legislation: The role of popular symbols in wealth tax policy' *Tax Law Review*, 51: 287–354.

Bourdieu, P. (1973) 'Cultural reproduction and social reproduction', in R. Brown (ed.) *Knowledge, Education, and Cultural Change: Papers in the Sociology of Education*, London: Tavistock Publications, pp. 71–112.

Bourdieu, P. (1986) 'The force of law: Toward a sociology of the juridical field', *Hastings Law Journal*, 38: 805–813.

Bourdieu, P. (1987) 'What makes a social class? On the theoretical and practical existence of groups', *Berkeley Journal of Sociology*, 32: 1–17.

Bourdieu, P. (1989) 'Social space and symbolic power', *Sociological Theory*, 14–25.

Bourdieu, P. (1990) *In Other Words: Essays Towards a Reflexive Sociology*, Stanford: Stanford University Press.

Bourdieu, P. (1997) 'Marginalia: Some additional notes on the gift', in A.D. Schrift (ed.), *The Logic of the Gift: Toward an Ethic of Generosity*, London: Routledge, pp. 231–241.

Bourdieu, P. (1998) *Practical Reason: On the Theory of Action*, Stanford: Stanford University Press.

Bourdieu, P. (1999a) 'Rethinking the state: Genesis and structure of the bureaucratic field', in G. Steinmetz (ed.), *State/Culture: State-formation after the Cultural Turn*, Ithaca, NY: Cornell University Press, pp. 53–75.

Bourdieu, P. (1999b) *The Weight of the World: Social Suffering in Contemporary Society*, Stanford: Stanford University Press.

Bourdieu, P. (2003) *Firing Back: Against the Tyranny of the Market*, New York: Verso.

Bourdieu, P. (2004) *Science of Science and Reflexivity*, Cambridge: Polity Press.

Bourdieu, P. and Nice, R. (1994) *Sociology in Question*, London: Sage Publications.

Bourdieu, P., Passeron, J.-C. and Saint-Martin, M. de (1996) *Academic Discourse: Linguistic Misunderstanding and Professorial Power*, Stanford: Stanford University Press.

Bourdieu, P. and Thompson, J.B. (1991) *Language and Symbolic Power*, Cambridge, MA: Harvard University Press.

Bourdieu, P. and Wacquant, L.G.D. (1992) *An Invitation to Reflexive Sociology*, Chicago: University of Chicago Press.

Bourdieu, P., Wacquant, L.J.D. and Farage, S. (1994) 'Rethinking the state: Genesis and structure of the bureaucratic field', *Sociological Theory*, 12(1): 1–18.

Bracewell-Milnes, B. (1989) *The Wealth of Giving: Every One in His Inheritance*, London: Institute of Economic Affairs Monograph.

Bracewell-Milnes, B. (1995) 'Unquoted companies and inheritance tax' *Intertax*, 614–615.

Bracewell-Milnes, B. (1997) 'The hidden costs of inheritance taxation', in G. Erreygers and T. Vandevelde (eds) *Is Inheritance Legitimate? Ethical and Economic Aspects of Wealth Transfers*, Berlin: Springer.

Bracewell-Milnes, B. (2002) *Euthanasia for Death Duties: Putting Inheritance Tax Out of its Misery*, London: Institute for Economic Affairs Monograph.

Brink, D.O. (1988) 'Legal theory, legal interpretation, and judicial review', *Philosophy and Public Affairs*, 17: 105–148.

Burns, J.F. and Landon, T. Jr. (2010) 'Britain unveils emergency budget,' *New York Times*, 22 June, Available www.nytimes.com/2010/06/23/world/europe/23britain.html?src=me (accessed 15 July 2010).

Campbell, J.L. (1993) 'The state and fiscal sociology', *Annual Review of Sociology*, 19: 163–185.

Cass, B. and Brennan, D. (2003) 'Taxing women: The politics of gender in the tax/transfer system', *eJournal of Tax Research*, 1(1): 37–63.

Clignet, R. (2009) *Death, Deeds, and Descendants: Inheritance in Modern America*, Piscataway, NJ: Aldine De Gruyter.

Coleman, J.S. (1974) 'Inequality, sociology, and moral philosophy', *The American Journal of Sociology*, 80: 741–764.

Copp, D. (1999) 'The idea of a legitimate state', *Philosophy and Public Affairs*, 28(1): 3–45.

Cronin, B., Snyder, H. and Atkins, H. (1997) 'Comparative citation rankings of authors in monographic and journal literature: A study of sociology', *Journal of Documentation*, 53: 263–273.

Dezalay, Y., Garth, B.G. and Bourdieu, P. (1998) *Dealing in Virtue: International Commercial Arbitration and the Construction of a Transnational Legal Order*, Chicago: University of Chicago Press.

Duff, D.G. (2005) 'Private property and tax policy in a libertarian world', *Canadian Journal of Law and Jurisprudence*, 18(1): 23–45.

Edwards, R.C. (1975) 'The social relations of production in the firm and labor market structure', *Politics & Society*, 5: 83–108.

Edwards, R.C. (1981) 'The social relations of production at the point of production', in M. Zey-Ferrell and M. Aiken (eds) *Complex Organizations: Critical Perspectives*, Glenview, IL, pp. 156–182.

Elliott, Larry (20 June 2010) 'George Osborne says emergency budget cuts will be "tough but fair"', *Guardian*, Available www.guardian.co.uk/politics/2010/jun/20/george-osborne-emrgencybudget-cuts (accessed 15 July 2010).

Elliott, Larry (22 June 2010) 'Budget 2010: George Osborne's austerity package haunted by spectre of 1981', *Guardian*, Available www.guardian.co.uk/uk/2010/jun/22/budget-budget-deficit (accessed 15 July, 2010).

Fiss, P.C. and Hirsch, P.M. (2005) 'The discourse of globalization: Framing and sense-making of an emerging concept', *American Sociological Review*, 70: 29–52.

Graetz, M.J. and Shapiro, I. (2005) *Death by a Thousand Cuts: The Fight Over Taxing Inherited Wealth*, Princeton, NJ: Princeton University Press.

Green, S. (2004) 'Cheating', *Law and Philosophy*, 23(2): 137–185.

Haslett, D.W. (1986) 'Is inheritance justified?', *Philosophy and Public Affairs*, 15: 122–155.

Hasseldine, J. and Li, Z. (1999) 'More tax evasion research required in new millennium', *Crime, Law and Social Change*, 31: 91–104.

Hurd, H.M. (2002) 'Liberty in law', *Law and Philosophy*, 21(4/5): 385–465.

Jaeger, J.C. and Cook, N.G.W. (1979) *Fundamentals of Rock Mechanics*, 3rd ed., London: Chapman & Hall.

Jinno, N. and DeWit, A. (1998) 'Japan's taxing bureaucrats: Fiscal sociology and the property-tax revolt', *Social Science Japan Journal*, 1: 233–246.

Lamanna, M.A. and Durkheim, É. (2001) *On the Family*, London: Sage Publications Inc.

Lefebvre, H. (1978) *The Survival of Capitalism: Reproduction of the Relations of Production*, London: Allison & Busby.

Levy, M.B. (1983) 'Liberal equality and inherited wealth', *Political Theory*, 11(4): 545–564.

Lowery, D. and Sigelman, L. (1981) 'Understanding the tax revolt: Eight explanations', *The American Political Science Review*, 75: 963–974.

Marx, K. and Lenin, V.I. (1932) *Capital: The Communist Manifesto and Other Writings*, New York: The Modern Library.

Mason, R. and Calvin, L.D. (1978) 'A study of admitted income tax evasion', *Law & Society Review*, 13: 75–77.

Massone, A. and Massone, C. (2001) *Should the Death Tax Die? And Should It Leave an Inheritance?*, POLIS papers, Available http://econpapers.repec.org/paper/ucaucapdv/22.htm.

McBarnet, D. (1988) 'Law, policy, and legal avoidance: Can law effectively implement egalitarian policies?' *Journal of Law and Society*, 15: 113–121.

McCaffery, E.J. (1994) 'The political liberal case against the estate tax', *Philosophy and Public Affairs*, 23(4): 281–312.

Menchik, P.L. (1980) 'Primogeniture, equal sharing, and the U.S. distribution of wealth', *Quarterly Journal of Economics*, 94(2): 299–316.

Mendenhall, G.S. (2008) 'Death and taxes', *Annals of Internal Medicine*, 149:822–824.

Mill, J.S. (1848) *Principles of Political Economy*, Boston: CC Little & J Brown.

Moore, M. (2004) 'Revenues, state formation, and the quality of governance in developing countries', *International Political Science Review/Revue Internationale de Science Politique*, 25(3): 297–319.

Muellbauer, J. and Murphy, A. (2008) 'Housing markets and the economy: The assessment', *Oxford Review of Economic Policy*, 24(1): 1–33.

Mullins, P. (2000) 'The line of descent in the intergenerational transmission of domestic property', *Housing Studies*, 15: 683–698.

Mumford, A. (2007) 'Inheritance in socio-political context: The case for reviving the sociological discourse of inheritance tax law', *Journal of Law and Society*, 34(4): 567–593.

Mumford, A. (2010) 'From Dahomey, to London, to DC', *Tax Law Review*, 63(1): 221–260.

Noble, T. (1980) 'Correspondence', *The British Journal of Sociology*, 31: 581.

Patterson, J. (2004) *The Bill of Rights: Politics, Religion, and the Quest for Justice*, Lincoln, NE: iUniverse Inc.

Picciotto, S. (2000) 'Liberalization and democratization: The forum and the hearth in the era of cosmopolitan post-industrial capitalism', *Law and Contemporary Problems*, 63:157–178.

Prabhakar, R. (2008) 'Wealth taxes: Stories, metaphors and public attitudes', *Political Quarterly*, 79: 172–178.

'Profile: George Osborne' (20 June 2010), *BBC*, Available www.bbc.co.uk/news/10343316 (accessed 15 July 2010).

'Profile: Gordon Brown' (10 May 2010), *BBC*, Available http://news.bbc.co.uk/1/hi/uk_politics/election_2010/8673575.stm (accessed 15 July 2010).

Ramp, W.J. (2001) 'Durkheim and the unthought: Some dilemmas of modernity', *Canadian Journal of Sociology/Cahiers Canadiens de Sociologie*, 26: 89–115.

Rawls, J. (1971) *A Theory of Justice*, Cambridge, MA: Harvard University Press.

Raz, J. (1985) 'Authority and justification', *Philosophy and Public Affairs*, 14(1): 3–29.

Sallaz, J.J., and Zavisca, J. (2007) 'Bourdieu in American sociology, 1980–2004', *Annual Review of Sociology*, 33: 21–41.

Schlachter, K.M. (1999) 'Repeal of the federal estate and gift tax: Will it happen and how will it affect our progressive tax system', *Virginia Tax Review*, 19: 781–824.

Stark, W. (ed.) (1952), *Jeremy Bentham's Economic Writings*, New York: B. Franklin.

Swartz, D.L. (1996) 'Bridging the study of culture and religion: Pierre Bourdieu's political economy of symbolic power', *Sociology of Religion*, 57(1): 71–85.

Swartz, D.L. (2003) 'From critical sociology to public intellectual: Pierre Bourdieu and politics', *Theory and Society*, 32(5): 791–823.

Swartz, D.L. and Zolberg, V.L. (2004) *After Bourdieu: Influence, Critique, Elaboration*, Norwell, MA: Kluwer.

Swedberg, R. (2003) 'The case for an economic sociology of law', *Theory and Society*, 32: 1–37.

Tiley, J. (2003) 'Euthanasia for death duties: Putting inheritance tax out of its misery, Barry Bracewell-Milnes', *British Tax Review*, 3: 255.

Tomes, N. (1981) 'The family, inheritance, and the intergenerational transmission of inequality', *Journal of Political Economy*, 89(5): 928–958.

Ventry, D.J. (2000) *Straight Talk About the 'Death' Tax: Politics, Economics, and Morality*, Available http://papers.ssrn.com/sol3/papers.cfm?abstract_id=251723.

Warren, T (2006) 'Moving beyond the gender wealth gap: On gender, class, ethnicity, and wealth inequalities in the United Kingdom', *Feminist Economics*, 12: 195–219.

12 From trustees to wealth managers

Brooke Harrington

Introduction

This chapter will address the question: why did trusteeship become a profession in its own right after centuries as a voluntary undertaking? The question ties into the core themes of this volume because trustees are central actors in the intergenerational transmission of wealth, and as a result, shape patterns of inequality (Harrington, forthcoming). Trustees – now more often known as wealth managers – create and oversee the structures that allow families to remain wealthy over multiple generations.

At present, the trustee is almost always a paid professional, but that is a relatively recent development. Throughout most of the history of trusts – that is to say, over centuries stretching back to the Middle Ages (Langbein, 1995) – family wealth has been entrusted to the care of unpaid friends and relatives. The legal recognition of this work as a distinct profession only began in the nineteenth century, and progressed so slowly that the group did not found a professional society until 1991.[1] Since then, there has been quick growth in the field, not just in the common law countries that recognize trusts, but worldwide: the professional association, known as the Society for Trust and Estate Practitioners (STEP), now represents over 17,500 members in 81 countries. How and why this change occurred will be the subject of this chapter.

In tracing the history of the profession, my argument will point out continuities between medieval and modern practice. This is not an original observation: Beckert (this volume) raises similar points in his 'Are We Still Modern?', and Haseler addresses the connection explicitly, arguing that the worldwide acceleration of wealth inequality 'is taking us back in time, back to the values and society of the feudal world' (2000: 72). However, this chapter contributes to the larger discussion by highlighting some sources of agency in the process: professional trustees, also known as wealth managers.

I will argue that not only are trusts themselves a holdover from the medieval period, but that the practices and norms that define the work of contemporary trustees remain closely tied to chivalric custom: an aristocratic code based on service, loyalty and honour, with the purpose of defending large concentrations of wealth and power from attack by outsiders. In the past, those large fortunes consisted primarily of land, and were defended by force of arms. Today, the fortunes are financial, and the 'income defense providers' (Winters, 2011: 219) use legal and organizational strategies as their weapons of choice. But the objectives and results of this activity have remained remarkably consistent: the maintenance of a highly-stratified social structure through the preservation of large private accumulations of wealth.

This historical continuity stems from the fact that trusts have themselves remained unchanged in important respects for seven centuries. Trusts emerged first in England as a means of avoiding the inheritance restrictions and taxes that were triggered by the death of a landowner. Wealthy individuals sought to preserve their estates by transferring title during their lifetime to a trusted relative or friend. The 'settlors' – so called because they had 'settled' land upon a trustee – continued to enjoy the use of their property as before the transfer. The real benefits of this arrangement did not become apparent until after a settlor's death. For one thing, there would be no tax due, because the legal owner of the land – the trustee – was still alive. More importantly, as a living landowner, the trustee could transfer title to a settlor's younger sons, or continue to hold the property in trust for a settlor's widow, daughters or minor sons, who would otherwise be dispossessed, since they could not inherit or own land in their own right. Thus, for private purposes (and now even in some commercial uses) trusts are 'essentially a gift, projected on the plane of time and so subjected to a management regime' (Rudden, 1981: 610). During the feudal period, when wills were not recognized as a valid means of transferring private property, trustees played an indispensable role in inheritance practices. Perhaps surprisingly, this remains true up to the present day, for reasons that will be discussed in greater detail below.

What *has* changed, radically, since the Middle Ages is the kind of assets trusts contain. And this, in turn, has driven significant changes in the nature of the 'management regime.' The trustee's original duties were quite simple: to hold (and possibly transfer) legal title to a piece of property. But as the impact of industrial capitalism changed the composition of wealth in the nineteenth century, a passive role for trustees was no longer tenable; when it came to managing financial wealth, they were obliged to take an active role. Thus, as trusts

> ceased to be a conveyancing device for land and became instead a device for holding a portfolio of financial assets. ... The transformation in the nature of wealth that led to the management trust brought about a parallel transformation in trusteeship.
>
> (Langbein, 2004: 53)

The development of trusteeship from a private, voluntary, amateur undertaking into a profession engaged with the public represents a point of inflection where the secretive world of wealthy families meets the workaday world of the professions. Analysing this process sheds light not only on professionalization, but also on socio-economic inequality.

The process occurred in two main phases. First, as wealth became more fungible, trusteeship changed from a passive activity – holding title to a piece of land – to one of active financial management. This development was made possible by legislative changes that acknowledged trustees as a 'putative professional class' (Marcus and Hall, 1992: 64), allowing them to be compensated for their work and to exercise increasingly wide discretion in the investment of trust assets. The second phase, which is still underway, has been characterized by collective action on the part of these professionals, including institution-building – such as the formation of STEP, and of university degree programs in wealth management – as well as lobbying to define and protect their jurisdictional boundaries (Freidson, 2001). These stages will be described in greater detail in the latter half of this chapter.

The trustee as kinsman and volunteer

The concept of exchanging land for service was not particular to trusts. In fact, the practice – known as *enfeoffment* – was common in feudal societies worldwide, from Europe to Central and East Asia (Yongjia, 2011; Barendse, 2003). The unique aspect of Anglo-Saxon practice was in allowing two modes of possession to apply to a single property simultaneously, distinguishing legal from beneficial ownership. This makes the trust 'the most distinctive achievement' of Anglo-American law (Maitland, 2011 [1909]: 23).

The central constitutive act of becoming a trustee was not the property transfer, but the pledge itself: the promise to own land without appropriating it for one's own benefit, and to honour the wishes of the settlor after his death. This practice was derived from the ceremonies of vassalage, in which a knight pledged loyal service to a lord in exchange for protection. Originally, there was no property involved in these vassalage ceremonies, but only a proffer of oaths, often made in the presence of sacred objects such as saintly relics, which made promises permanent, irrevocable and secured by divine authority (Cervone, 2011).[2] Despite the absence of written contracts (which were often distrusted in any case – see Gurevich, 1977) spoken promises were sufficient to enact a trust. Indeed, as Barendse (2003) observes, they were sufficient to uphold the social structure itself: 'The act of entrusting oneself was thus critical to feudalism' (2003: 515).

Becoming a trustee of land, then, was one of several 'performative utterances' (Austin, 1961) through which medieval life was enacted – another example being the quintessential feudal speech act, 'I dub thee knight' (Beale, 2009). As we know from the work of MacKenzie *et al.* (2007), these speech performances remain vitally important in constituting present-day capitalist societies. Austin himself pointed to inheritance as one of the most significant occurrences of the phenomenon in contemporary practice. Among the very first instances he offers to define a speech act is: 'I give and bequeath my watch to my brother' (Austin, 1961: 5).

For the original trustees of the Middle Ages, land could *only* be put into trust by means of performative utterances because the law did not recognize the arrangement as a binding contract. Until the development of chancery courts in the fourteenth century, there was no way to enforce such pledges legally (Friedman, 2009). As far as the medieval common law was concerned, whoever held the title owned the land and could use it as he wished. Complaints against 'faithless feoffees' – trustees who broke their pledge and appropriated land entrusted to them for their own use – are recorded as early as 1390 (Langbein, 1995). But a betrayed trust beneficiary could do no more than lodge a complaint and hope that the Lord Chancellor (who governed the Chancery Courts) would provide justice. Beyond that, anyone who put a property into trust 'had to depend on literal trust and community opinion to ensure that the trustees discharged their duties' (Marcus, 1983: 231).

Remarkably, this honour system worked well enough to preserve many great fortunes in England, America and other common law countries[3] until well into the nineteenth century. The work of trusteeship was undertaken almost as an act of class solidarity against laws that threatened to dissipate dynastic wealth through onerous tax burdens (known as 'feudal incidents') and the dispossession of all but eldest males in a family through enforced primogeniture – a catastrophe for landowners without sons, as dramatized in the novels of Jane Austen (notably *Pride and Prejudice* [1813] and *Persuasion* [1818]). Solidarity among the Anglo-Saxon elites meant that trustees were often 'friends and relatives of the same social class' as the settlor and beneficiaries (Stebbings, 2007: 3). Thus, even into the twentieth century, '[a]lmost every well-to-do-man was a trustee' (Maitland, 1936: 175). Elite solidarity, honour and oaths figured as prominently under capitalism as they did among feudal landholders.

The effect, then as now, was to assert the rights – particularly the heritable property rights – of elites against governing authorities. In medieval England, knights were instrumental in creating a society in which aristocrats appropriated nearly all the wealth and 'became more powerful than any central institution' (Barendse, 2003: 511). They protected the interests of landed elites at a time when one's position in the social structure was dependent upon property ownership. This is how the term 'estate' – which first appeared in English in 1230, with the meaning of condition or standing in the world – came by 1439 to mean property and possessions.[4] During the same period, trustees helped their peers and fellow landowners deprive the Crown both of taxes and of its jurisdiction over land, which had formerly been absolute (Waugh, 1986). As one authority on the history of trusts put it, 'Trustees of old were unpaid amateurs, that is, family and community statesmen who lent their names and their honour to a conveyancing[5] dodge' (Langbein, 1995: 638). Contemporary trustees, as I argue elsewhere, stand in much the same relation to the present-day distribution of financial wealth: preserving the concentration of assets and the socio-economic status of an elite seeking to assert their autonomy from governance institutions (Harrington, forthcoming a). But now, the governance institutions include the bureaucratic nation-state and trans-national bodies such as the Organisation for Economic Co-operation and Development (OECD), which has attempted to curtail elites' use of tax havens to evade taxation, inheritance rules, and other laws (Sharman, 2006).[6]

However, I would argue that the effectiveness of honour and oaths in permitting trusteeship to endure as a voluntary undertaking suggests that there is more at stake here than a 'conveyancing dodge'. This is not to downplay the materialist aspects of the role and its significant impact on wealth inequality (see Harrington, forthcoming a). Rather, I argue that the specific practices and norms that govern trustees are the products of medieval mores and culture. Ultimately, the ideal and the material aspects of their work are inextricable and mutually reinforcing, as has been observed of other feudal relationships: 'The idea of feudal service was therefore *inseparable from that of spending and the distribution of wealth*: it was impossible otherwise to conceive of friendship and loyalty between knights' (Gurevich, 1977: 19, emphasis added).

The many obvious differences between the two eras make it easy to overlook some important similarities in the socio-economic roles of knights and trustees. Although trusteeship is now a paid profession in the main, the essential normative demands of honour, selfless service, prudence and loyalty – however often they may be violated in practice – remain unchanged in many respects from their origins in the relations among feudal nobles. Pledges and elite solidarity are still critical to the functioning of the socio-economic system (for a discussion of this in contemporary financial markets, see Greenspan 1999). Just as the structure of feudal society and the distribution of wealth was held together by 'a web of oaths' (Barendse 2003: 515), observers of modern capitalism have noted that 'Wealth, in a commercial age, is made up largely of promises' (Pound, 1922: 236) – promises made and kept by the professional class of wealth managers. Formerly, the standards of conduct for these actors were enshrined in ceremonies or in texts such as *Le Chanson de Roland* and the *Canterbury Tales*; now, they are written into statutes and codes of professional ethics.[7]

Consider, for example, the case of fiduciary laws, which – along with powers legislation – represent the two general rules governing trustee activity. Whereas powers legislation defines what trustees have the power to *do* (invest, vote securities, operate a business, litigate, employ agents, and so forth) fiduciary laws regulate *how* they do it: that is, they set behavioural standards. 'Fiduciary' is a general term describing a relationship that exists not only between trustees and beneficiaries, but also between attorneys and clients, as well as corporate officers and shareholders. In the language of principal-agent theory, such relationships are 'characterized by unusually high costs of specification and monitoring. The duty of loyalty replaces detailed contractual terms' (Easterbrook and Fischel, 1993: 426–7).

For trustees, the basic standards of fiduciary duty are loyalty and care, and their purpose is to set conditions on the exercise of the trustee's powers (Langbein, 1995). In this context, loyalty means putting the best interests of the beneficiaries first in all decisions, avoiding self-dealing or conflicts of interest (Fuller, 2005). Until legal changes in the Victorian era, the ban on self-dealing meant that trustees could not be paid for their work except in the rare instances where compensation was stipulated by the settlor and written into the trust instrument. As a late eighteenth-century treatise explained, 'The courts of equity look upon trusts as *honorary*, and as a burden upon the *honor* and *conscience* of the person intrusted [the trustee], and not [to be] undertaken upon mercenary motives' (Sanders, 1791: 194; emphasis and spelling in original). This created a formidable, and intentional, barrier to professionalization.

The duty of care, formalized in statutes such as the Uniform Prudent Investor Act in the United States, requires trustees to act with 'reasonable care, skill and caution' and to 'manage trust assets as a prudent investor would' (American Bar Association, 1994: 5).[8] The standards are intentionally broad and open to interpretation, precisely because of the risk and uncertainty involved in trust administration. Included here are not only the risks of losses from investments, but the unknowns that arise over the long time frames attendant upon multi-generational property transfers. These are certainly not equivalent to the risks and uncertainties that medieval knights faced in defending the property of their feudal lords, but the analogies between the two conditions mean that in both cases, terms of service cannot be specified beyond a general code of conduct.[9]

Perhaps the most famous statement of the code was provided in 1928 by Justice Benjamin Cardozo, then serving on the highest court of the state of New York. Cardozo, who was later elevated to the Supreme Court of the United States, wrote for the majority in *Meinhard v. Salmon*,

> A trustee is held to something stricter than the morals of the market place. Not honesty alone, but the punctilio of an honor the most sensitive, is then the standard of behavior ... the level of conduct for fiduciaries [has] been kept at a level higher than that trodden by the crowd.

These are precisely terms that characterize medieval knights: punctilio (a regard for formalities and etiquette); honour; honesty; and a sense of being above the crowd, bound to a duty 'stricter than the morals of the marketplace'. In fact, it reads like a contemporary description of the pilgrim knight in Chaucer's *Canterbury Tales*, who 'loved chivalry, truth, honour ... and all courtesy' (1994[1478]: 2).

The medieval becomes modern

But these historical continuities also raise the question: why did an adaptation to feudal conditions survive the Middle Ages? That is, once feudal taxes and inheritance restrictions were lifted, what need did landed elites have for trusts and trustees? By the end of the seventeenth century, land could be 'devised by will', meaning that it was legally valid to transfer real property (not just money or goods) to one's heirs through a testamentary document (Langbein, 1995: 638). Furthermore, the development of offshore financial centres in the twentieth century has made it possible for corporations based in places like the Caribbean to offer most of the tax shelter functions once provided by trusts. These two factors would seem to make the practice of putting assets into trust as obsolete as the broadsword in an age of automatic weapons.

Yet trusts remain a popular tool for wealth management – seemingly more popular than ever before. Because trusts conceal the amount and ownership of assets (Chester, 1982), the precise number of trusts and the value they contain is unknown; unlike corporations, their existence is not a matter of public record (Sharman, 2006). However, we do know that trusts are considered a mainstay – even a necessity – of financial planning for wealthy families and individuals (Collier, 2002; Hughes, 1997). And their use appears to be growing, possibly connected to the steep increase in the fortunes of the world's wealthiest people, even after the 2008 financial crash (Cap-Gemini, 2011; Davies *et al.*, 2008). For example, since 2009, the number of billionaires in Russia and the Ukraine has tripled; during that period, trusts linked to those individuals and their families have purchased over $1 billion in American real estate, including some of the most expensive residential properties ever sold (Barrionuevo, 2012). Of the $84 billion in capital flight from Russia in 2011 – driven, apparently, by fear of asset seizure by the government – much has gone into trusts that purchase not only US real estate, but also yachts, art collections and other valuables, all made impervious to confiscation by situating legal ownership with the trustee in a jurisdiction whose laws are aligned with the beneficial owner's objectives.

In the event that trust structures are exposed to public scrutiny, as happens in some court cases, their number and complexity are often staggering. For example, a 2002 lawsuit revealed that the $15 billion fortune of Chicago's Pritzker family was held in 2,500 different trusts, as well as 60 companies (Jaffe and Lane, 2004). More recently, documents related to tax evasion charges filed by the US Securities and Exchange Commission against the billionaire Wyly brothers of Dallas revealed that they held at least $750 million of their fortune in 'an elaborate sham system of trusts and companies' based in the Isle of Man and the Cayman Islands (Wyatt, 2010: B1). These structures allowed the Wylys to control their companies without paying the taxes associated with legal ownership; in addition, they enjoyed the beneficial use of mountain ranches in Colorado, as well as a multi-million dollar collection of art, jewellery and antiques all legally owned by the trusts – again, avoiding millions in taxes.

These cases point up another puzzle of the longevity of trusts: why haven't corporations supplanted them as asset-holding structures? Clearly, wealthy people like the Pritzkers and the Wylys *do* use corporations to some extent, but the evidence suggests that they and other families continue to rely heavily on trusts to contain their fortunes. Moreover, rather than corporations replacing trusts, firms have taken to using trusts themselves. In fact, Langbein (1997) estimates that commercial trusts now outnumber personal trusts by a factor of nine to one. As he writes elsewhere,

> Although feudal law no longer needs evading, the trust has endured because it has changed function. The trust has ceased to be a conveyancing device for holding freehold land and has become instead a management device for holding financial assets.
>
> (1995: 637)

The advantages of the trust structure are compelling enough that trusts are now the central organizational tool underlying pension funds, mutual funds, bond issues, and even regulatory compliance, such as the resource pools created to pay for decommissioning nuclear plants.

What are these advantages? One or more of the following considerations usually come into play:

1   *Taxation*. In some cases, trusts remain a more effective way to avoid taxes – both for individuals and corporations – than alternative structures. In most onshore jurisdictions, assets held in corporations are subject to two rounds of taxation. The first is corporate tax, which the firm pays. The second round, known as capital gains tax, is triggered when an individual takes profits from the corporation, for example by selling stock. In many jurisdictions, trusts are not taxed as entities, so their assets are subject to taxation only when a beneficiary receives a distribution.[10]

2   *Privacy*. In most onshore jurisdictions, corporations must be registered publicly, and are subject to regulations – such as the requirement to audit accounts – which increase administrative costs (cutting into profits) and expose the firm to scrutiny from outsiders. Trusts are not subject to these rules. This reduces management costs compared to corporations, increases their value as a tax avoidance mechanism (assets that are not visible to regulators are difficult to tax), and affords a measure of political protection. For wealthy people who live in unstable countries, holding assets in trust can reduce their visibility as targets of extortion and kidnapping attempts. For businesses, trusts 'obscure concentrations of economic power, which arouse alarm, suspicion and public odium' (Gadhoum *et al.*, 2005: 342).

3   *Inheritance*. Once it became legal in the late seventeenth century to transfer property by testament (Langbein, 2004), there was still the problem that women could not own property in their own name; this left widows and unmarried daughters of landowners in danger of losing their homes and livelihoods if the male head of a family died. Thus, some of the restrictions that gave rise to trusts in the first place remained significant for elites. As an eminent scholar of the common law wrote, 'And now we come to the origin of the Trust ... the Englishman would like to leave his land by will. He would like to provide for his daughters and younger sons. That is the root of the matter' (Maitland, 1936: 157). In addition, some landowners were concerned for their married daughters, whose assets became property of their husbands; to protect a married woman financially, her father might put her share of the family fortune into trust, making it untouchable by a spendthrift husband or his creditors (Sanders, 1791). Trusts are still used as a workaround by citizens of countries that do not permit women equal inheritance rights with men, or which mandate forced heirship, such as the German *Pflichtteil* (Beckert, 2007). Finally, the twenty-first-century prevalence of long-term cohabitation, same-sex partnerships and multiple marriages (which may each produce children and step-children), have given trusts increasing

importance in bridging the gap between law and practice. Trusts can be used to secure the inheritance rights of unmarried partners who might otherwise receive nothing, as well as to sort out the claims of children from multiple relationships (Walker, 2008).[11]

Thus, even despite the rise of corporations and the legalization of property transfers by will, neither trusts nor trusteeship died out. In essence, the trust structure proved extremely flexible as a tool for contending with changes in the nature of capitalism itself. As wealth became more fungible, with property increasingly superseded by financial assets, trusts provided elites with a means of control that was not easily duplicated through contracting or incorporation. But trusts require trustees, and it is to the changes demanded of them that we shall turn now.

Stage one: from voluntarism to professionalization

During the nineteenth century, processes that had been underway in economic history since the Age of Exploration produced great merchant fortunes in Europe and North America. The basis of wealth shifted decisively from land to capital – a more fungible source of wealth requiring a different kind of attention and maintenance than landed estates. In England, the nineteenth century saw the repeal of the Bubble Act, allowing corporations – and corporate investment – to flourish as never before. Suddenly, trustees had tremendous amounts of cash to manage, and hundreds of joint stock companies in which to invest. Yet they did not have the right to buy those securities unless specifically authorized to do so by the trust instrument. Most trust instruments, in the interests of protecting beneficiaries from 'faithless feoffees,' gave no such powers, leaving the trustee to act simply as a passive title holder for real estate.

A major step forward in the professionalization process occurred when the courts stepped in to expand trustees' powers of investment. In the UK, where trust law originated, this did not occur until the Trustee Investment Act of 1889, which allowed trustees to invest in English land or government bonds, even if the trust instrument did not confer powers of investment. As investment opportunities expanded, trustees were offered options sanctioned by the courts and the legislature for putting trust capital to work. These so-called 'legal lists' remained limited to local real estate and government bonds. The limitations did not cause as much consternation as might be supposed, since the failure of the South Sea Company in 1720 (Harrington, 2012) continued to cast a long pall over trust finances, such that 'Trust practitioners argued that it was imprudent for a trustee to invest trust funds in equities on the stock market, even if he had power to do so' (Parkinson and Jones, 2008: 111). Thus, when granted the express power to invest in stocks later in the nineteenth century and early in the twentieth century, trustees frequently played it safe by eschewing stocks on the 'legal lists' in favour of the old standbys: land and bonds. It took more than a century – until the Trustee Act of 2000 – before the UK courts awarded trustees full discretion to invest in equities, as if they were the beneficial owners of the assets (Parkinson and Jones, 2008).

These limitations on the autonomy of trustees were matched by the requirement of full personal liability for any losses to the wealth held in trust. That is, a trustee was required by law to repay from his own personal assets any loss in the value of the trust caused by his actions and decisions – even if the loss was incurred by accident and in good faith (Stebbings, 2007). The risk of personal bankruptcy kept many trustees from investing in stocks, particularly since the courts maintained that trustees should neither be paid nor delegate any decision-making to specialists, such as accountants. In sociological terms, the role of the trustee was governed by the logic of the gift rather than the logic of compensation (Zelizer, 1996). Indeed, because trusts originate legally in the concept of the gift (see Rudden, 1981), the ordinary requirements of 'consideration' (i.e. payment) to establish a contract did not apply (Langbein, 1997). Trustees were thus 'economically celibate' (Hall, 1973: 282), barred from earning a fee for their efforts on behalf of settlors and beneficiaries. This, combined with the burdens of full liability and limited investment discretion, helped maintain the 'the whole tradition of the trust as a personal relationship' (Stebbings, 2007: 7), grounded in moral obligation and voluntarism, as opposed to professional service.

The process of acknowledging professional characteristics in the role of the trustee – specifically, autonomy and expertise (Freidson, 2001) – began almost 60 years earlier in the US, when the Supreme Court of Massachusetts established the 'prudent man rule' in the *Harvard College* v. *Amory* decision of 1830. On the one hand, the rule simply codified the heretofore informal practices of elite solidarity, since 'prudence' was defined by the courts in terms of the behaviour of 'businessmen from the upper circles of Boston society' (Friedman, 2009: 115). But the decision also represented a substantive and historical advance in the professionalization process. By acknowledging that trustees could exercise some independence and expert judgement in deploying trust assets, the Massachusetts courts provided an essential element in the constitution of all professions: recognition by the state (Macdonald, 1995).

The timing and location of this first public acknowledgement of trustees as an emergent professional group was not coincidental: the American northeast, unlike Great Britain and continental Europe, had no history of land being tied up for generations in the hands of hereditary nobility or by plantation farming. Instead, the region grew wealthy through whaling, as well as through the global trade in textiles, rum and slaves. These businesses generated a huge profit, and with it, the need for advice on the disposition of cash reserves greater than most families could spend in a generation.

In other words, the profession of trust and estate planning emerged concurrently with the transformation of capitalism itself. In some respects, the trustees employed by nineteenth century Brahmin families had the same goals and motives as their medieval counterparts – notably, the maintenance of class solidarity. Not only were trustees generally men of the same rank as the families they served, but they were instrumental in creating a network of self-reinforcing elite institutions:

> As managers of private capital, they served a critical role as mediators who funneled the wealth of private fortunes into key Boston financial institutions. ... The professional trustee – private or corporate – completes the institutional integration of a stable capitalist class.
>
> (Marcus and Hall, 1992: 65)

Despite this continuity of aims, however, trustees faced significant new demands under industrial capitalism. As wealth took on new forms, moving from material property to merchant capital, the need for expert assistance in managing wealth increased as well. The job required time and expertise far beyond those demanded of the traditional, unpaid trustee of real property. Thus, as the remnants of the old feudal economic system gave way to a new mode of creating wealth, trusteeship became a very different kind of job. After centuries of stability, major transformations occurred within a few decades:

> the typical trustee at the end of the Victorian period was quite different from that at the beginning of the reign. He had become the manager of a fund, of a portfolio of investments, rather than the guardian of a family's landed estate. ... It was a skilled occupation undertaken for profit.
>
> (Stebbings, 2007: 4)

The mobility of present-day wealth means that assets belonging to a single cluster of related individuals may be spread all over the world, subject to multiple regimes of taxation, inheritance rules and other regulations. In this context, the wealth manager's job becomes finding the optimal mix of organizational structures, legal strategies and financial planning to meet the client's needs. Those needs may involve intergenerational transfers or tax reduction, but are often much broader than that, encompassing the long-term (as in dynastic trusts designed to endure far beyond the settlors lifetime), as well as issues of culture and religion – particularly important matters for those living on the Arab peninsula, who are not taxed, but who are instead subject to the restrictions of Shari'a law on investment and on the rights of women (Nasr, 2009).

Thus, the job of the trustee has been transformed by the increasing complexity of elites' investments, tax sheltering strategies and organizational structures for holding assets (Beaverstock *et al.*, 2004). Over the past 20 years – coincident with the creation of STEP – the business of hiding wealth from tax and other regulatory authorities has become 'multifaceted and global in its operation' (Winters, 2011: 219). Over the same period, there has been a dramatic increase in coordination among disparate industries offering products and services designed to help the wealthy stay that way, including banks, law firms, accounting agencies and insurance providers, as well as numerous boutique firms and individual practitioners (US Senate, 2003).

This global expansion and coordination demands a new kind of professional expertise, as 'transnational' and 'hypermobile' (Bauman, 2000; Sklair, 1997) in its orientation as the capital and clientele it serves. If, as Marcus and Hall write, the trustee is 'the concrete human incarnation of this abstract functioning of law and money' (1992: 70), it was perhaps inevitable that the internationalization of capital would drive professional transformation (Fourcade, 2006). If the trustee was the creation of the nation-state – a consequence of the trust laws designed to protect and perpetuate elites (Marcus and Hall, 1992) – then wealth management is the product of the supra-national space created and inhabited by the world's wealthiest families.

Stage two: from trustees to wealth managers

While the initial phase of professionalization was driven by lawyers – who still make up more than half of STEP's current membership – it later received a significant assist from accountants, who constitute about 20 per cent of the professional society's members. Indeed, the first step toward collective action as a profession was taken by Liverpool accountant George Tasker. Despite the increasing professional recognition trustees enjoyed in the nineteenth and twentieth centuries, most practitioners were isolated from one another, and their work was seen as one of the 'havens for age and obscurity' in the financial sector (STEP, 2006: 1). Tasker decried this state of affairs in a November 1990 letter to the editor of *Trusts & Estates* magazine – at the time, the only publication linking the diverse group of professionals engaged in wealth structuring and management. His letter drew hundreds of responses, with many suggesting that readers meet to share experiences and best practices. In early 1991, 82 practitioners attended the inaugural meeting of the Society for Trust and Estate Professionals in central London. One year later, STEP enrolled its 1,000th member.

From these initial steps have sprung a host of other institution-building activities and political activism, both behalf of the profession and for its wealthy clients. For example, STEP is active in lobbying and legislation, and has been working with UK lawmakers to shut down amateur – or 'cowboy' – will writers by restricting the trade to professionals, such as STEP members (Devine, 2011). The Society is also very active in offshore jurisdictions, where members regularly cooperate with elected officials to draft financial laws (Palan *et al.*, 2010). On the global front, STEP has been a key player in the struggle tax havens have waged against blacklisting by the OECD; the Society's members crafted some of the rhetoric that won the battle of words, forcing a retreat on the part of the OECD, which had proposed sanctions against some jurisdictions (Sharman, 2006).

As STEP's membership has grown, the organization has also been increasingly active in establishing its boundaries as a knowledge system. Because most of those who practice trust and estate planning are also members of other professions, STEP has developed the TEP certification – short for Trust and Estate

Practitioner – to designate those specializing in services to wealthy clients. This has become the de facto standard credential in the profession, recognized worldwide, much like the CPA for accountants (Harrington, forthcoming).[12] The TEP also serves symbolically to unite a global profession (Fourcade, 2006): a necessity given the wide range of backgrounds among STEP's 17,500 members, spread across 81 countries. The credential is earned through a series of five week-long seminars, which are as much a socialization process as a knowledge-delivery system.

The ties between the profession and higher education are still developing. While professional knowledge is distinctively 'centered in and allied with the modern university' (Larson, 1977: 50), formal degree programs in trust and estate planning have only been established recently. Law schools, of course, have offered specialized courses on trust law for decades. But it was not until the Autumn of 2011 that a university offered a degree devoted to the subject. The University of Manchester, in cooperation with STEP, will confer the first BSc degrees in Management of Trusts and Estates in the Spring of 2013, representing another milestone in the professionalization process.

Since the boundaries around professional identity are still being established, the names used to define the profession are also in flux. Some, like the founders of STEP, emphasize their historical roots by calling themselves 'Trust and Estate Practitioners,' thereby associating themselves with the feudal traditions of trusts and estates. Yet contemporary practice for STEP members often involves not only trusteeship but oversight of family businesses, coordination of many different types of income-generating assets around the world, and the ever-important consideration of the tax consequences attendant upon ownership and trading. As a result, one practitioner put it, the job requires one to be: 'part lawyer, part tax adviser, part accountant and part investment adviser rolled into one' (Parkinson and Jones, 2008: 20; see also Langbein, 1995, 2004).

Thus, members of the emergent profession sometimes refer to themselves as 'tax planners', 'private bankers', 'family office managers', or 'wealth preservation specialists'. In many cases, the job combines features of all those terms, including tax planning, private banking, family office services (coordination and distribution), and long-term preservation. In the few scholarly references to the emergent profession, some use the term 'transaction planners' (Langbein, 1995: 630), while others prefer the more politically pointed 'income defence providers' (Winters, 2011: 219). However, consensus seems to be developing around the term 'wealth managers' (for example, Del Col *et al.*, 2003), even among many STEP members (for example, Pexton, 2010).

A much-discussed article in the *STEP Journal* stated the case for the new nomenclature, beginning with a definition of wealth management as comprising: 'the whole spectrum of the client's assets and other financial affairs. Wealth management is seen as the overarching role pulling together the advice of various investment, tax, and other experts into a coherent plan' (Sternberg and Maslinski, 2008: 29). The article then alludes to the considerable overlap in terminology within financial services, and the larger struggle for legitimacy (and profits) among the banks, trust companies and individual practitioners competing for the business of wealthy clients. In a pointed jurisdictional claim (Abbott, 1988), Sternberg and Maslinski write:

> It is perhaps debatable whether private bankers and other so-called wealth managers are actually better equipped to deliver this service – the term 'wealth management' sits more comfortably with the remit of the traditional responsibilities of a trustee.
>
> (2008: 29)

With the erosion of client confidentiality in many of the world's historic wealth management centres – such as Switzerland and Liechtenstein – wealth management may itself give way to another, more up-to-date term. While trusts are expected to remain in widespread use, they may be applied to new ends, as they have been in the past. As tax avoidance becomes more difficult to accomplish within the bounds of the law, trusts may be used to move wealth around the world for other purposes, such as coordinating payments to and from large international work projects involving expatriate staff from many different countries of origin – a task of surprising complexity, given the patchwork of banking and tax laws globally. Another potential future for the profession is expansion into the management of elites' social capital, protecting reputations and 'good names' as part of a family legacy, in addition to financial wealth; this has led to speculation that the title 'trusted adviser' will supplant that of wealth manager (McKenzie, 2010). Finally, wealth managers will likely play a leading role in one of the fastest-growing areas in the financial industry: Islamic finance, which requires practitioners to blend the intricacies of Shari'a law with those of modern Western finance. In this case, the goals are not tax-related but rather geared to the avoidance of religious improprieties, such as lending or borrowing money at interest, or interactions between women and men who are not related to each other; the latter constraint opens up a significant market for female wealth managers in the Islamic world (Nasr, 2009; Maurer, 2005).

Conclusion

As the essays in this volume illustrate, inheritance of wealth poses a major challenge to post-Enlightenment ideals of justice and meritocratic achievement. In the *Communist Manifesto*, 'abolition of the right of inheritance' ranks third on Marx and Engels' list of the ten most important steps necessary to realize 'the forcible overthrow of the whole extant social order' (1978[1848]: 499).[13] This high ranking is a measure of the significance of inherited wealth in sustaining and reproducing the socio-economic order of capitalism. It also suggests why resistance to change in the right of inheritance has been so robust. Despite the many changes capitalism has undergone since publication of the *Manifesto* in 1848 – co-opting much of Marx and Engels' social programme, including the creation of a graduated income tax, child labour laws and free public education – the right of inheritance retains an almost unique position as a vestige of the Middle Ages in the modern era.

This chapter has focused on the professionals who enact and embody these medieval traditions. Known first as trustees, and now by a variety of other names reflecting their new responsibilities, they have much in common with the feudal knights whose code of chivalric service and loyalty became the basis for the fiduciary role essential to trusts. The historical continuities also include the similar impact of knights and trustees on maintaining elite solidarity and socio-economic inequality. Both sets of actors have been instrumental in enabling wealthy families to maintain and transmit their fortunes intergenerationally, without submitting to taxation or other regulatory restrictions.

Trusts remain indispensable as devices for managing inheritance and main-taining the autonomy of private fortunes; but they are now part of a much larger portfolio of undertakings that require coordination across multiple domains. Rather than making the job of the trustee obsolete, these changing conditions in the economic and legal environment have led to professionalization of a role for-merly occupied by amateurs and unpaid volunteers. In response to the increasing complexity of the world's largest private fortunes, trustees have moved from what was once a tightly constrained role with no reliance on outside experts per-mitted, to a much broader set of responsibilities commonly known as wealth management, which requires oversight of many different structures and types of wealth, along with coordination of other professionals' contributions into a cohe-sive global strategy. The formerly passive work of the trustee has evolved into a form of relational contracting whose aims are long-term, complex and carry unforeseen consequences.

The change might more properly be called a 'revolution' (Langbein, 1995: 644), since it paralleled developments in capitalism itself, such as the trans-formation of wealth from real property to financial assets, and the 'emancipa-tion' of trustees and corporations from legal restrictions. At the beginning of the nineteenth century, both trustees and corporations were held in close check by the courts and legislatures. Modern capitalism only came into being when law-makers granted 'corporations legal powers almost coextensive with those of natural persons … to engage in any lawful line or lines of business' (Clark, 1986: 676). Trustees, who received legal recognition as a profession at about the same time, were instrumental in financing these firms – establishing a capital circuit between elites' private and corporate wealth (Zelizer, 2005). If, as Zelizer theorizes, a circuit is a set of transactions occurring within and dependent upon a closely bounded set of social ties, contemporary wealth managers form a sort of human chain linking the themes central to this volume: inheritance, inequality and the contemporary economic system. But paradoxically, they also link us to a feudal past that is in many ways incompatible with the political and social ideals of the present. The difficulties of resolving this conflicted position are apparent in the profession's struggle to name and define itself – a process shadowed by the increasing public discourse on the injustice of escalating global inequality.

Acknowledgements

This work was supported by a grant from the European Research Council (#263741-PIPES), as well as a Fernand Braudel Fellowship from the European University Institute. The author would like to thank William Fuller, John Harper and Prof. John Langbein for their contributions to her understanding of trusts, trustees and taxation.

Notes

1 ACTEC, the American Council of Trust and Estate Counsel, was founded in 1949, but represents only lawyers in North America – both a professional and geographical subset of the trustee population; as of 2011, its membership base included just 2,600 individuals.

2 In reality, of course, such oaths were famously and repeatedly violated. One of the best known examples is depicted in the Bayeux Tapestry, which shows the English Earl Harold Godwinson swearing an oath on sacred relics to support William of Normandy's claim to succeed Edward the Confessor as King of England; Harold's violation of this oath by claiming the English Crown for himself is portrayed in the Tapestry as the catalyst for the Battle of Hastings (Terkla, 1995).

3 Trusts are not recognized by the civil law governing continental Europe, as well as much of South America and the Middle East; however, citizens of civil law countries can (and often do) establish trusts in common law jurisdictions.

4 'estate, n.' *OED Online*, March 2012, Oxford University Press, Avalaible www.oed. com/viewdictionaryentry/Entry/64556 (accessed 23 March 2012).

5 A legal term for the transfer of title to a property.

6 This struggle endured for centuries, long past the Middle Ages; in the sixteenth century, for example, Henry VIII proposed the Statute of Uses to put elites' landholdings back within absolute royal control, and thus within the Crown's revenue system. We are now witnessing a similar back-and-forth between international governing bodies and global socio-economic elites, in which ownership and taxation rights over primarily financial assets are at stake.

7 The medieval imprint continues to be visible in the language of trusts. For example, the notion of 'indenture' – an instrument used by a lord to retain the services of an aide (Waugh, 1986) – carries over into the present-day 'trust indenture'. See, the Trust Indenture Acts in US law, which govern commercial trusts containing bonds and other debt instruments.

8 Fiduciary administration of trusts is also governed by many subrules, including the duty to keep and render accounts, enforce and defend claims against trust assets, and to minimize costs (Langbein, 1997).

9 Despite their breadth, the rules remain meaningful and enforceable, as evidenced by the many successful lawsuits brought against trustees for breach of fiduciary duty; for several interesting cases, see Harper (2010).

10 In some countries, such as the United States, trusts can be taxed as entities, although they may still enjoy tax-favoured status compared to alternative structures (Patterson, 2005). Generally speaking, trusts are not taxed in the civil law countries. However, tax laws are changing rapidly, driven in part by nation-states' need for revenues following the 2008 global financial crisis and the ensuing European debt crisis. For example, France passed a law in 2011 taxing trusts benefiting French residents, or containing assets situated in France (Innocent, 2012).

11 This occurs even in countries that are otherwise among the most legally progressive. A recent and much-publicized case concerns the late Swedish author Stieg Larssen,

author of the best-selling Millennium trilogy. His partner of 32 years, Eva Gabriels-son, received nothing upon his death because Swedish law does not grant inheritance rights to unmarried partners. Instead, the multi-million dollar estate went to the only heirs recognized by the state: Larssen's father and brothers. Since Larssen's death in 2004, Gabrielsson and his family have been locked in increasingly costly and bitter litigation over the inheritance (McGrath, 2011).

12 While there are other accreditations available for wealth management, none are as widely held or as widely recognized as the TEP. This is in part because many of the other credentialing programs are offered by firms rather than professional societies, and are open only to those who already hold law or accounting degrees. Credentials that seek to cover similar intellectual territory as the TEP certificate include: the Accredited Wealth Management Adviser, offered by the College for Financial Planning; the Certified Estate and Trust Specialist, offered by the Institute of Business and Finance; and the Chartered Trust and Estate Planner, offered by the American Academy of Financial Management. More information on credentials available in wealth management can be found on the website of the US Financial Industry Regulatory Authority (FINRA): http://apps.finra.org/DataDirectory/1/prodesignations.aspx.

13 By the time of the Basle Congress of the First International in 1869, Marx had changed his mind, shifting his attention 'upstream' of inheritance rights to private property in general. Abolish private ownership, he argued, and the problem of inheritance 'would die of itself' (Cunliffe, 1990: 229).

References

Abbott, A. (1988) *The System of Professions: An Essay on the Division of Expert Labor*, Chicago: University of Chicago Press.

American Bar Association (1994) *Uniform Prudent Investor Act*, Chicago: ABA. Available www.law.upenn.edu/bll/archives/ulc/fnact99/1990s/upia94.pdf.

Austen, J. (1813) *Pride and Prejudice*, London: T. Edgerton.

Austen, J. (1818) *Persuasion*, London: John Murray.

Austin, J. (1961) 'Performative utterances', in *Philosophical Papers*, Oxford: Oxford University Press, pp. 233–252.

Barendse, R.J. (2003) 'The feudal mutation: Military and economic transformations of the ethnosphere in the tenth to thirteenth centuries', *Journal of World History*, 14: 503–529.

Barrionuevo, A. (2012) 'Time to sell penthouse. The Russians have cash', *New York Times*, 3 April, p. A1.

Bauman, Z. (2000) *Community: Seeking Security in an Insecure World*, Cambridge: Polity.

Beale, W. (2009) *Learning from Language: Symmetry, Asymmetry, and Literary Humanism*, Pittsburgh, PA: University of Pittsburgh Press.

Beaverstock, J., Hubbard, P. and Short, J. (2004) 'Getting away with it? Exposing the geographies of the super-rich', *Geoforum*, 35: 401–407.

Beckert, J. (2007) *Inherited Wealth*, Princeton, NJ: Princeton University Press.

Cap-Gemini (2011) *World Wealth Report*, Paris: Cap-Gemini, Available www.capgemini.com/insights-and-resources/by-publication/world-wealth-report-2011/?d=BCD137B0–8001–3261–87C2–98873EFF1DF0.

Cardozo, B. (1928) *Meinhard* v. *Salmon*, 164 N.E. 545 (N.Y. 1928), at 546.

Cervone, A. (2011) *Sworn Bond in Tudor England: Oaths, Vows and Covenants in Civil Life and Literature*, Jefferson, NC: McFarland & Company.

Chaucer, G. (1994 [1478]) *Canterbury Tales*, Mineola, NY: Dover.

Chester, R. (1982) *Inheritance, Wealth and Society*, Bloomington, IN: Indiana University Press.

Clark, R. (1986) *Corporate Law*, New York: Aspen Publishers.

Collier, C. (2002) *Wealth in Families*, Cambridge, MA: Harvard University Alumni Affairs and Development Communications.

Cunliffe, J. (1990) 'Intergenerational justice and productive resources: A nineteenth century socialist debate', *History of European Ideas*, 12: 227–238.

Davies, J., Sandström, S., Shorrocks, A. and Wolff, E. (2008) *The World Distribution of Household Wealth*, Helsinki: UNI-WIDER, World Institute for Development Economics Research, Discussion Paper 2008/03.

Del Col, M., Hogan, A. and Roughan, T. (2003) 'Transforming the wealth management industry', *Journal of Financial Transformation*, 9: 105–113.

Devine, S. (2011) *REVEALED: Incompetence and Dishonesty of Cowboy Will Writers*, London: STEP, Available www.step.org/news/press_releases/2011/revealed_incompetence_and_dis.aspx?link=rightLink.

Easterbrook, F. and Fischel, D. (1993) 'Contract and fiduciary duty', *Journal of Law and Economics*, 36: 425–438.

Fourcade, M. (2006) 'The construction of a global profession: The transnationalization of economics', *American Journal of Sociology*, 112: 145–194.

Freidson, E. (2001) *Professionalism: The Third Logic*. London: Polity.

Friedman, L. (2009) *Dead Hands: A Social History of Wills, Law and Inheritance*, Stanford: Stanford University Press.

Fuller, W. (2005) 'Restatement of trysts', *Chicago Review*, 50: 241–258.

Gadhoum, Y., Lang, L. and Young, L. (2005) 'Who controls US?' *European Journal of Financial Management*, 11: 3: 339–363.

Greenspan, A. (1999) *Commencement Address*, Washington, DC: Federal Reserve Board. Remarks delivered June 10th at Harvard University in Cambridge, MA., Available www.federalreserve.gov/boarddocs/speeches/1999/199906102.htm.

Gurevich, A. (1977) 'Representations of property in the high Middle Ages', *Economy and Society*, 6: 1–30.

Hall, P. (1973) *Family Structure and Class Consolidation Among the Boston Brahmins*, PhD dissertation, State University of New York, Stony Brook.

Harper, J. (2010) 'The ethical trustee', *STEP Journal*, September, p. 17

Harrington, B. (forthcoming) 'Trust and estate planning: The emergence of a profession and its contribution to socio-economic inequality', *Sociological Forum 27*.

Harrington, B. (2012) 'The sociology of financial fraud', in K. Knorr-Cetina and A. Preda (eds) *The Oxford Handbook of the Sociology of Finance*, Oxford: Oxford University Press, pp. 393–410.

Haseler, S. (2000) *The Super-Rich: The Unjust New World of Global Capitalism*, New York: Palgrave.

Hughes, J. (1997) *Family Wealth: Keeping It in the Family*, Princeton Junction, NJ: NetWrx Inc.

Innocent, R. (2012) 'Taxation of trusts in France', *Law Society Gazette*, 3 January, Available www.lawgazette.co.uk/in-practice/practice-points/taxation-trusts-france (accessed 19 April 2012).

Jaffe, D. and Lane, S. (2004) 'Sustaining a family dynasty: Key issues facing multi-generational business- and investment-owning families', *Family Business Review*, 17(1): 5–18.

Langbein, J. (1995) 'The contractarian basis of the law of trusts', *Yale Law Journal*, 105: 625–675.

Langbein, J. (1997) 'The secret life of the trust: The trust as an instrument of commerce', *Yale Law Review*, 107: 165–189.

Langbein, J. (2004) 'Rise of the management trust', *Trusts & Estates*, 142: 52–57.

Larson, M. (1977) *The Rise of Professionalism: A Sociological Analysis*, Berkeley: University of California Press.

Macdonald, K. (1995) *The Sociology of the Professions*, London: Sage.

MacKenzie, D., Muniesa, F. and Siu, L. (2007) *Do Economists Make Markets? On the Performativity of Economics*, Princeton, NJ: Princeton University Press.

Maurer, B. (2005) *Mutual Life, Limited: Islamic Banking, Alternative Currencies, Lateral Reason*, Princeton, NJ: Princeton University Press.

McGrath, C. (2011) 'Eva Gabrielsson: The girl who cast a Viking spell', *New York Times*, 21 June, p. C1.

McKenzie, C. (2010) 'Vision of the future', *STEP Journal*, May.

Maitland, F. (2011[1909]) *Equity: A Course of Lectures*, Cambridge: Cambridge University Press.

Maitland, F. (1936) *Selected Essays*, ed. by H. Hazeltine, G. Lapsley and P. Winfield, Cambridge, UK: Cambridge University Press.

Marcus, G. and Hall, P. (1992) *Lives in Trust: The Fortunes of Dynastic Families in Late Twentieth-Century America*, Boulder, CO: Westview Press.

Marx, K. and Engels, F. (1978[1848]) 'Manifesto of the Communist Party', in R. Tucker (ed.), *The Marx-Engels Reader*, New York: Norton, pp. 469–500.

Nasr, S.V.R. (2009) *Forces of Fortune: The Rise of the New Muslim Middle Class and What It Will Mean for Our World*, New York: Free Press.

Palan, R., Murphy, R. and Chavagneux, C. (2010) *Tax Havens: How Globalization Really Works*, Ithaca, NY: Cornell University Press.

Parkinson, M. and Jones, D. (2008) *Trust Administration and Accounts*, 4th Edition, Birmingham, UK: Central Law Training.

Patterson, J. (2005) *The Income Taxation of Trusts and Estates*, New York: American Institute of Certified Public Accountants, Available www.aicpa.org/InterestAreas/Tax/Resources/TrustEstateandGift/Trusts/DownloadableDocuments/IncomeTaxTrust Estates.pdf (accessed 19 April 2012).

Pexton, P. (2010) 'Fast forward: 2015', *STEP Journal*, April.

Pound, R. (1922) *An Introduction to the Philosophy of Law*, New Haven, CT: Yale University Press.

Rudden, B. (1981) 'Book Review of *The Restatement of Trusts. Modern Law*', *Review*, 44: 610.

Sanders, F. (1791) *An Essay on the Nature and Laws of Uses and Trusts, Including a Treatise on Conveyances at Common Law and Those Deriving Their Effect from the Statute of Uses*, London: E. & R. Brooke.

Sharman, J. (2006) *Havens in a Storm: The Struggle for Global Tax Regulation*, Ithaca: Cornell University Press.

Sklair, L. (1997) 'The transnational capitalist class', in J.G Carrier and D. Miller (eds), *Virtualism. A New Political Economy*, Oxford: Berg, pp. 135–159.

Stebbings, C. (2007) 'Trustees, tribunals and taxes: Creativity in Victorian law', *Amicus Curiae*, 70: 2–8.

Sternberg, A. and Maslinski, M. (2008) 'Trustees: The true wealth managers', *STEP Journal*, 16: 27–29.

STEP (2006) *STEP: The First Fifteen Years*, London: Society of Trust and Estate Practitioners.

Terkla, D. (1995) 'Cut on the Norman bias: Fabulous borders and visual glosses on the Bayeux tapestry', *Word and Image*, 11: 264–290.

US Senate (2003) *US Tax Shelter Industry: The Role of Accountants, Lawyers, and Financial Professionals*, Washington, DC: US Government Printing Office, Available www.gpo.gov/fdsys/pkg/CPRT-108SPRT90655/html/CPRT-108SPRT90655.htm.

Walker, R. (2008) 'Which side "ought to win"? Discretion and certainty in property law', *STEP Journal*, July.

Waugh, S. (1986) 'Tenure to contract: Lordship and clientage in thirteenth-century England', *English Historical Review*, 101: 811–839.

Winters, J. (2011) *Oligarchy*, Cambridge: Cambridge University Press.

Wyatt, E. (2010) 'Billionaire brothers long suspected of tax evasion', *New York Times*, July 30, p. B1.

Yongjia, L. (2011) 'Stranger-kingship and cosmocracy; or, Sahlins in southwest China', *The Asia-Pacific Journal of Anthropology*, 12: 236–254.

Zelizer, V. (1996) 'Payments and social ties', *Sociological Forum*, 11: 481–495.

Zelizer, V. (2005) 'Circuits within capitalism', in R. Swedberg and V. Nee (eds), *The Economic Sociology of Capitalism*, Princeton, NJ: Princeton University Press, pp. 289–321.

13 To give or not to give?

Inter vivos gifts of mobile property and donor profile before and after the 2004 Flemish Gift Tax Reform

Carine Smolders

Introduction

In Belgium gift and inheritance taxes are levied by the Regions. The Special Financing Law (13 July 2001) gave the regional governments the power to set tax rates and change the tax base of both inheritance and gift taxes. Particularly in the Flemish and the Brussels Region the governments launched a series of initiatives to decrease taxes and create tax systems more apt to civil law changes (for example, related to stepchildren, adopted children).

In this study we focus on a specific Flemish reform. Since January 2004 different tax rates apply in the Flemish Region to gifts of mobile property and gifts of building lots. Tax rates on mobile property decreased considerably. Former progressive tax schemes were reduced to flat taxes for registered gifts. Since the reform a Flemish donor pays a 3 per cent tax for gifts to children and grandchildren and amongst spouses and civil partners. Gifts to others are taxed at 7 per cent. Tax rates on real estate gifts remained the same, except for building lots. For gifts of building lots to children, grandchildren, spouses and civil partners, the rates were reduced with 2 per cent for the tax brackets below €150,000. Other beneficiaries pay 10 per cent for the share of the transfer inferior to €150,000 (see Tables 13.1 and 13.2). Another important feature of the reform is related to the fact that registered gifts are removed immediately from the inheritance once the gift tax is paid.[1]

The tax reform wanted to increase revenues from gift taxes and to increase the number of registered gifts.[2] Yet, a third important purpose of the reform was to speed up gifts. Much as in France, Italy and Germany, Belgian savings are quite considerable. According to planning experts wealth is largely concentrated in the older age cohorts, while younger generations experience difficulties in financing an affordable home. Estate experts confirm that inheritances are received more often in later stages of life. By lowering gift tax rates, the government wanted to encourage early transfers. This policy is in line with the French and US evidence on the tax sensitivity of gifts (Arrondel and Laferrère, 2001; Bernheim *et al.*, 2001) and with the results of studies specifically focusing on home acquisition through gifts (Mayer and Engelhardt, 1996; Guiso and Jappelli, 2002; Duffy and Roche, 2007; Cirman, 2008; Yukutake *et al.*, 2010).

Table 13.1 Tax rates for gifts and inheritances in direct line and to spouses and partners (%)

Tax brackets in €	Gift tax before the reform	Gift tax on building lots after the reform	Gift tax on mobile property after the reform	Inheritance tax
0–12,500	3	1	3	3
12,500–25,000	4	2	3	3
25,000–50,000	5	3	3	3
50,000–100,000	7	5	3	9
100,000–150,000	10	8	3	9
150,000–200,000	14	14	3	9
200,000–250,000	18	18	3	9
250,000–500,000	24	24	3	27
>500,000	30	30	3	27

Table 13.2 Tax rates for gifts and inheritances between siblings (%)

Tax brackets in €	Gift tax before the reform	Gift tax on building lots after the reform	Gift tax on mobile property after the reform	Inheritance tax
0–12,500	20	10	7	30
12,500–25,000	25	10	7	30
25,000–75,000	35	10	7	30
75,000–125,000	50	10	7	55
125,000–150,000	50	10	7	65
150,000–175,000	50	50	7	65
>175,000	65	65	7	65

In the Flemish region especially tax income significantly increased from 2004 to 2006, as Figure 13.1 demonstrates.[3] In 2007 and 2008 monthly revenues stabilized round €20 million. The lower level in 2009 presumably results from the 2008 financial crisis.

Though the revenues and the number of gifts definitely revealed an upward shift in the post reform years, it was not clear who was giving. However, from a policy point of view this is important information, necessary to evaluate the reform. Contrary to other OECD countries, no wealth-related micro data were available that allowed the profile of the donors to be established and to establish changes in the characteristics of the gifts before and after the reform.[4]

This study adopted two distinguished data strategies to increase knowledge concerning the profile of donors and the changes in gifts before and after the reform. First, data were gathered from a natural experiment, including face-to-face interviews registered with randomly chosen respondents visiting a fair for people aged 50 or older. This study allowed testing differences in gift behaviour related to gender, income, age, education, motives, planning behaviour and appreciation concerning transfer taxes. Logistic regression reveals important

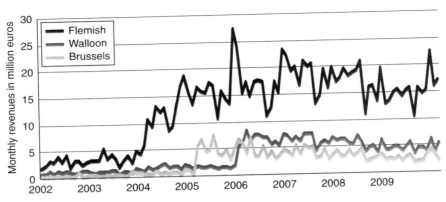

Figure 13.1 Monthly revenues from gift taxes in the Flemish, Walloon and Brussels regions (in million €).

elements of the probability of giving. Second, 4,708 deeds registered in 9 registry offices were screened. Next to donor characteristics like age and gender, these data give the opportunity to distinguish between the number of beneficiaries, the type of gifts and the conditions attached to the gift before and after the reform.

The remaining part of the chapter is organized as follows: first, a brief overview of the literature is provided focusing on donor profiles. Next the methodology applied to gather the survey data is presented. The following sections discuss the variables tested and the results of the logistic regression. The next part reports on the data gathered in the registry offices and presents the results from the bivariate and multivariate analyses. Finally, the most important findings are summed up in the conclusion.

The literature on *inter vivos* gifts and donor profiles

Several authors have studied the profile of donors in other countries. Most attention is given to personal characteristics of donors, attributes of the family, income and wealth status. We briefly go through the main results of the studies.

Donors' age

Poterba (1998) finds that the probability of giving increases when the household head is over the age of 65. McGarry and Schoeni (1995), Page (2003) and Joulfaian and McGarry (2004) suggest that older parents have a higher probability of making a gift. This holds too for the analysis in Hochgeurtel and Ohlsson (2000). Arrondel and Laferrère (2001) did not find an effect of age on the probability of giving. Yet age did seem to matter if the probability of the intention to give was estimated. The effect was positive and concave. However, Eggebeen (1992) found that those aged 75 and more, are less likely to donate compared to those aged less than 45. Hong *et al.* (2003) confirm this negative effect of age. Several researchers (Berry, 2001; Cooney and Uhlenberg, 1992) confirm that as parents reach advanced age, the adult child receives less support. Joulfaian (2005) is positioned in between and states that age positively affects the likelihood of giving but at a declining rate.

Donors' gender

Gender differences have been observed in giving patterns in previous research. Some studies present evidence that men are less likely to receive gifts (Eggebeen, 1992; Pezzin and Schone, 1999). Hong *et al.* (2003) find that compared to the single female households, a somewhat higher share of single male households gave to their children. The amount of money given by them was also slightly higher. A higher percentage of single male parents gave to daughters than to sons, but the amount given was about the same. Berry (2001) however, found that single parents are more likely to give to children of the same gender.

Generation skipping gifts show larger variations. Both single males and single females give more frequently to their daughter's children. However, males are giving more to their son's children; females are giving more to their daughter's children. The probability of giving was positively related to household income and home equity (for giving to daughters) and to liquid assets and health (for giving to sons). Kohli and Künemund (2003), Joulfaian and McGarry (2004) and Joulfaian (2005) find that women are likely to donate more. Finally, Hochgeurtel and Ohlsson (2000) did not find evidence of gender driven giving in the US.

Cox (2003) resorts to some prominent themes in reproductive biology like the paternity uncertainty and reproductive and economic prospects of male versus female offspring. He shows that grandmothers who are exclusively maternal provide more hours of childcare than grandmothers who are exclusively paternal. As for money transfers, the results are the opposite: paternal grandparents are more generous with transfers of money.

Donors' health

Joulfaian and McGarry (2004) find that health status significantly affects the probability of giving. Cooney and Uhlenberg (1992), McGarry and Schoeni (1995) and Feinstein and Ho (2000) report that parents in good health make more transfers than parents in poor health. Hochgeurtel and Ohlsson (2000) also report a significant positive impact of health status on the probability of giving, but not on the amount given.

Donors' income and wealth

Dahan and Gaviria (1998) find that the distribution of resources between children varies across income groups. Due to efficiency concerns, poor and middle-income families will be inclined to direct their scarce resources to a few children whereas richer families are more likely to allocate resources more equally.

Poterba (1998, 2001) argues that transfers rise with household net worth and with the liquidity of the assets. Income and wealth has been found to be positively associated with transfers of financial assistance in other research (Altonji *et al.*, 1996; McGarry, 1999; Pezzin and Schone, 1999; Hochgeurtel and Ohlsson, 2000; Page, 2003; Villanueva, 2003; Altonji and Villanueva, 2003; Kohli and Künemund, 2003; Joulfaian, 2005). Arrondel and Laferrère (2001) find a positive effect from wealth and an even more important positive effect from taxable wealth, but not from income when estimating the probability of giving. A paper by Joulfaian and McGarry (2004) confirms that the probability of *inter vivos* gifts rises with the amount and liquidity of assets. They also report that business ownership has a positive, though imprecisely measured effect on giving.

Related to wealth is the impact of having received a gift or from having inherited before. In Arrondel and Laferrère (2001) this seems to positively affect the willingness to give, whereas in Bernheim *et al.* (2004) it has no effect.

Donors' education level

Hong *et al.* (2003) find a positive effect of parents' education level on the probability of giving. Eggebeen (1992), McGarry (1999), Hochgeurtel and Ohlsson (2000) and Kohli and Künemund (2003) also came up with this positive influence of parents' education on making lifetime donations. In Arrondel and Laferrère (2001), on the contrary, this is not the case.

Household size and marital status

Family structure influences intergenerational transfer patterns (Berry, 2001; McGarry, 1999; Eggebeen, 1992). However evidence is diffuse. Page (2003), Kohli and Künemund (2003) and Joulfaian (2005) report that single households have a higher probability of donating than married ones, whereas Eggebeen (1992), McGarry (1999) and Joulfaian (2005) demonstrate that the number of children has a positive effect on donating.

Joulfaian and McGarry (2004) and Joulfaian (2005) find donators more likely to be widowed, contrary to Villaneuva (2003) whose results for the US and West Germany suggest that the amount transferred by mother widows is inferior to that of other parents. This is also the case for divorced parents in the US.

Donor's sensitivity to inheritance taxes

Poterba (1998; 2001) finds support for the link between giving and the federal inheritance tax threshold: the probability of making a gift is higher for households whose net worth exceeds the level at which their estates would become taxable. This was also the case in Bernheim *et al.* (2004) who studied reactions of donators at the occasion of the TRA97 reform in the US relying on 6 household surveys. Page (2003) and Joulfaian (2005) find a positive relation between inheritance tax rates and both the probability and level of lifetime gifts. This effect is larger for households with a household head who is over 65. Taxable estate did not influence the probability of *inter vivos* transfers in McGarry (1999).

Donor's wish to support children's home acquisition

As Mayer and Engelhardt (1996), Guiso and Jappelli (2002), Duffy and Roche (2007) and Cirman (2008) suggest, gifts of parents very often are meant to relax down payment constraints at the time children are buying a house. Gifts may also result in buying more expensive dwellings or reduce the children's saving for a house. Whether parents do this because they are altruistic is not totally clear. In the literature many studies suggest that the exchange motive has higher explanatory power.

Methodology

Transfer behaviour is obviously a delicate matter. First, gifts, bequests and income issues are preferably kept private. To get individuals to fully cooperate, guaranteeing discretion is necessary. Second, surveys very soon become complicated, due to the technicality of civil and fiscal law. Ill-informed respondents require extra information to be included in the questionnaire, in order to rule out misunderstandings or false interpretations of the law. An appropriate tool to cope with these concerns is the face-to-face interview. Due to the direct interaction between the interviewer and interviewee information flaws can be taken care of and the mutual discretion and reliability stressed.

A third issue concerns the sampling of donors. Donors could not be identified *a priori*, unless through the tax files of the government, to which there was no free access at the time of the research. Contrary to other countries no health, aging or wealth related longitudinal panels revealing gift behaviour were available in 2007.

From discussions with estate planners it was learned that gifts do not occur frequently before donors reach middle age. To contact this part of the population, a stand was rented at an event in Ghent focusing on the life of persons aged 50 and older. Visitors were invited randomly to participate to the research in exchange for a package containing a small gift and some official leaflets on gift and inheritance taxes. The average interview took 30 to 40 minutes and was based on a semi-structured survey. After nine days 212 questionnaires were collected. Thirty-one per cent of respondents had already made a gift, 12.3 per cent had been the beneficiary of one. In 95 per cent of the cases, gifts were directed to relatives in direct line; in 90 per cent of the cases mobile property was transferred. Compared to the Flemish population, citizens older than 65 were slightly underrepresented, whereas the health status of the average participant was superior to the Flemish average. The survey mainly reached the midrange incomes. Summary statistics of the variables can be found in Table 13.3.

In 2008 the research team was allowed to cross check the results of the survey, through the collection of data from 4,708 deeds. These were all the deeds available in 10 registry offices spread throughout the Flemish region. Compared to the face-to-face interviews the information collected was much more restricted. Only gender, age, the type of gift, the relationship between donor and beneficiary, and the time of giving were to be extracted from these deeds. Yet, as deeds were screened from 2000 up to 2007, the effect of the 2004 reform could be investigated.

The specification tested with the data obtained from the face-to-face interviews

The data collected through the face-to-face interviews were used to estimate the following relation:

$GIFT_i = f(IDENTITY_i, APPRECIATION_i, MOTIVE_i, PLANNING_i,$
$FISCALRESPONSIVENESS_i)$

Table 13.3 Summary statistics

	N	Minimum	Maximum	Mean	Std. deviation
$CIVIL_i$	212	0.00	1.00	0.09	0.29
$GENDER_i$	210	0.00	1.00	0.29	0.45
$HEALTH_i$	212	0.00	1.00	0.03	0.17
$OWNER_i$	211	0.00	1.00	0.92	0.25
$CHILD25D2_i$	208	0.00	1.00	0.24	0.43
$CHILD25D3_i$	208	0.00	1.00	0.33	0.47
$CHILD25D4_i$	208	0.00	1.00	0.17	0.38
$EDUD2_i$	210	0.00	1.00	0.15	0.36
$EDUD3_i$	210	0.00	1.00	0.29	0.45
$EDUD4_i$	210	0.00	1.00	0.28	0.45
$EDUD5_i$	210	0.00	1.00	0.11	0.31
$EDUD6_i$	210	0.00	1.00	0.06	0.25
$AGED2_i$	212	0.00	1.00	0.22	0.41
$AGED3_i$	212	0.00	1.00	0.26	0.44
$AGED4_i$	212	0.00	1.00	0.12	0.33
$AGED5_i$	212	0.00	1.00	0.07	0.26
$AGED6_i$	212	0.00	1.00	0.03	0.17
$INC5000_i$	178	0.00	1.00	0.03	0.19
$GIFTREC_i$	212	0.000	1.00	0.15	0.35
APPRECT1	163	−3.88	0.85	0.00	1.00
APPRECT2	163	−3.57	2.61	0.00	1.00
$HOUSE_i$	184	1.00	2.00	1.19	0.39
$HELP_i$	212	0.00	1.00	0.25	0.43
$PLAN_i$	212	0.00	1.00	0.57	0.49
$PLANFAMILY_i$	212	0.00	1.00	0.23	0.42
$RESPT_i$	188	0.00	1.00	0.59	0.49

The dichotomous explanatory variable $GIFT_i$ is set equal to 0 for respondents that have not donated yet. It equals 1 for those who have donated at least once already.

$IDENTITY_i$ contains a set of dummy variables covering for the donor's civil status, gender, health status, ownership status, number of children at the active age, education level, age, income and received gifts:

$CIVIL_i$: civil partnership = 1, else = 0

$GENDER_i$: female = 1, male and couple = 0

$HEALTH_i$: good and very good health = 1; else = 0

$OWNER_i$: owning a house = 1; else = 0

$CHILD25D1_i$: no children in the age group 25–45 years = 1, else = 0 (= reference group)

$CHILD25D2_i$: one child in the age group 25–45 years = 1, else = 0

$CHILD25D3_i$: two children in the age group 25–45 years = 1, else = 0

$CHILD25D4_i$: three children in the age group 25–45 years = 1, else = 0

$EDUD1_i$: only primary education degree = 1; else = 0 (= reference group)

$EDUD2_i$: lower secondary education degree = 1, else = 0

$EDUD3_i$: higher secondary education degree = 1, else = 0

$EDUD4_i$: higher education, short term degree = 1, else = 0

$EDUD5_i$: higher education, long term degree = 1, else = 0

$EDUD6_i$: university degree = 1, else = 0

$AGED1_i$: 50–55 years = 1; else = 0 (= reference group)

$AGED2_i$: 56–60 years = 1, else = 0

$AGED3_i$: 61–65 years = 1, else = 0

$AGED4_i$: 66–70 years = 1, else = 0

$AGED5_i$: 71–75 years = 1, else = 0

AGED6$_i$: 76–80 years = 1, else = 0

INC5000$_i$: income > €5,000 = 1, else = 0

GIFTREC$_i$: donor received at least once a gift = 1; else = 0

We expect to find positive coefficients for the variables representing income and health. Higher degrees of education, higher age groups and donors having already received a gift are also expected to increase the probability of giving. Females are expected to give more than males, but respondents living in civil partnership are expected to be in a lesser position to donate. Having children in the active age group is expected to stimulate gifts, but it is not clear *a priori* whether this depends on the number of children too.

APPRECIATION$_i$ refers to the respondent's appreciation of the inheritance tax system (APPRECT1$_i$ and APPRECT2$_i$). These two variables result from a varimax principal component analysis implemented on 6 items in the questionnaire.[5] We expect respondents finding inheritance rates rather high to be more inclined to transfer wealth through *inter vivos* gifts.

MOTIVE$_i$ represents the respondent's motives to give. Though the questionnaire contained a large list of motives the respondents were able to indicate, a large number of them were hardly chosen. Therefore the analysis is restricted to two motivations:

HOUSE$_i$: the gift is meant to support ownership of the children = 1; else = 0

HELP$_i$: the gift is meant to help children in general = 1; else = 0

For both variables positive signs are expected, presuming that these motives increase giving.

PLANNING$_i$ clusters two dummy variables measuring whether the respondents invest in estate planning for themselves (PLAN$_i$) of for members of their family (PLANFAMILY$_i$). These variables are interpreted as proxies for knowledge concerning inheritance law and specific attention for estate planning. They might also be a secondary indicator of the wealth level of the respondent. Again, a positive sign is expected.

Finally the respondents were asked whether taxes are important to them. FISCALRESPONSIVENESS$_i$ (RESPT$_i$) is rescaled into a dummy variable. A positive sign is expected.

Results from the estimation based on the data obtained from the face-to-face interviews

Several specifications were tested applying a logistic regression model (Table 13.4). The likelihood ratio shows that the models are statistically relevant. Simultaneous introduction of the variables generates coefficients different from

Table 13.4 Results from the logistic regression (dependent = GIFT$_i$) (significance level: * = 10%, ** = 5%, *** = 1%)

Variables in the equation	Logit 1 odds ratio	Wald	Sign.	Logit 2 odds ratio	Wald	Sign.	Logit 3 odds ratio	Wald	Sign.	Logit 4 odds ratio	Wald	Sign.	Logit 5 odds ratio	Wald	Sign.
CIVIL$_i$	0.407	0.997		0.437	0.699		0.000	0.000		0.353	1.237		0.533	0.447	
GENDER$_i$	3.244	6.894	***	3.778	5.809	**	2.513	3.084	*	3.095	6.133	**	4.468	8.878	***
HEALTH$_i$	0.153	1.139		0.000	0.000		0.640	0.092		0.150	1.377		1.290	0.038	
OWNER$_i$	9.032	3.275	*	2.51E+09	0.000		8.003	2.503		7.514	2.712		7.409	2.578	
CHILD25D2$_i$	6.049	3.859	**	3.366	1.411		16.808	4.246	**	7.122	4.566	**	12.146	3.931	**
CHILD25D3$_i$	18.269	11.510	***	15.324	8.242	***	60.695	9.346	***	21.763	12.451	***	42.095	9.593	***
CHILD25D4$_i$	6.352	3.688	*	4.842	2.160		18.689	4.133	**	6.509	3.666	*	13.112	4.006	**
EDUD2$_i$	1.216	0.051		1.109	0.010		1.732	0.330		1.448	0.181		0.778	0.074	
EDUD3$_i$	0.805	0.076		0.598	0.263		0.928	0.007		0.870	0.030		0.603	0.366	
EDUD4$_i$	1.151	0.030		1.036	0.001		2.856	1.260		0.970	0.001		1.443	0.185	
EDUD5$_i$	2.036	0.582		1.582	0.185		3.244	1.161		1.863	0.425		1.651	0.248	
EDUD6$_i$	2.093	0.462		1.235	0.024		5.019	1.796		1.899	0.332		1.718	0.227	
AGED2$_i$	1.661	0.644		1.656	0.392		1.421	0.225		1.432	0.308		1.886	0.832	
AGED3$_i$	2.003	1.290		2.201	1.003		1.397	0.211		1.963	1.174		1.729	0.578	
AGED4$_i$	1.553	0.340		2.100	0.615		1.768	0.402		1.825	0.622		2.300	0.959	
AGED5$_i$	3.973	2.762	*	5.414	2.333		4.766	2.408		2.819	1.423		5.048	2.923	*
AGED6$_i$	13.063	4.755	**	36.382	6.063	**	37.582	5.137	**	17.807	5.695	**	15.153	3.532	*
INC5000$_i$	6.519	2.878	*	5.706	2.109		7.815	3.075	*	7.968	3.479	*	4.002	1.146	
GIFTREC$_i$	0.260	2.985	*	0.186	3.258	*	0.274	2.235		0.206	3.676	*	0.298	2.184	
APPRECT1	/	/	/	1.066	0.074		/	/	/	/	/	/	/	/	/
APPRECT2	/	/	/	1.272	0.891		/	/	/	/	/	/	/	/	/
HOUSE$_i$	/	/	/	/	/	/	0.859	0.049		/	/	/	/	/	/
HELP$_i$	/	/	/	/	/	/	4.613	8.669	***	/	/	/	/	/	/
PLAN$_i$	/	/	/	/	/	/	/	/	/	3.075	5.306	**	/	/	/
PLANFAMILY$_i$	/	/	/	/	/	/	/	/	/	0.460	2.066		/	/	/
RESPT$_i$	/	/	/	/	/	/	/	/	/	/	/	/	0.913	0.039	
Constant	0.003	12.690	***	0.000	0.000		0.001	10.745	***	0.002	13.860	***	0.001	11.904	***
Number of Obs.	175			137			154			175			155		
−2 Log likelihood	163.724			119.333			127.992			157.679			135.241		
Nagelkerke R^2	0.381			0.462			0.494			0.416			0.394		
Cox–Snell Adj. R^2	0.273			0.333			0.355			0.297			0.274		
% correctly predicted	75.40%			78.80%			80.50%			77.10%			78.10%		

zero. The Cox–Snell R^2 vary between 0.27 and 0.35, and the adjusted Nagelkerke R^2 range from 0.38 to 0.49. The specifications produce a concordance between true and predicted answers of 75 to 80 per cent. The standard multicollinearity tests (VIF, tolerance) show that the explanatory variables are sufficiently independent.

The Wald-χ^2-statistic indicates which coefficients are significant. For each model, odds ratios were included in the first column. Model (1) contains all the IDENTITY$_i$ variables that are introduced in each of the models tested. The significance of the gender variable (GENDER$_i$) indicates that the probability of giving is higher amongst women than amongst men. The coefficients of the dummies CHILD25D2$_i$, CHILD25D3$_i$ and CHILD25D4$_i$ are significant too and have the expected sign. An increase in the number of children between 25 and 45 from 1 to 2 raises the probability of donating. The odds ratio is the highest for the group having 2 children in the active age. The health variable (HEALTH$_i$) is not significant. Neither are the set of dummy variables representing the educational level (EDUD$_i$) of the donor or the civil status (CIVILi). Age increases the probability of donating. From all age groups, respondents older than 70 (AGED6$_i$) are expected to donate more frequently than others. Income and home ownership is important too. Respondents earning more than €5,000 a month (INC5000$_i$) or owning a house, are more prepared to give than others. Denote that the coefficients of these variables are only significant at the 10 per cent-level. Having received a gift in the past (GIFTREC$_i$) increases the willingness to donate additionally.

Next to the IDENTITY$_i$-variables, Model (2) includes variables representing the appreciation of the inheritance tax system. None of the variables introduced is significantly related to the probability of giving.

Model (3) is the best performing model, adding the donor's motives to the IDENTITY$_i$ variables. It is generally believed that parents predominantly donate money to their children to help them acquire a house. Yet, the results of this estimation do not support this hypothesis. Rather we find that helping children in general is an important drive to donate.

Model (4) takes into account the donor's involvement in estate planning. Especially planning the own estate (PLAN$_i$) is significantly related to the willingness to donate. Respondents engaged in estate planning for their family did not donate more often. The same holds for the variable RESPT$_i$ added to Model (5). Whether or not the respondents are sensitive to taxes does not influence their behaviour as a donor.

Results from the screening of the deeds

In 2008 permission was received from the Federal Government to study deeds in 10 registry offices. These offices were located in three different counties. According to the Federal Finance Administration these offices are representative of the Flemish part of Belgium with regard to the amount and types of gifts. All the deeds related to the period 2000–2007 were looked into. The database contains information from in total 4,708 deeds. More specifically, the donor's and the beneficiary's gender and age, the number of beneficiaries, the amount given and the type of gift was derived from each contract. Related to the beneficiary, gender, age and the relationship with the donor were retraced. However, no indication of income or wealth level was present, and no information was available on the family composition of either donators or beneficiaries of gifts.

The purpose of the investigation was to offer the government a second study concerning the donors' and beneficiaries' profiles. In addition, the analysis aimed to clarify the effects from the 2004 reform of the gift taxes. As pointed out in the introduction, in January 2004 the government switched from the former progressive tax schemes to a flat rate tax system for registered gifts of mobile property. The aim of this tax reform was threefold: to increase the number of official gifts, to increase the revenues from gift taxes and to stimulate giving at a younger age in order to reactivate savings that otherwise are left unused for several decades.

To obtain reliable and meaningful results, outliers were identified and removed from the sample.[6] Gifts were expressed as an amount per donor. Initially cross-tab analysis and t-tests were implemented to reveal changes in the number of gifts, the amount given and the characteristics of donors and beneficiaries. These clearly indicated significant differences between the period ex-ante (2000–2003) and ex-post the reform (2004–2007):

- On average total gifts per donor increased from €57,712 to €137,924 ($t = 17.9$; $p < 0.001$; $n = 2,469$). Gifts per donor of mobile property also increased significantly after the reform (from €28,955 to €144,112 ($t = 10.1$; $p < 0.001$; $n = 2,469$).
- Before the reform only 112 deeds were including cash, stocks, bonds or other financial assets. For the last four years 2,358 gifts of mobile property were identified, implying a multiplier of 21 ($\chi^2 = 29.4$; d.f. $= 7$; $p < 0.001$).
- During the period preceding the reform, gifts of mobile property mainly consisted of cash (79.5 per cent of all cases). Since 2004 stocks, bonds, derivatives, gold and other financial assets have become increasingly important (from 8 per cent to 26.8 per cent of all gifts), as is the case for mixed gifts (14 gifts in the pre-reform era versus 138 gifts after the reform) ($\chi^2 = 27.2$; d.f. $= 3$; $p < 0.001$).
- In the pre-reform era only a very small number of the gifts were registered by a notary; in 83 per cent of the cases the deeds were cash gifts, for which no registration fees were paid. The registered deeds mainly concerned the transfer of real estate. From 2004 onwards, the officially registered deeds for which the notary intermediated became the dominant group (56 per cent) ($\chi^2 = 65,27$; d.f. $= 1$; $p < 0.001$).
- From the 112 deeds registered before 2004 only seven contained gifts to brothers, sisters, nieces or nephews, distant relatives or total strangers; in the post reform era deeds to others than those belonging to the direct line represented 48.1 per cent of all the deeds ($\chi^2 = 75.4$; d.f. $= 1$; $p < 0.001$).

- In 56.6 per cent of the cases only one beneficiary was appointed; for gifts to brothers, sisters, nieces en nephews or to total strangers more beneficiaries were counted.
- No significant differences in the gender of the donor were found; women were representing 48.1 per cent of the sample before the reform and 49.3 per cent afterwards ($\chi^2 = 0.59$; d.f. = 1; $p = 0.8$).
- Donors[7] donated on average at age 79; only 1 per cent of the donors was younger than 50; the age group 51–70 years represented on average 16 per cent of the total sample. Donors in direct line started giving at an earlier point in life. The cross-tab analyses reveal that in comparison with the pre-reform era the gifts of the youngest group of donors became less important. Before the reform these gifts made up 4.5 per cent of all gifts; in the post-reform period they only represent 0.8 per cent. In addition, the gifts done by the two following generations also became less important in time. Clearly, the reform was mostly appealing for the older cohorts. The number of gifts done by citizens older than 80 years, increased from 26 to 1,377 ($\chi^2 = 120$; d.f. = 3; $p = 0.0$).
- Beneficiaries on average were age 50; only 15 per cent of them were younger than 36; beneficiaries older than 50 years received 50.9 per cent in the post reform era versus 16.8 per cent before ($\chi^2 = 115.1$; d.f. = 3; $p < 0.001$).
- Only a minority of the cases contained conditions (e.g. usufruct, return to the donor in case the beneficiary dies early, etc.).

Next to the bi-variate analyses, an OLS estimation was established. The following specification was tested:

$$\text{TOTGIFT}_{i,t} = f(\text{DONOR IDENTITY}_{i,t}, \text{BENEFICIARY IDENTITY}_{i,t}, \text{TYPE OF THE GIFT}_{i,t}, \text{TAX REFORM}_{i,t})$$

The dependent variable $\text{TOTGIFT}_{i,t}$ indicates the total amount donated in the deed per donor.

$\text{DONOR IDENTITY}_{i,t}$ contains a set of dummy variables covering the donor's gender ($\text{GENDERDONOR}_{i,t}$: female = 1, male and couple = 0).

$\text{BENEFICIARY IDENTITY}_{i,t}$ is related to the difference in age between the first beneficiary and the donor ($\text{AGEDIF}_{i,t}$), to the first beneficiary's gender ($\text{GENDERDONEE}_{i,t}$) and to the total number of beneficiaries ($\text{NDONEES}_{i,t}$). The relationship between donor and donee is indicated by $\text{DL}_{i,t}$ which is a dummy variable equal to 1 in case the beneficiary is part of the direct line and equal to 0 in all other cases. The dummy variable $\text{MIXED}_{i,t}$ is equal to 1 if the gift is distributed between beneficiaries in direct line and others.

$\text{TYPE OF THE GIFT}_{i,t}$ regroups the following variables:

$\text{NOTARY}_{i,t}$: = 1 in case the deed was registered by a notary; else = 0

$\text{ESTATE}_{i,t}$: = 1 if the gift contains real estate property; else = 0

CASH%$_{i,t}$: the amount of transferred cash as a percentage of the gift

FINASSETS%$_{i,t}$: the amount of financial assets (stocks, bonds, other financial assets) transferred as a percentage of the gift

COND1$_{i,t}$: = 1 if the deed contains the condition that the gift is to be returned to the donor in case the beneficiary dies before the donor; else = 0

COND2$_{i,t}$: = 1 if the deed contains the condition that the beneficiary is expected to pay a rent to the donor; else = 0

COND3$_{i,t}$: = 1 if the deed contains other conditions (e.g. usufruct).

TAX REFORM$_{i,t}$: = 1 for the period 2004–2007; else = 0

The amount given per donor is expected to be positively related to the variables DL$_{i,t}$, NOTARY$_{i,t}$, ESTATE$_{i,t}$, and TAX REFORM$_{i,t}$. The transfer is equally expected to be more substantial if it includes real estate (ESTATE$_{i,t}$). In addition, female donors are expected to give larger amounts confirm Kohli and Künemund (2003), Joulfaian and McGarry (2004) and Joulfaian (2005). In line with Eggebeen (1992) and Pezzin and Schone (1999) we expect men (GENDERDONOR$_i$) to receive smaller gifts. Negative signs are also expected for the variable indicating cash transfers (CASH%$_{i,t}$). As to the conditions added to the deeds, the signs are a priori inconclusive (COND1$_{i,t}$, COND2$_{i,it}$ and COND3$_{i,t}$). Taking up conditions can lead to more substantial gifts as the donor is somehow insured against undesired behaviour of the beneficiary or his relatives. However, conditions might also be an indication of distrust, which in the first place might have reduced the transfer.

The results from Table 13.5 are based on 2,252 valid cases. Due to multicollinearity, the variable ESTATE$_{i,t}$ was left out of the estimation. The variance-inflation test indicates that after removing this variable, multicollinearity was no longer the case. The Durbin–Watson value of 1.88 is fairly close to 2.00, suggesting the absence of problematic serial autocorrelation. The variables included in the estimation explain 22 per cent of the variance of the dependent variable.

In general, the results match very well with the expectations. Except for GENDERDONEE$_{i,t}$ and the three variables representing the conditions in the deed (COND1$_{i,t}$ to COND3$_{i,t}$) all the coefficients are significantly different from zero. Yet, though insignificant, the sign of GENDERDONEE$_{i,t}$ is positive as presumed, stating that men receive smaller gifts than women. Women donate more and the amount transferred is higher in the case of multiple beneficiaries or in the case of gifts to direct relatives. It is also more substantial in the case of deeds which were established with the cooperation of a notary. Gifts containing financial assets like stocks, bonds or derivatives are on average larger, whereas cash transfers are smaller. Conditions seem not to be related to the magnitude of the gift.

Table 13.5 Results from the OLS regression (dependent = TOTGIFT$_{i,t}$ (in €))

	B	*t*	*Sig.*	*VIF*
(Constant)	24,324.391	2.232	**	
GENDERDONOR$_{i,t}$	17,865.568	3.952	***	1.073
GENDERDONEE$_{i,t}$	3,844.233	0.878		1.013
AGEDIF$_{i,t}$	−445.544	−2.164	**	1.023
NDONEES$_{i,t}$	7,666.979	7.261	***	1.024
DL$_{i,t}$	22,305.346	3.705	***	1.215
MIXED$_{i,t}$	−14,426.801	−2.526	**	1.170
NOTARY$_{i,t}$	10,554.691	2.152	**	1.118
CASH%$_{i,t}$	−525.239	−9.206	***	1.654
FINASSETS%$_{i,t}$	419.545	3.968	***	1.231
COND1$_{i,t}$	−5,425.101	−0.612		1.006
COND2$_{i,t}$	−968.081	−0.093		1.026
COND3$_{i,t}$	4,258.433	0.830		1.048
TAX REFORM$_{i,t}$	126,010.773	19.992	***	1.646
Number of Obs.	2,252			
R²	22.2			
R² adj.	21.7			
Durbin–Watson	1.88			

The difference in age between the donor and the beneficiary decreases the amount given. In general this means that younger beneficiaries receive smaller gifts than older ones. This might well be due to the fact that donors are more confident in relatives which they have observed for much longer time. This might lead them to believe that the gift will not be wasted.

Finally, considering the tax reform dummy, the coefficient shows a positive sign. For the period starting in 2004, the constant is increased by €126,010,773. As such the regression line is considerably shifted upwards, confirming the change in *inter vivos* giving in the post-reform era. Though this might be due to unidentified changes in the financial status of the citizens involved, definitely some part of the shift in gifts is attributable to the tax reform. More detailed analysis of the structural break reveals that the important increase in officially registered deeds intermediated by a notary and the significant shift concerning the gifts to other relatives clearly starts in 2004 and not in preceding or succeeding years.

Conclusions

In this study the profile of Flemish donors was examined. In addition the study aimed to reveal differences in gifts before and after the 2004 Flemish reform of the gift tax. As no wealth, income or health panel data were available, the analysis first was based on 212 face-to-face interviews. Second, information from 4,708 deeds registered in the period 2000–2007 in nine registry offices spread over three Flemish counties lead to some additional insights. These contracts provided more information about the beneficiaries and covered a much larger number of cases of individuals donating at a relatively advanced age (70 years or more).

Concerning the donor profile, both studies reveal that women are more inclined to donate than men. The logit analysis based on the face-to-face interviews confirms that having grown up children facing financial needs is also an important indicator. In addition, income and wealth (proxied by home-ownership) increase the willingness to give. Having received a gift proves reproductive. However, health status does not seem to matter. Neither does the set of dummy variables representing the educational level or civil status. Housing acquisition is not an explicit motive of donors, though the need for finance might already be captured by the variables representing the number of children aged 25 to 45. Results suggest that donors are altruistic and that they care about the welfare of their children and grandchildren. Whether they have strategic motives for behaving that way could not be inferred from the data used. Finally, estate planning, which might correspond to a more profound knowledge concerning inheritance law is also positively related to the probability of giving. Satisfaction with the inheritance tax burden, however, does not seem to have an impact.

The analysis based on the registered deeds identifies 2004 as a structural break, indicating that the tax reform clearly influenced citizens. The number of gifts as well as the amount given increased significantly from 2004 onwards. Gift composition changed too: gifts definitely became more diversified. Donors and beneficiaries more often decided to register the deed officially and distant beneficiaries are far more present in the deeds since the reform.

Yet, the tax reform did not persuade donors to start giving earlier. Though it was an explicit aim of the government to activate savings at a much younger age, the deeds documented that the average age to give was 79 years. Only 1 per cent of the donors were aged 50 or younger. The probability of giving was higher for donors in the age group of 70–80 or older over the total period. Yet, compared to other age groups, the number of gifts by donors age 80 or older increased exponentially after the reform (+479 per cent versus +33 per cent for the cases in the age group 50–70 years). The higher propensity to give might be related to a better financial position of the elder generations. It might also be due to the fact that at the age of 80, donors estimate that they will not live much longer and as such do not need to keep up savings at previous levels. As most individuals face a higher risk of becoming ill or physically dependent, they might also act more strategically. As such, they might be giving to relatives in exchange for care. As for the younger generations, the lower propensity to donate might also be related to the financial needs of many individuals wanting to lead an active life while retired. Additionally, precautionary savings might explain the rather modest number of officially registered gifts for this age group. As the face-to-face interviews suggested, family structure (and more specifically the number of children at an active age), might be of importance too. Finally, donors might rather be inclined to transfer wealth by means of unregistered cash gifts. Given their age, a life expectancy of at least three years is seen as plausible, which is the time period needed to keep the donation from being subjected to the inheritance tax. Unfortunately, the data available do not allow us to check these plausible explanations. Further investigation is needed to unravel why and when the older generations choose to donate *inter vivos*.

Acknowledgements

The author gratefully acknowledges the support of the Steunpunt Fiscaliteit & Begroting, financed by the Flemish government. The views expressed in this article are the personal responsibility of the author.

Notes

1 For gifts of real estate the so called 'progressievoorbehoud' still holds. This implies that gifts will still be taxed in the inheritance tax if the donator dies within the period of three years after the gift.
2 Though not compulsory, donors were advised to arrange the gift with the intermediation of a notary.
3 Tax income and the number of gifts in direct line increased by 74 per cent and 135 per cent respectively. Gifts to more distant relatives or to total strangers increased with 84 per cent generating 32 per cent of extra tax revenues in 2006 when compared to 2004.
4 Neither the SILC survey nor the PSHB budget survey provided detailed data about gifts made or received. The SHARE database that today contains data for Belgian respondents, was not yet available to the researchers in 2007.
5 Respondents were asked to evaluate tax rates in general and top bracket rates specifically for the inheritance tax applying to the direct line, applying to brothers and sisters and applying to all other heirs. The items were scored on a five point scale ranging from '1 = very low' to '5 = very high'.
6 The removal of outliers reduced the sample for the individual variables to maximum 2,470 deeds; the multivariate analysis is based on 2,252 valid cases. Most cases dropped due to the screening of the dependent variable. For the identification of the outliers, the SPSS 'explore' procedure was applied. In addition all cases superior to the 95th percentile were deleted.
7 In 63 per cent of the cases deeds were registered by only one donor; the average age of unique donors was 71 years.

References

Altonji, J., Hayashi, F. and Kotlikoff, L. (1996) *The Effects of Income and Wealth on Time and Money Transfers Between Parents and Children*, NBER Working Paper No. 5222.

Altonji, J. and Villanueva, E. (2003) *The Marginal Propensity to Spend on Adult Children*, NBER Working Paper No. 9811.

Arrondel, L. and Laferrère, A. (2001) 'Taxation and wealth transmission in France', *Journal of Public Economics*, 79: 3–33.

Bernheim, B.D., Lemke, R.J. and Scholz, J.K. (2001) *Do Estate and Gift Taxes Affect the Timing of Private Transfers?*, NBER Working Paper No. 8333.

Bernheim, B.D., Lemke, R.J. and Scholz, J.K. (2004) 'Do estate and gift taxes affect the timing of private transfers?', *Journal of Public Economics*, 88: 2617–2634.

Berry, B. (2001) *Financial Transfers from Parents to Adult Children: Issues of Who Helped and Why*. Population Studies Center Report No. 01–485. R.

Cirman, A. (2008) 'Intergenerational transfers as a response to changes in the housing market in Slovenia', *European Journal of Housing Policy*, 8: 303–315.

Cooney, T. and Uhlenberg, P. (1992) 'Support from parents over the life course: The adult child's perspective', *Social Forces*, 71: 63–84.

Cox, D. (2003) *Private Transfers within the Family: Mothers, Fathers, Sons and Daughters*, Boston College, Economics Department, Working Papers in Economics.

Dahan, M. and Gaviria, A. (1998) *Parental Actions and Siblings' Inequality*, Inter-American Development Bank, Office of the Chief Economist.

Duffy, D. and Roche, M.J. (2007) *Getting a Helping Hand: Parental Transfers and First-Time Homebuyers*. National University of Ireland – Maynooth, Economics, Finance and Accounting Department, Working Paper Series No. 1740507.

Eggebeen, D. (1992) 'Family structure and intergenerational exchanges', *Research on Aging*, 14(4): 427–447.

Feinstein, J.S. and Ho, C. (2000) *Elderly Asset Management and Health: An Empirical Analysis*, NBER Working Paper No. 7814.

Guiso, L. and Jappelli, T. (2002) 'Private transfers, borrowing constraints and the timing of homeownership', *Journal of Money, Credit and Banking*, 34: 315–339.

Hochguertel, S. and Ohlsson, H. (2000) *Compensatory Inter Vivos Gifts*, Göteborg University, Department of Economics, Working Paper No. 31.

Hong, G., Bhargava, V. and Palmer, L. (2003) 'Intergenerational transfer behavior of single senior households: Does gender matter?', *Consumer Interests Annual*, 49.

Joulfaian, D. (2005) 'Choosing between gifts and bequests: How taxes affect the timing of wealth transfers', *Journal of Public Economics*, 89(11–12): 2069–2091.

Joulfaian, D. and McGarry, K. (2004) 'Estate and gift tax incentives and inter vivos giving', *National Tax Journal*, 57(2): 429–444.

Kohli, M. and Künemund, H. (2003) 'Intergenerational transfers in the family: What motivates giving?', in V.L. Bengtson and A. Lowenstein (eds) *Global Aging and Challenges to Families*, New York: Aldine de Gruyter, pp. 123–142.

Mayer, C. and Engelhardt, G.V. (1996) 'Gifts, down payments, and housing affordability', *Journal of Housing Research*, 7(1): 59–77.

McGarry, K. (1999) 'Inter vivos transfers and intended bequests', *Journal of Public Economics*, 73: 321–351.

McGarry, K. and Schoeni, R. (1995) *Transfer Behavior within the Family: Results from the Asset and Health Dynamics Survey*, NBER Working Paper No. 5099, revised.

Page, B. (2003) 'Bequest taxes, inter vivos gifts, and the bequest motive', *Journal of Public Economics*, 87(5–6), 1219–1229.

Pezzin, L. and Schone, B. (1999) 'Parental marital disruption and intergenerational transfers: An analysis of lone elderly parents and their children', *Demography*, 36(3), 287–297.

Poterba, J. (1998) *Estate and Gift Taxes and Incentives for Inter Vivos Giving in the United States*, NBER Working Paper No. 6842.

Poterba, J. (2001) 'Estate and gift taxes and incentives for inter vivos giving in the United States', *Journal of Public Economics*, 79: 237–264.

Villanueva, E. (2003) *Intervivos Transfers and Bequests in Three OECD Countries*, Second draft for 'Economic Policy', submitted for consideration for the 40th October Panel in Amsterdam.

Yukutake, N., Iwata, S. and Idee, T. (2010) *Strategic Interaction between Inter Vivos Gifts and Housing Acquisition*, Paper presented at the 57th RSAI meeting, Denver.

Index

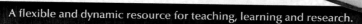